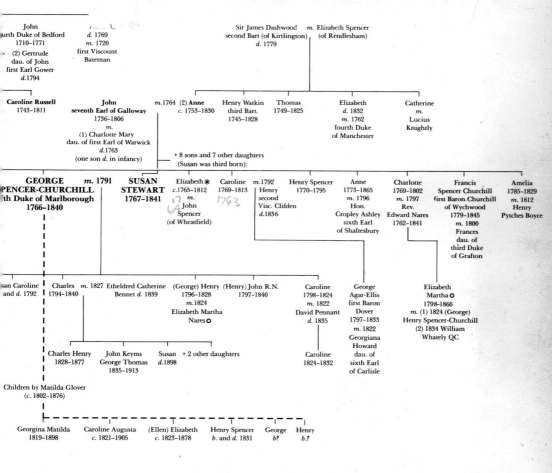

John urth Duke of Bedford 1710–1771 - (2) Gertrude dau. of John first Earl Gower d.1794	?..... L d. 1769 m. 1720 first Viscount Bateman			Sir James Dashwood second Bart (of Kirtlington) d. 1779	m. Elizabeth Spencer (of Rendlesham)			

| Caroline Russell
1743–1811 | John
seventh Earl of Galloway
1736–1806
m.
(1) Charlotte Mary
dau. of first Earl of Warwick
d.1763
(one son d. in infancy) | m.1764 (2) Anne
c. 1753–1830 | Henry Watkin
third Bart.
1745–1828 | Thomas
1749–1825 | | Elizabeth
d. 1832
m. 1762
fourth Duke
of Manchester | Catherine
m.
Lucius
Knightly |

+ 8 sons and 7 other daughters
(Susan was third born):

| GEORGE m. 1791
PENCER-CHURCHILL
th Duke of Marlborough
1766–1840 | SUSAN
STEWART
1767–1841 | Elizabeth ✳
c.1765–1812
m.
John
Spencer
(of Wheatfield) | Caroline
1769–1813
1763 | m.1792
Henry
second
Visc. Clifden
d.1836 | Henry Spencer
1770–1795 | Anne
1773–1865
m. 1796
Hon.
Cropley Ashley
sixth Earl
of Shaftesbury | Charlotte
1769–1802
m. 1797
Rev.
Edward Nares
1762–1841 | Francis
Spencer Churchill
first Baron Churchill
of Wychwood
1779–1845
m. 1800
Frances
dau. of
third Duke
of Grafton | Amelia
1785–1829
m. 1812
Henry
Pytches Boyce |

| san Caroline
and d. 1792 | Charles m. 1827 Etheldred Catherine
1794–1840 Bennet d. 1839 | (George) Henry
1796–1828
m.1824
Elizabeth Martha
Nares ○ | (Henry) John R.N.
1797–1840 | | Caroline
1798–1824
m. 1822
David Pennant
d. 1835 | George
Agar-Ellis
first Baron
Dover
1797–1833
m. 1822
Georgiana
Howard
dau. of
sixth Earl
of Carlisle | Elizabeth
Martha ○
1798–1866
m. (1) 1824 (George)
Henry Spencer-Churchill
(2) 1834 William
Whately QC | |

| Charles Henry
1828–1877 | John Keyms
George Thomas
1835–1913 | Susan
d.1898 | + 2 other daughters | | Caroline
1824–1832 |

Children by Matilda Glover
(c. 1802–1876)

| Georgina Matilda
1819–1898 | Caroline Augusta
c. 1821–1905 | (Ellen) Elizabeth
c. 1823–1878 | Henry Spencer
b. and d. 1831 | George
b? | Henry
b.? |

THE PROFLIGATE DUKE

By the same author

CLEMENTINE CHURCHILL

CHURCHILL FAMILY ALBUM – A PERSONAL ANTHOLOGY

THE
PROFLIGATE
DUKE

George Spencer-Churchill,
fifth Duke of Marlborough,
and his Duchess

MARY SOAMES

COLLINS
8 Grafton Street, London W1
1987

William Collins Sons & Co. Ltd
London · Glasgow · Sydney · Auckland
Toronto · Johannesburg

First published in 1987
Reprinted 1987

Text copyright © Mary Soames

ISBN 0 00 216376 4

Set in Monophoto Baskerville by
Ace Filmsetting Ltd, Frome, Somerset
Made and printed in Great Britain by
Butler & Tanner Ltd, Frome

FOR SUNNY AND ROSITA

Contents

Illustrations

A full list of picture credits will be found overleaf.

PICTURE CREDITS

We should like to express our deep gratitude to the following for kind permission to reproduce illustrations in this book.

The Alden Press, Oxford, no. 16; the Ashmolean Museum, Oxford, no. 14; Mrs Susan Bernstein for the Marshall Papers, nos. 62, 65, 66, 77; Birmingham Museums and Art Gallery, no. 74; the British Museum Department of Prints and Drawings, nos. 2, 26, 27, 34, 53, 54, 56, 57, 60; the Duke of Marlborough, nos. 1, 4, 5, 6, 7, 12, 13, 15, 28, 32, 40, 42, 49, 50, 51, 67, 68, 69, 70, 71, 72, 73, 75, 78, 79; the Lady Juliet de Chair and the Trustees of the Olive, Countess Fitzwilliam's Chattels Settlement Trust, no. 41; the Courtauld Institute, no. 19; Dover Publications Inc, New York, no. 63; the Henry E. Huntingdon Library and Art Gallery, California, no. 11; the Controller of Her Majesty's Stationery Office, no. 9; Her Majesty the Queen, no. 10; the Metropolitan Museum of Art, New York, no. 59; the National Gallery of Ireland, Dublin, no. 25; the National Portrait Gallery, London, nos. 33, 35, 36, 38, 76; the University of Reading, nos. 30, 31, 43, 44, 45, 46, 61; the RIBA Library, London, no. 52; the Royal Botanic Gardens, Kew, no. 37; Mr and Mrs Andrew Stewart, nos. 17, 18; the Marquess of Tavistock and the Trustees of the Bedford Estates, no. 8; the City of Westminster Libraries, no. 21; private collections, nos. 20, 22, 23, 24, 29, 47, 48.

The following illustrations appear in books now out of copyright: No. 39 in *Self-Instruction for Young Gardeners* by J. C. Loudon, London, 1845; no. 55 in *Mary Russell Mitford and Her Surroundings* by Constance Hill, London, 1920; no. 58 in *A Versatile Professor* by G. Cecil White, London, 1903; and nos. 3 and 64 in *A Description of Blenheim* by W. F. Mavor, Oxford, 1835.

Author's Note
and Acknowledgements

This book is about unimportant people, but I have found my *dramatis personae* every bit as interesting in their characters and emotions, in the complexities of their relationships, and in the events of their lives, as those of the greater folk who are central figures in the history of the Marlborough dynasty. My characters are only details in this tapestry, but they are an intrinsic part of the whole design.

My principal sources of information have been the following books and archives: the late David Green's *Blenheim Palace*; A. L. Rowse's *The Later Churchills*; Thomas and Barbara Hofland's account of the gardens and house at Whiteknights; the Blenheim Papers; and the Marshall Papers. For further details and other sources and publications used, readers are invited to consult the Source Notes and Bibliography.

I am grateful to my kinsman, the eleventh Duke of Marlborough, who encouraged me to write about his forebears, the fifth Duke and Duchess of Marlborough, and who has given me such ready help at all times. He has allowed me to use some of the beautiful flower paintings by Susan Blandford, later fifth Duchess of Marlborough, and has put me in the way of the invaluable Marshall Papers which came to his knowledge so recently. In addition, the Duke has enabled me to reproduce many pictures and prints at Blenheim Palace, and allowed me access to his Library.

I wish to thank most warmly Mr Paul Duffie, the Administrator at Blenheim Palace, for his ready help and patience on numerous occasions in answering my queries and those of my picture researcher, Joy Law. My thanks are also due to Mr H. Fawcus, the Schools' Liaison Officer at Blenheim, for translating the Latin inscription of the fifth Duchess's memorial tablet, and for hunting out (with the assistance of the Rev. George de Burgh-Thomas) details of burials at Ardley Churchyard. My thanks also to Mr Paul Hutton, the former Blenheim Estate Agent, for his help and advice on a number of matters. I wish to record my gratitude also to the late Mr David Green, who, from my first tentative steps, gave me so generously of his unrivalled knowledge of Blenheim.

Many documents vital to my purpose, including the rare and beautiful book on Whiteknights by the Hoflands, are in the Library of the University of Reading, and I owe a special debt of gratitude to Dr J. A. Edwards, the Keeper of Archives and Manuscripts there when I began my researches, who accorded me access to the archives, and gave me invaluable help; his kindness has been continued by Mr Michael Bott, who succeeded him on his retirement. My first tour of the campus of Reading University, formerly the site of the Marquess of Blandford's (later the fifth Duke of Marlborough) famous Whiteknights' gardens, was made in the winter of 1981 in the company of Mr R. W. Rutherford, Superintendent of the Plant Science Botanic Gardens and the Glasshouses, and of Mr Gordon Rowley, then a lecturer in Agricultural Botany at the University. Mr Rutherford has also kindly advised me on the modern nomenclature of the species and varieties of plants mentioned in the Hoflands' book, or elsewhere; and Mr Rowley's excellent plans of various parts of the grounds were invaluable in making the overall map of Whiteknights. In the winter of 1984, Mr Ian Cooke, the Superintendent of Grounds at the University, conducted me once again round the area of the former gardens and Wilderness, showing me the remarkable work of restoration which has recently been undertaken by his department, and I have benefitted greatly from their suggestions. Dr T. A. B. Corley, Senior Lecturer in Economics, kindly checked the manuscript letters of Mary Russell Mitford at Reading Central Library for me, for which I am most grateful.

I am indebted to members of the Galloway family for their help with regard to their ancestress, Lady Susan Stewart (later fifth Duchess of Marlborough); my thanks to the Earl of Galloway, and to Lady Antonia Dalrymple. And I wish particularly to thank Mr and Mrs Andrew Stewart, who answered my questions and allowed me and my picture researcher access to Cumloden, near Newton Stewart, Wigtownshire; and I am most grateful to Mr Andrew Stewart for permission to use several of the pictures there as illustrations.

I owe a special debt of thanks to Mr Gavin J. H. Johnston Stewart, whose family is a branch of the Galloway Stewarts, and who allowed me to read his most interesting thesis, 'From Out the Storied Past', about the Galloway family and their houses, from which I gleaned much useful information; he also put me in touch with other valuable sources, and elucidated numerous points for me. To Mr and Mrs Edward Strutt, I wish to express my warm thanks for their help and hospitality, both to myself and my picture researcher. Mr Strutt was, until recently, the owner of Galloway House, and lives nearby, and I greatly enjoyed and profited from his guided tour of the house and gardens. And in further connection with information about the Galloways, I would like to thank Mrs Rosemary Bigwood; Professor R. H. Campbell; and Mr D. S. Ross of Cowan & Stewart, Solicitors in Edinburgh.

Shortly before I began to write this book, Mrs Susan Marshall Bernstein had drawn to the Duke of Marlborough's attention the letters in her family's possession written by George, fifth Duke of Marlborough to her ancestress, Matilda Glover. I am most grateful to Mrs Bernstein for allowing me to use these letters and other papers in her possession, and also the portraits of Matilda Glover and her daughters; and I wish to thank her and her husband for their enthusiastic help, and delightful hospitality.

I wish to record my warm thanks to the many people who have supplied information or other help, some of them in response to my appeal in the press asking for material: Mrs Douglas Bell, for drawing my attention to her article about the Hoflands at Richmond and for her help with illustrations; Mr Denis Butts, for information drawn from his thesis, and for facts about the Hofland pictures of Whiteknights; the Duke and Duchess of Devonshire and the Archivist at Chatsworth for assistance in connection with the letters of George Agar-Ellis, first Baron Dover, to the sixth Duke of Devonshire; Mrs Dorothy Howell-Thomas, who sent me her excellent book, *Lord M's Susan*, on which I based my account of Susan Churchill; Mr R. S. Lea, for information about the Galloway family's houses; Mr Anthony Lister, for possibly relevant material in the Spencer papers at Althorp; Mr T. R. Millman, for drawing my attention to his life of Charles James Stewart, Bishop of Quebec; Mr P. W. Montague-Smith, for lending me E. W. Dormer's book on the Parish and Church of St Peter, Earley, near Reading; the Duke of Northumberland and the Archivist at Syon House, for information concerning Syon Hill House; Lady O'Neill, for sending me her most interesting articles on seventeenth- and eighteenth-century plant collectors, and one on Humphry Repton; the Royal Society, for permission to quote from their Misc. MSS 6.67; Mrs Swainston, for referring me to a relevant letter in the Library of the Linnean Society; Mr Igor Vinogradoff, for sending me the interesting extracts from the journal of his ancestress, Countess de Wassenaer; and finally, Miss E. Willson, for her useful information on Mary Russell Mitford.

I am indebted to the staffs of the following libraries who have afforded my researcher, Ann Hoffmann, and myself assistance, and I would like to thank them: Bodleian Library, Oxford; British Library Department of Manuscripts; British Museum (Natural History), Department of Botany Library; Greater London Record Office Library; London Library; Reading Central Library; Westminster Public Libraries.

I am most grateful to the County Archivists and their staffs at the following Record Offices for their help: Berkshire; Cambridgeshire; Dorset; Hertfordshire; Northamptonshire; Oxfordshire; Oxford University Archives; Warwickshire. We have received special help from the following: Miss S. J. Barnes, Oxfordshire County Archivist; Mr David J. Brown of the Historical Search Room, Scottish Record Office; Miss Pamela Clark, Assistant Registrar, Royal Archives, Windsor; Miss S. M. D. Fitzgerald, Chief Librarian and Archivist, Royal Botanic Gardens, Kew; Mr A. D. K. Hawkyard, Archivist at Harrow School; Miss Hilary Morris, Assistant Librarian at Kew; and Miss Daphne Phillips, Principal Librarian (Local Studies), Reading Central Library.

At my publishers, Collins, my thanks go to Robin Baird-Smith, whose initial enthusiasm for the book was so encouraging; to my editors Carol O'Brien and Ariane Goodman, and to Ron Clark and Vera Brice, who designed the book with such skill and patience.

And now, my 'home team': I want to record my gratitude to my husband who gave me constant encouragement and help, and who with other members of my family toiled in the kitchen at times of stress, that I might spin. My grateful thanks also to my secretary, Judy Meisenkothen, who, apart from endless letters, telephone calls and visits to the photo-copier, has borne with equanimity various literary crises.

I have been lucky enough to have had Joy Law's expert assistance in finding, verifying and preparing the illustrations for this book. It has been a most stimulating experience to collaborate with her, and I offer her my warm thanks.

As with my life of Clementine Churchill, Ann Hoffmann, of Authors' Research Services, has once again assisted me. She has undertaken the arduous and long research for this book: she has a keen 'nose' for where nuggets may be found. Miss Hoffmann has also typed my manuscript, and prepared the source notes, bibliography and the index. Her excellent advice and criticism, her good humour and enthusiasm for the task are boundless; and once more it is with pleasure that I record my true gratitude to her.

In addition there are several people who gave me assistance who do not wish to be publicly acknowledged; to them, and to any others I may unintentionally have omitted, I give my thanks.

One last note: in all quotations throughout the book, except for reasons of clarity, the original spelling and punctuation have been preserved.

I

Heritage

I N THE GREAT HALL at Blenheim Palace beneath the bust of John, first Duke of Marlborough are inscribed these lines:

Behold the man to distant nations known,
Who shook the Gallic, fix'd the Austrian throne.
New lustre to Britannia's glory gave;
In councils prudent as in action brave.
Not Julius more in arms distinguish'd shin'd,
Nor could Augustus better calm mankind.

But when this account of later and littler generations begins, the Great Duke had been dead for nearly half a century. His tremendous Sarah had battled on for twenty-one years before she (contentious to the last) was immured with her husband in the chill chapel at Blenheim, beneath the storied sculptured tomb she had caused Rysbrack to raise in his heroic memory.

The glittering cluster of titles which John Churchill had earned by his service and his sword – Duke of Marlborough, Prince of the Holy Roman Empire, Prince of Mindleheim, Marquess of Bland-ford, Baron Churchill of Sandridge – had passed, by special Act of Parliament, through the female line (John and Sarah's sons having pre-deceased their father) through the eldest of their four daughters, Henrietta, Countess Godolphin. Her son also not surviving, it then passed through Charles Spencer, fifth Earl of Sunderland, son of her sister Anne, the wife of the third Earl : thus were united the Churchill and the Spencer families, bringing an artistic, intellectual strain to mingle with the dynamic stream of Churchill blood.

Caparisoned with worldly honours, yet John and Sarah had

spanned triumph and disaster in the parts they had played in politics and war. Shiningly steadfast in their love and loyalty to each other, in their family life they had known bitter grief in the loss and early deaths of four of their six children, and much disappointment and strife in Sarah's relationships with the two surviving daughters – Henrietta, Countess Godolphin and Mary, Duchess of Montagu. These two quarrelled endlessly with their mother: no doubt her stormy, dictatorial nature was much to blame, but both daughters come down to us as difficult, and Mary Montagu as cold-hearted. The great General, who may have been the scourge of his country's enemies, was essentially peaceable and urbane in social and political intercourse and in family relations, and his daughters were ever on good terms with him. But a sad letter to Mary Montagu survives, the postscript written in his own hand the year before he died: 'I am not well enough to write so long a letter with my own hand; and I believe I am the worse to see my Children Live so ill with a Mother for whom I must have the greatest Tenderness and regard.'[1]

Anne Sunderland had been Sarah's favourite child, and great was the grief of her parents when she died aged thirty-two in 1716. Thereafter Sarah lavished love on her four motherless Spencer grandchildren, and when their father too died six years later, the old Duchess took over the entire care of the young orphans and the management of the family finances. Charles Spencer (in his twenties when he succeeded first his brother as fifth Earl of Sunderland, and then, in 1733, his Aunt Henrietta as third Duke of Marlborough) was a spendthrift, and had his grandmother, as a trustee of the first Duke's estate, not kept strict control over all money matters, he would surely have squandered the family seedcorn. As it was, in the years between his succession as Duke and the death of his grandmother in 1744 he piled up considerable debts, borrowing large sums against his future fortune: but the inheritance, wisely guarded, was able to stand the strain.

Although under the firm tutelage of his formidable grandmother so far as financial affairs were concerned, Charles took his own line

---

1. The monument in the Chapel at Blenheim, designed by William Kent and built by John Michael Rysbrack, commemorates the first Duke and Duchess of Marlborough and their two sons, who died young.

G.W.A.DELAMOTTE del.   C.JEWITT.del.sc.

in personal matters, making a lastingly happy marriage to Elizabeth Trevor in 1732. The match was deeply disapproved of by Sarah, since the bride's father, Lord Trevor, had been among those raised to the peerage for the purpose of passing through Parliament the infamous Treaty of Utrecht in 1713. Since Sarah had the life tenancy of Blenheim, Charles and Elizabeth in 1738 bought Langley Park in Buckinghamshire; curiously enough, the previous owner had been Lord Masham, widower of the reviled Abigail (Sarah's cousin – a sly-boots who supplanted her in the Queen's affections). The Marlboroughs lavished money on the place, rebuilding the house, making a park and a lake, and planting woodland. For the next fifty years Langley Park was to remain a favourite home of the family.

His spendthrift ways apart, Charles, Duke of Marlborough was an ambitious and successful soldier, but his military career was cut short in 1758 when, newly appointed as Commander-in-Chief of British Forces, he died of fever at Münster in Westphalia, aged fifty-two.

George, Marquess of Blandford was nineteen when he succeeded his father; he was handsome, virtuous, and well-intentioned – and, being unwed, the object of the attentions of society's matchmakers. At first he philandered with Lady Sarah Lennox, erstwhile flame of the young King, until he was made to marry Princess Charlotte of Mecklenburg. But presently the Duke's serious attentions fixed upon Lady Caroline Russell, the 21-year-old only daughter of the fourth Duke of Bedford by his second wife, Gertrude, daughter of the first Earl Gower: she was, by all accounts, a disagreeable, managing woman. The Duke of Bedford's first wife had been the beloved 'Lady Di' – old Duchess Sarah's favourite Spencer grandchild, who had died aged only twenty-six: Bedford was thus Marlborough's uncle by marriage. Duchess Gertrude was a determined matchmaker, and the young Duke of Marlborough and Lady Caroline Russell were married in 1762.

As a girl, the new Duchess had been judged by Horace Walpole to be 'extremely handsome';[2] she does not appear, however, to have

2. High Lodge, an engraving from John Boydell's *Views*, 1752
3. High Lodge engraved by W. A. Delamotte, in Mavor's *Description of Blenheim*, 1835

possessed a pleasing personality – perhaps she had too much of her mother in her. Horace Walpole (1717–97), fourth Earl of Orford and youngest son of Sir Robert Walpole, the English statesman, was a prolific and witty correspondent and noted commentator of the day, from whose letters we will often have cause to quote. He reported that the Duke felt a 'vast repugnance' [3] to the match – not on account of his bride, with whom he was in love, but because he thoroughly disliked her mother. The young people's affections, however, surmounted this difficulty and, as time went on, they were acknowledged by all the world to be an unusually close and mutually devoted couple. Caroline Russell made a good wife and chatelaine for her Duke – and her health must have been splendid, for she bore him eight children, despite the perils of eighteenth-century childbed. At the time of their marriage – well born, rich, good-looking, and in high favour with the King and his new Queen – the young Marlboroughs were a glamorous and much-sought-after couple.

From the first days of their marriage, George and Caroline were to make Blenheim their home and habitation. The Great Duke, for whom this amazing prize and monument had been built, had lived there only for the last few years of his life : the idea and the reality of the great Palace were equally pleasing to him, representing the esteem of his Queen and countrymen – although he had forfeited the favour of the first some time before the magnificent mark of her pleasure became habitable. Sarah, from the first, had thought the whole conception exaggerated and impractical, and she had quarrelled without respite with the architect Sir John Vanbrugh (1664–1726), summarily dismissing him in 1716.

When he died in 1722, Marlborough left Blenheim to Sarah for her life, and thereafter she 'laboured like a pack horse' (her own words) to see the great pile finished – which at last it was, nearly thirty years after its conception in the heady aftermath of the Great Duke's immortal victory. But Duchess Sarah spent only a few weeks of each year at Blenheim – enough time to chivvy the workmen and supervise the works generally; she herself preferred to live at Marlborough House in London (one of Wren's last works) or at Holywell House in St Albans, which had been John and Sarah's first real home together; or at the Lodge at Windsor Great Park which was her 'perk' as Ranger of the Great Park (a life appointment bestowed on her by Queen Anne) – it was here that the Marlboroughs liked best of all to live, and where he died. Finally, she was busy house-building at a new property in Wimbledon, bought after her husband's death.

During the fourteen years the third Duke, Charles, and his Duchess reigned at Blenheim, they made no alterations either to the Palace or to the gardens and park – indeed, none seemed to be called for, and they had spent a great deal of money on works at Langley. But they lived splendidly in the great house, enjoying it all at last in its full splendour – as those for whom it had been created had not been destined to do. From now on Blenheim was to become the dominating theme in the lives of those who succeeded to the dukedom, casting its spells and toils about them for generations to come.

Unlike his father, George Spencer came into his inheritance full of ideas and plans for the further adornment of Blenheim. Sir William Chambers (1726–96) carried out decorative improvements to the house, and embellished the park with a temple of Diana, a Tuscan gate, and a bridge (the New Bridge) over the Glyme at Bladon. But the man who wrought for his young patron and for posterity the most sensational changes was Lancelot ('Capability') Brown (1715–83), then at the height of his fame and the leading exponent of the fashionable 'Back-to-Nature' school, of which the Duke was an enthusiastic admirer. Indeed, he had called in Brown to advise and work at Langley Park in the 1760s, but anything carried out there was eclipsed by the larger and more important undertaking at Blenheim. From 1764 for ten years Capability Brown held sway in the gardens and Great Park at Blenheim, creating the fine and fitting setting for the great jewel of a house which we see in its fulfilment today. The most immediate of Brown's achievements was the flooding of one hundred acres of the valley below the house, which enhanced and gave meaning to Vanbrugh's Grand Bridge; this noble structure at first straddled the Glyme (a comparatively insignificant stream) and some marshy land; later, under Sarah's direction, there had been three canals and a cascade, but now the vast shining lake put it in splendid proportion. Brown's bold stroke of genius was hailed with admiration by all the *cognoscenti*. Elsewhere Capability ordained tree-plantings in his 'belt and clump' style. Today Palace, lake, island, bridge and forest trees create a memorable scene of broad, majestic beauty.

Nor did Brown's confident and sweeping arm stop at flooding valleys and planting trees – buildings too had to bow before the floodtide of fashion. He would have liked to add crenellations to the Palace and park walls (there are sketches), but here even his bounding confidence and visionary zeal were stayed. There had to be some tribute paid, however, to the spirit of historical romance. High Lodge, so called on account of its prominent position on a hill overlooking the park and lake, was – before Capability gave it a new incarnation – a middle-sized gentleman's country residence of straightforward end-of-seventeenth-century style; the favourite haunt and scene of the early death in 1680 of the brilliant and scandalous second Earl of Rochester, it was included in Queen Anne's gift of Woodstock Park to Marlborough. Sarah had added a wing to the house, and she and the Duke lodged there from time to time while Blenheim was a-building. Brown caused High Lodge to be pulled down and in its place raised a new dwelling, a toy fort whose 'Gothick' crenellations could be glimpsed from the Palace, rising through the trees. At this distance of time it is possible, from contemporary illustrations, to admire both versions of High Lodge, but one is reminded of that excellent French saying : '*Le mieux est l'ennemi du bien.*'

One cannot help but feel a strong pang of regret that the unique military garden to the south of the Palace was swept away by Brown a mere half-century later, to be replaced by greensward. This six-sided 77-acre plot had been enclosed by stone-built curtain walls, interrupted by eight great bastions. Within these military-type fortifications, Henry Wise (1653–1738), gardener to Queen Anne, had, with Blenheim's architect, created a vast formal garden, where the intricate patterns were traced by box and punctuated with box, laurel, yew and bay, with a groundwork of coloured sands that contrasted with the dark tracery. There were parterres and fountains, and raised walks from which the visitor could admire the farther prospect. Over this triumph of the art of formal gardening was ensconced a colossal bust of Louis XIV, taken from the gates of Tournai. (The 'Sun King' would no doubt have appreciated Mr Wise's magnificent layout more than the sea of sheep-nibbled grass which rolled up to the Palace steps after Mr Lancelot Brown had had his will.)

In her day, despite strong protests from Vanbrugh, Duchess

Sarah had caused the beautiful, historic shell of old Woodstock Manor to be swept away; her practical, impatient mind saw no virtue in a romantic ruin which obstructed the view from the Palace. Fifty years later, her great-grandson permitted the vast garden created by the most eminent architect and gardener of their generation also be obliterated. David Green, the chronicler of Blenheim, has commented: 'It was an "improvement" which, for sheer vandalism, ranked second only to the erasure of Woodstock Manor.'[4] But even had the fourth Duke stayed Capability's sweeping arm, Wise's masterpiece might have succumbed to later changing fashions and economic pressures, especially as the military garden must have needed an army of gardeners to maintain it. As it is, the setting Brown wrought for Blenheim remains among his most admired work.

Nor did the Duke confine his enthusiasm and energy to the improvement and embellishment of his Palace and Park: like many of his contemporaries, he was a keen collector. In his day, the Great Duke had accumulated – largely by gift – a magnificent collection of works of art, among which a series of Rubens's canvases was housed in a special gallery; and there was Van Dyck's equestrian portrait of King Charles I (now in the National Gallery), and the fabulous tapestries depicting Marlborough's victories. His great-grandson, the fourth Duke, starting in his early twenties, added to this already rich and varied collection by acquiring the Zanetti gems and cameos, bought in Venice from the connoisseur and art collector, Conte Antonio Maria Zanetti; later, he was to be presented with an important collection of porcelain by a Mr Spalding, to house which he had a special gallery constructed near the Home Lodge, at the Woodstock entrance to the Park. The Duke's enjoyment of his works of art must have been somewhat hampered by the fact that he was colour-blind and, according to both Horace Walpole and Fanny Burney (who was told it by the King), could not distinguish scarlet from green.[5] Another of his interests was astronomy, an occupation which, in later years, was to be the solace of this shy man's lonely existence: in the 1780s we learn of the fitting up of observatories in two of the Palace towers.[6]

These divers activities were immensely expensive, and the years of lavish spending were to be followed by times of retrenchment: Langley Park, for instance, so much loved by his parents, was sold in 1788. But the various measures of economy did not diminish the Marlboroughs' mode of life, which – even to contemporary eyes – was regarded as princely. Moreover, although Blenheim was their main base, the Duke owned several other residences: in London, there was Marlborough House (where Sir William Chambers also effected additions and embellishments); at Brentford, Syon Hill House, where the Duke built another observatory; and at Brighton for summer visits, another Marlborough House, close by the Royal Pavilion. Early autumn saw the Marlboroughs installed at Bath, to take the waters, and until it was sold, Langley Park made another port of call. The family on the move must have been a sight to behold – a veritable caravan with all their children, and a troupe of sixty servants.

Although immensely rich and grand, this Duke and Duchess shunned the fashionable scene; they were completely bound up with each other and with their growing brood of children – three boys and five girls. One of the Duke's sons-in-law, the Reverend Edward Nares (of whom we shall hear more anon), was to write many years later of 'how little the family mix'd with the world at large. Highly connected as both the Duke and Duchess were, the company they received at home was, of course, for the most part of the first rank: and they never went from Blenheim, but to other houses belonging to the Duke . . .'.[7]

Marlborough's mother, Duchess Elizabeth, had had the most sanguine expectations for her eldest son: writing to a tutor after her husband's death in 1759, she expressed the desire that the young Duke should 'apply himself to the Modern History of Europe and Laws of his own country in which he is born to be a principal actor, and I make no doubt a very shining and exemplary one.'[8] Elizabeth Marlborough died in 1761, three years after her husband, and therefore did not live to see the very middling role her boy was to play in his country's political history. He had started out well enough: a mild Tory, at twenty-two years old he was appointed Lord Chamberlain, and became a Privy Councillor in 1762; but it is thought that this court appointment did not suit His Grace, for he soon relinquished it – perhaps he needed to be in attendance too frequently. However, in George Grenville's administration (1763–5) he held the much more important office of Lord Privy Seal. One assumes that he did not relish these few years in *haute politique*, for although he was pressed by the King to stay in government, he never accepted office again.

The high-watermark of the fourth Duke's political ambition was the acquisition of the Garter, but for this accolade he had to wait until 1768. From then on he merely shilly-shallied on the sidelines of the political scene, frequently fussed by the actions and opinions of his brothers: Lord Charles held various minor offices and was generally busy in public affairs; while Lord Robert, an inveterate gambler, was active as a Foxite Whig, and a lifelong boon companion of Charles James Fox. The tenth Earl of Pembroke (1734–94), married to the Duke's sister Elizabeth, referred sarcastically to Marlborough in a letter to his son, George Herbert, as 'Your Oyster Uncle, and my Oyster brother in Law . . .';[9] two years earlier, in 1779, the Earl had told his son: '. . . entre nous, the D. of M. takes a very silly, indecisive part for which he gets abused, justly enough I must say though I am sorry for it, in the News Papers, at which he is very sore.'[10] Nevertheless, the Duke's support was canvassed by ministers on a number of measures, and his approval sought for sundry appointments. Dr Rowse has commented on 'the amount of time and energy expended in this aristocratic age on places and pensions, providing for younger sons, the consideration for great families, keeping them sweet, keeping them together.'[11]

Not only did the Duke increasingly eschew politics, but, although a personal friend of the Sovereign, after his tenure as Lord Chamberlain, neither he nor the Duchess held any court appointments. This must have been a personal choice, for in earlier days as Lady Caroline, the Duchess had been a bridesmaid to Princess Charlotte when she married the King, and the Marlboroughs' third daughter, Charlotte, born in 1769 and a favourite royal godchild, was a bridesmaid to Princess Caroline of Brunswick at her ill-fated marriage to the Prince of Wales in 1795. The Duke and Duchess attended court functions when courtesy demanded, but otherwise were not easily lured.

The King would write to the Duke on divers occasions asking for his support or intervention – support which was not always forthcoming to the extent desired, so reluctant was Marlborough to involve himself in anything the least bit troublesome. Yet the relationship between Sovereign and nobleman, formed in their younger days, remained; and each held the other in true regard. In a letter dated 12 March 1789 to his friend the statesman and diplomatist William Eden, later first Baron Auckland (1744–1814), the Duke gave a touching account of a visit he had paid to the King, then recovering from his first serious bout of madness:

> He [the King] sent for me to Kew the other day, and I found him just as I could wish as to health and spirits. He was very kind to me indeed. I fear I behaved like a fool twice, whilst I was with him, but the account of his feelings &c., moved me so much that I could not help it, and he took it very kindly, and was a good deal affected himself.[12]

The King gave his friend an astronomical watch and, to mark his beloved Sovereign's restoration to health, the Duke dedicated one of the garden temples at Blenheim as the Temple of Health.

Standing aside as they did from court, society and politics, the Marlboroughs were a remarkably self-absorbed couple. They gradually withdrew more and more into a world encompassed by the park walls at Blenheim and the mechanics of their stately progress between their regular ports of call in London, Brighton and Bath; the great events of their time filtered through to them at second hand.

There were occasions, however, when His Grace was galvanized into action: one instance was in 1799 when, during the course of the American War of Independence, news was received of the successful defence of Savannah against the French and the Duke was moved to instruct his agent at Blenheim: 'I think there should be a bonfire in the Park and some beer given out . . .'.[13] It was of course much easier then than now to ignore the events of a troubled world: Jane Austen's novels were written at the height of the Napoleonic Wars, when the invasion of this country was for a period of time a very real

---

4. Blenheim in 1748 from the south-west, before the making of the lake by Alexander Cozens.

5. Vanbrugh's Grand Bridge at Blenheim before the 'improvements' and flooding by William Hannan.

6. *Overleaf*: The fourth Duke and Duchess of Marlborough and their family in 1777, by Sir Joshua Reynolds (detail). By his father stands George, Marquess of Blandford; in the foreground (*l. to r.*) are Charlotte, Henry and Anne; behind stand the two elder girls, Elizabeth (*l.*) and Caroline. Francis and Amelia were not yet born.

threat – yet she depicts a society composed not of eccentric dukes and duchesses but of small-town or country gentry and the prosperous middle classes, apparently pursuing their absorbing lives at a time of universal peace.

Our Duke and Duchess's main contact with the affairs of the outside world was through a delightful and valued friend – John Moore, a former tutor of the Duke's younger brothers. Born in fairly humble circumstances, Moore had gone from grammar school to Pembroke College, Oxford, later taking orders. In 1770 he married (*en deuxième noces*) Catherine Eden, sister of the Marlboroughs' close friend, the future Lord Auckland. He rose swiftly from Prebend at Durham to Canon at Christ Church, and was Archbishop of Canterbury from 1783 until his death in 1805. Throughout this time he remained in communication with his former pupils' family. Both George and Caroline Marlborough looked to this remarkable, wise and likeable man not only for news and comments on the affairs of the world, which they had chosen for the most part to shun, but also for advice on their private and family life, which their own amazing lack of self-confidence or nous seems to have rendered them quite incapable of resolving for themselves.

Such was Dr Moore's standing with his friends at Blenheim that he sometimes adopted a 'headmasterly' tone: 'The truth is the Duke of Marlborough need never want employment, nor either of your Graces society. But both will be wanted till the Duke resolves not to be afraid of a little employment and both your Graces resolve not to be afraid of society . . .'.[14] Commenting on the Duke's reluctance to take part in parliamentary affairs, Dr Moore wrote to his brother-in-law, William Eden: 'He [the Duke] will be at the House today. It is a pity he had not nerves to move the address.'[15] At the time of the peace discussions with the American Colonies, Moore (by then Bishop of Bangor) wrote gravely to the Duke that this was a time 'too important in my opinion for a man who has such a stature as yours in the country to allow himself to be absent from this great scene of business.'[16] Even this cajolement failed to budge His Grace.

---

7. George, fourth Duke of Marlborough in his Garter robes, by George Romney.
8. Lady Caroline Russell, fourth Duchess of Marlborough, by Thomas Gainsborough.

A great fluster was caused at Blenheim when King George and Queen Charlotte, accompanied by the Princesses, were due to make an official visit to Oxford in the summer of 1786; prodded by Dr Moore (now Archbishop of Canterbury), the Duke extended an invitation to Their Majesties to visit Blenheim. Afterwards the Duchess wrote an account of it all to their friend and mentor:

> Considering the shortness of the notice, it all went off very well. They stayed here from eleven till six. We had breakfast for them in the library and, after they returned from seeing the park, some cold meats and fruit . . . We were just an hour going over the principal floor, as they stopped and examined *everything in every room*; and we never sat down during that hour or indeed very little but while we were in the carriages, which fatigued me more than anything else as I was not at all well at the time. Lord Harcourt [presumably in waiting on the King] told the Duke of Marlborough that he had been full-dressed in a bag and sword every morning since Saturday; but the Duke of Marlborough could not follow his example in that, as he had no dress-coat or sword in the country. He desires me to tell you that he had no misgivings. All the apprehensions were on my side. Nobody could do the thing better or more thoroughly than he did.[17]

The King was very gracious, remarking, 'We have nothing to equal this', a compliment which gave great pleasure. Being also much interested in astronomy, the King and the Duke had hived off to inspect the observatory then in course of installation in one of the towers: later that year the King presented his friend with a very fine telescope made by the German astronomer, Dr Herschel. But after this enormous effort the Marlboroughs retreated once more into their shell.

In 1778, Sir Joshua Reynolds (1723–92) painted the Duke and Duchess with their children. It is a splendid picture: the children, aged at that time between fifteen and five years old, look attractive and full of vitality. They were a gifted family, music and artistic accomplishments coming to them through their Spencer blood. The boys had clever and sometimes distinguished tutors, and later went to Eton and Oxford, in the family tradition; proper attention was also paid to the girls' education which as well as 'drawing and music and other elegant accomplishments'[18] included history and philosophy. United and affectionate, they must have made a lively company.

We get a charming glimpse of them in the diary of Mrs Lybbe Powys, who paid a visit to Blenheim in 1778:

> The environs of Blenheim have been amazingly improved by Brown since I was last there, many rooms furnish'd and gilt, and as there are many fine pictures, must be always worth seeing. A fine ride round the park of five miles which we went, and afterwards three round the shrubbery. The Duke, Duchess, and many of their children, with other company, were driving about in one of those clever Dutch vehicles call'd, I think, a *Waske*, a long open carriage holding fifteen or sixteen persons. As forms are placed in rows so near the ground to step out, it must be very heavy, but that, as it was drawn by six horses, was no inconvenience, and 'tis quite a summer machine without any covering at the top. [A precursor of the mini-bus, apparently.][19]

Not only the gardens and park but also the Palace were open to visitors at stated times, even when the family was in residence. In the fourth Duke's time the house could not be visited before three o'clock because 'the little Ladys are continually in the Appartments except the hours that the house may be show'd.'[20] Visiting stately homes was as much an eighteenth-century diversion as it is today: travellers of repute regarded it as a matter of course that they should be allowed to view the seats of the aristocracy and gentry, and contemporary letters and journals abound in descriptions of visits to notable houses. In an age of elegance and creative taste, those who owned beautiful properties were proud and gratified for them to be shown to a small but discriminating public. The conducted tour was usually guided by the housekeeper, but for visitors to Blenheim there was a lyrically written and elegantly illustrated guidebook entitled *A New Description of Blenheim*. This was the handiwork of Dr William Fordyce Mavor (1758–1837), for many years Rector of Bladon-with-Woodstock, Headmaster of Woodstock Grammar School, and ten times mayor of that borough. Born in Aberdeen, he had come as a very young schoolmaster to Burford, moving later to Woodstock. Employed to tutor the fourth Duke's

children, he got to know the whole family, greatly admiring his
patron, the Duke, and falling forever beneath the spell of the great
house and its splendid surroundings; he was also the author of
numerous books on divers learned and educational subjects. Dr
Mavor brought out the first edition of *A New Description of Blenheim*
in 1789; running into many editions, it was to be the guidebook to
Blenheim for almost fifty years, and from 1791 there was also a
French translation. Its flowery style may raise a smile on the lips of
twentieth-century readers, and the adulatory fashion in which the
succeeding incumbents of Blenheim are addressed may jar on the
ears of more democratic generations, but those who care to do so
can follow through the good Doctor's pages the changes wrought at
Blenheim, both in the Palace and in the grounds, from soon after
'magician' Brown had waved his wand up to the 1840s, when a
posthumous edition was published in the time of the sixth Duke.

The Marlboroughs were conscientious parents who took a great
interest and part in their children's upbringing; Duchess Caroline,
however, had the reputation of being a cold and difficult mother.
In August 1807, Mrs Frances Calvert, recording in her diary a visit
from the Duchess who had brought with her Amelia, her youngest
daughter, aged twenty-two, noted that the girl was rather pretty,

> but looks formal and not at her ease. They say the Duchess
> has always been a most disagreeable mother, indeed, some
> go as far as to say an unnatural one, but a common ac-
> quaintance as I am, can see nothing of it. She is the best
> bred woman I ever saw, and has great suavity of manners,
> but there cannot have been so much smoke without fire,
> and she is proverbial for unkindness to her family. [21]

Nevertheless, life at Blenheim in the 1770s and 1780s must have
been agreeable, with a troupe of noisy young people to liven up the
great house with their games and squabbles, while outside the Park
offered every kind of activity, and a chance to escape from a censorious Mama or tiresome tutors. But perhaps distance has lent
enchantment to the view, for we have a less than enthusiastic appreciation from the Reverend William Coxe (1747–1828), who was the
young Marquess of Blandford's tutor and chaplain at Blenheim for
two years, from 1773–5. He subsequently went to the Pembroke

family (we have already seen that the tenth Earl was married to the Duke's sister, Elizabeth), and accompanied their son, Lord Herbert, on the Grand Tour. The Duke had expressed himself as being highly delighted with the young man and, according to William Coxe himself, had hinted not only at further employment in his own family, but also at a 'leg-up' in his ecclesiastical career. However, except that Dr Coxe was often a guest at Blenheim, where he always received a most cordial welcome from the Duke and Duchess, the promised preferments remained in the realm of hope (or imagination?). Happily, Coxe was a clever scholar and an agreeable companion, and the course of his life was not impeded by the lack of boosting by the Marlboroughs; he almost certainly had a freer and a more interesting time away from kind but claustrophobic Blenheim. His lot fell among cultivated people, he travelled widely, became an Archdeacon, married well, wrote lively letters and historical works, and enjoyed a lifetime of friendship with the Herbert family. Nevertheless, disappointment in his ducal patron at the time may well be reflected in a letter Coxe wrote to Lord Herbert in 1781 :

> I passed a week at Blenheim; the place is delightful. I wish I could say as much of those who possess it. Though wonderfully civil and obliging yet I did not regret my having declined the honour of domesticating myself in the family, wh wd have been ennui itself. I cd bear it no longer than a week, & so made the best of my way to my sister's at Winchester . . .[22]

One cannot resist the thought that an element of 'miff' may have entered into the ambitious young man's verdict. For it is hard to believe that, with all Blenheim had to offer, life can have been 'ennui itself'. Take the theatricals, for instance.

We first hear of amateur theatricals at Blenheim towards the end of the Great Duke's life, when the instigators were John and Sarah's grandchildren, and plays were performed in the Bow Window Room; these included Dryden's *All for Love* and Rowe's *Tamerlane*. The Duke, a sad figure since his stroke, was greatly diverted; Sarah kept a sharp eye on propriety and, according to a Miss Cairnes who took part in the plays, 'scratched out some of the most amorous speeches, and there was no embrace allowed . . .'.[23]

Over half a century later, a new generation found occupation and entertainment in play-acting. Amateur dramatics were all the rage in the 1780s, and in several great houses plays were performed regularly to quite large audiences, notably at Hinchingbrook (the Earl of Sandwich's house) and at Sir Watkin William Wynn's home at Wynnstay in Cheshire. So popular did these 'home-made' theatricals become, that winter bookings at Bath were said to be seriously affected by the rival dramatic attractions at various noble houses in the neighbourhood.

When the fourth Duke's children began their play-acting at Blenheim, they probably used one of the rooms as a theatre (perhaps the Bow Window Room, as in former days); but as they grew older and more enthusiastic they also became more ambitious. In December 1786 the Blenheim 'company', which consisted almost entirely of the Spencer children and their close relations, presented Goldsmith's *She Stoops to Conquer* and two other plays on three successive evenings. Parts were taken by Lord Blandford (twenty years old), Lord Henry Spencer (aged sixteen), the Ladies Caroline and Elizabeth (in their early twenties), the Duke's brother, Lord Charles Spencer, and the Duchess's brother, Lord William Russell. These performances were a great success, and the Duke and Duchess were so enthusiastic that they decided to convert Vanbrugh's conservatory (engagingly referred to as a 'greenhouse' in contemporary parlance) into a theatre, where up to two hundred people could be accommodated. The stage was large, and fitted with no less than ten changes of scenery, devised and executed by Michael Angelo Rooker (1743–1801), the engraver and water-colour painter who for some years was chief scene painter at the Haymarket Theatre; the lighting was of the newest type. The theatre was painted dove grey, with the niches and friezes in pale blue, the pilasters and other ornamentation in white: Dr Mavor described it all in his *New Description of Blenheim*, adding: 'The whole has a grand and pleasing effect.' The Doctor was so much excited by the new venture that he composed a lengthy poem to celebrate the opening of the theatre, entitled 'To His Grace the Duke of Marlborough, on converting his Green-House into a Private Theatre'.

In October 1787 the first performance was given in the new theatre: Lady Charlotte Spencer (aged eighteen) and a first cousin,

Lord John Spencer, were family additions to the cast; some friends and neighbours took part, and the Duke's porter earned high praise in a walk-on role. The 'season' was for six consecutive nights, and the repertoire consisted of four plays: *False Delicacies*; *Who's the Dupe?*; *The Guardian* and *The Lyar*. The audience was drawn from a wide circle; among those invited were the corporations of Oxford and Woodstock with their wives, and tickets were available generally and were in great demand, people coming from quite far away.

The Duke and Duchess were hospitable and affable to all and sundry, and refreshments were provided on a lavish scale. The newspapers carried long, colourful accounts of the Blenheim 'season', warmly praising the theatre, the actors and the costumes, as well as the graciousness of Their Graces (who also got marks for promoting 'this elegant, and instructive mode of entertaining their family and friends' in preference to racing and gambling!). But a less fulsome view of the acting was taken by a visiting dramatist, Frederic Reynolds, who, with two friends, an actor and an author, procured tickets for one of the performances: Reynolds found he was 'unable to hear one line out of twenty which these really *private actors* uttered' (a common criticism, one may add, of amateur actors of all centuries). All three men, however, were much struck by the beauty and freshness of the three Ladies Spencer, and impressed by the 'elegant and expensive dresses they wore'. They also much commended Lady Charlotte's singing, and 'a dance by the characters was executed so elegantly, as to attract the attention and applause of the whole audience . . .'.[24]

The Blenheim theatricals continued to be a great feature of life there and, in spite of the criticisms, a source of enjoyment to the neighbourhood in the last years of the 1780s. It must all have been great fun and absorbing of time and talent to the group of family and friends who took part; they were certainly hardworking, for they put on two seasons a year of four, five and six nights. To drama was added romance: in 1790 Elizabeth Spencer married her first cousin, John, the son of Lord Charles Spencer; living not far from Blenheim, at Wheatfield, John was a regular member of the acting group. This match can have caused no flutter in the Blenheim dovecote, but another romance – a direct result of the theatricals – was to cause a drama indeed.

Lord Henry Spencer, the Duke's second son, was an under-graduate at Christ Church, Oxford, where he had made friends with a 27-year-old don, the Reverend Edward Nares, son of a distinguished judge. Looking for a recruit for the theatricals at Blenheim, Lord Henry invited Nares to join the group. He at first refused out of shyness and diffidence, but, on being urgently pressed by both the Duke and the Duchess, eventually gave in, and thereafter took part regularly in the play-acting. 1789 saw the last theatrical season there, as the family troupe was breaking up – within the next few years Blandford, Elizabeth and Caroline were all to be married, and Lord Henry posted abroad in the diplomatic service. Further-more, sinister shadows cast by events in France served to depress high spirits: play-acting was at an end. But by this time Edward Nares had become a great favourite with the family, and in succeed-ing years he was a welcome guest not only at Blenheim and with the cousins at Wheatfield, but also at Marlborough House and at Syon Hill. The outcome of his frequent visits is not hard to guess: he and Lady Charlotte (the one who sang so charmingly) fell in love and sought the permission and blessing of her parents to their marriage. The Duke and Duchess were surprised and outraged (although they must have been purblind not to have seen what was going on be-neath their noses) – and, it seems to a later generation, unreasonable and unkind, particularly as Charlotte was in her late twenties. But eighteenth-century dukes looked to their daughters to marry grandly (or richly); clever young dons in orders – albeit of respectable birth, and however kind and charming – simply would not do.

Presently the Duke and Duchess accepted that Charlotte's heart and mind were unchangeable, and they ceased to oppose the match: she and Edward Nares were married quietly at Henley-on-Thames in April 1797, his widowed sister having fetched the bride from Blenheim in her own carriage; none of her relations was present. Soon after their marriage the Duke's steward wrote to Lady Char-lotte, informing her that her father would give her an allowance of £400 a year. After a lapse of time, she was invited to visit Blenheim,

9. Marlborough House, St James's Park, 1754.

10. The marriage of the Prince of Wales and Princess Caroline at St James's Palace on 8 April 1795, with John Moore, the Archbishop of Canterbury, officiating, by Henry Singleton.

but since the invitation did not include her husband she preferred not to accept, and she never again set foot in her old home. Most of her relations, however, ignored the Duke and Duchess's embargo (which was generally regarded as unreasonable) and welcomed Edward Nares with as much pleasure and warmth as a relation as they had done erstwhile as a friend.

Charlotte felt the disapproval and unkindness of her parents deeply, but she was happy with Edward Nares, a kind and clever man whose career prospered; he was now the Rector of Biddenden in Kent. They had three children, of whom only one survived infancy – Elizabeth Martha, born in 1798. But Charlotte and Edward were destined to know only five years' happiness together: she became ill and, in 1801, so weak that her husband took her to Bath, hoping that there she might get stronger. It was not to be. Softened by their daughter's illness, the Marlboroughs sent word that they hoped she might visit them at Marlborough House when she returned to London. But it was too late for visits – Charlotte Nares died, her husband's hand in hers, in January 1802. The Duke asked that his daughter's body might be brought to Blenheim, to be buried in the family vault at nearby Ardley beside her brother Henry (the one who had brought Edward Nares into the Blenheim circle), who had died a few years before; Nares acceded to the Duke's wish. Many people thought the Marlboroughs' conduct towards their daughter and her husband had been reprehensible, and they received a number of hostile anonymous letters; Nares himself, however, would never listen to any criticism of his parents-in-law, preferring only to remember their welcoming kindness in former days; he must have been a true Christian.

Most of Charlotte's relations were warm in their sympathy for the heartbroken widower, and felt deeply the pathos of her fate; her aunt, the Duke's sister, Lady Diana Beauclerk, wrote: 'Poor thing,

---

11. 'The Little Fortune Teller', showing Lord Henry and Lady Charlotte Spencer as children, by Sir Joshua Reynolds.

12. George, Marquess of Blandford at the age of eleven, with one of the cases of Zanetti gems in his arms. His father, the fourth Duke, holds a cameo portrait of the Emperor Augustus. Detail from the family group by Reynolds.

13. Theatricals at Blenheim Palace with Lord Henry Spencer, Lady Elizabeth Spencer, John Spencer and Miss Peshall, by J. Roberts, 1788.

the story is too horrid to write. Her husband behaved with the utmost affection during her illness (others not so!); there are sad hearts about the world . . .'. And in a later letter: 'Her parents' hard-heartedness helped to break her heart I fear – they really are become callous to all (but themselves), when I say 'they' I mean more particularly the female.'[25]

Charlotte's Spencer kin rallied round to cherish the four-year-old Elizabeth Martha, who after her mother's death was a frequent visitor both to her grandparents and her other relations. But Edward Nares was not invited to Blenheim until two years after Duchess Caroline's death in 1811; he was then bidden to accompany his daughter on a visit to her grandfather. It would seem that it had been the Duchess who had been the more unforgiving. At any rate, it is pleasant to be able to record that Edward Nares and his father-in-law were reconciled, and that thereafter Nares became once more a welcome guest. He was by then quite eminent in the academic world, having just been appointed Regius Professor of Modern History at Oxford. He married again not long after Charlotte's death, but her family did not waver in their friendship, and in after years received the new Mrs Nares with kindness.

When the old Duke died in 1817, he made financial provision for Elizabeth Martha and, as if in atonement, added a codicil to his Will desiring that his daughter Charlotte's body should be brought from Ardley to rest beside his own in the vault in the Chapel at Blenheim Palace: so Charlotte Spencer came home at last. Old hurts were further healed when, in 1823, Elizabeth Martha married her first cousin, Lord Henry Spencer-Churchill, the third son of the fifth Duke.

Perhaps the last theatrical performances given at Blenheim signalled the ending of the happy, carefree times for that generation. In 1789, when the curtain rang down, the six elder children ranged in age from twenty-six to sixteen years old; those 'bigger ones' would have been the 'fun makers' (Francis, aged ten, and little Amelia, four years old, were still in nursery or schoolroom); and now 'real' life beckoned for most of them. The first to marry was Elizabeth, who wed her cousin John Spencer in 1790; George Blandford, the heir, followed suit the following year, marrying Lady Susan Stewart, and Caroline married Lord Clifden in 1792. But 1795 brought sorrow to the family circle when Henry, the diplomat son so full of promise (in contrast to his elder brother), died in Berlin, *en poste*, aged twenty-four. With all these departures, life at Blenheim – always so self-contained, so self-sufficient – must have become a good deal quieter and even more isolated.

The Duke, from early on in his life, was remarkable for his silent disposition. In 1777 the Duchess went with some friends to visit the old actor, David Garrick, with whom they had kept in touch following his farewell performance on the London stage the previous year. Afterwards, Mrs Elizabeth Montagu, one of the ladies in the party, reported to her friend, Mrs Vesey: 'The Duchess is in hopes to bring the Duke into such Company next Winter in hopes to make him speak; that will fall to your lot, at least you will make him listen, which is the best preparation to furnishing a part of conversation . . .'.[26] As time went on, however, the Duke's silences became longer, and it was reported from the congenial, easy-going circles of the Jockey Club that Marlborough 'was sullen and overbearing in his general demeanour.'[27] Perhaps these characteristics had their root in an unconquerable shyness. Yet we know the Duke could be a most affable host, as when receiving and entertaining the audiences who attended the theatricals; and he was habitually surrounded by large family gatherings at Blenheim for Christmas and other festive occasions.

Time seems to have accentuated the Duke's eccentricities, and in particular with regard to the outside world. A diverting example was the occasion in July 1802 when Admiral Lord Nelson, accompanied by Sir William and Lady Hamilton, arrived unexpectedly to view Blenheim. Nelson, fresh from his glorious victory in the previous year at Copenhagen, had on 22 July been received in Oxford, where City and University had bestowed upon him their highest accolades of honour and distinction. That night he and his friends stayed at a Woodstock inn, and the next morning proceeded to Blenheim, to survey the recompense given to a victorious general by his grateful Queen. Neither Lord Nelson nor Sir William Hamilton were personally acquainted with the Duke of Marlborough, but no doubt they expected that when the arrival of such a national hero was announced, His Grace would welcome them with alacrity. No such reaction resulted – although, after a long pause, it was announced that refreshments would be supplied to Lord Nelson and his party in the Park. This at-arm's-length hospitality caused grave offence, and was indignantly refused. Carola Oman has expressed the theory that the Duke's curious behaviour may have stemmed from the mortifying publicity of the previous year, occasioned by a lawsuit brought by Mr Charles Sturt against the Marquess of Blandford, accusing him of adultery with his wife: the newspapers had been full of the sordid details of the case and the embarrassing and ridiculous letters from Blandford to his lady love. The arrival, unannounced, at Blenheim, of persons (however eminent) linked publicly by scandal may have been more than the Duke could face.[28]

While the carriages were summoned, Lady Hamilton sought to soothe her hero's offended sensibilities by saying that Blenheim Palace had been Marlborough's reward because his sovereign was a woman, and 'women have great souls'; had she, Emma, been a queen, her tribute to Nelson would have been a principality on such a scale that Blenheim would seem only a kitchen garden by comparison. Nelson, the story goes, was touched to tears. One sees how Emma got where she did.[29]

Life within the sheltering walls of Blenheim was not immune from grief or mortification: Lord Henry's death in 1795 had been a heavy sorrow to bear; the deaths of two of the Marlboroughs' daughters – Charlotte in 1802, and Elizabeth in 1812 – cast sombre shadows; and the continuing worry and shame of Blandford's follies, extravagance and indebtedness must all have served to deepen the Duke's morose and taciturn attitude to life, and to further sour the Duchess. In 1805, the Marlboroughs lost their great friend Archbishop Moore; they would miss so much his accounts of important events – and to whom could they now turn for sage and sensible advice?

In 1811 the Duchess died. Queen Caroline had once said that she and Lady Carlisle were 'the two haughtiest and proudest women in England . . .';[30] one doubts the Queen meant this wholly as a compliment. Caroline Marlborough may have been a cold and difficult mother, but for nearly half a century she had made a good wife and chatelaine for her morose Duke, and he must have missed her close and constant companionship. She has left her own memorial at Blenheim: a pleasant row of almshouses for widows along the approach to Woodstock from Oxford, which she built and endowed in 1797.

A year or two after they had married, Horace Walpole had written of George and Caroline Marlborough that 'they are so inseparable, than when one goes, t'other will'. [31] In fact, the Duke was to survive his wife by six years; but after her death he withdrew further into ever-deepening silence. He had always been interested in astronomy, and now contemplating the galaxies became his chief occupation. He died very suddenly – he was found dead in bed on 30 January 1817, in his seventy-eighth year – and was succeeded by his middle-aged son, George, Marquess of Blandford, who is the principal subject of this book.

II

George

IT WAS INTO THIS WORLD within a world that George Spencer was
born on 6 March 1766, probably in London at Marlborough
House, for he was baptized at St Martin-in-the-Fields on 3 April.
As the eldest son, from birth he bore the courtesy title of Marquess
of Blandford. He was George and Caroline Marlborough's third
child – his sisters Caroline and Elizabeth being three and two years
old respectively at the time of his birth. He was never therefore a
solitary child; moreoever, sisters and brothers arrived with regularity
to swell the numbers in the Blenheim and Marlborough House
nurseries.

We first hear of George when he was between seven and nine
years old, during which period the Reverend William Coxe (who,
as we saw in the last chapter, was to judge life at Blenheim as 'ennui
itself') was his tutor. Evidently he was a tiresome charge, and
disciplining him was made harder by the fact that for a year or so,
when he was nine or ten, he was ill on and off. A long letter early in
1775 to the Duchess from that sage family counsellor, Dr Moore (at
this time, Dean of Canterbury), refers to 'Lord Blandford's fits'.[1]
Naturally, the Marlboroughs were greatly worried, and, as usual,
invoked their friend's advice: a personal servant of Lord Blandford
had been cheeky, and Mr Coxe seems to have been lacking in firmness
and presence of mind. Dr Moore had sensible and reassuring advice
to give, and, happily, the child's health improved. The Duke overall
had apparently been well satisfied with the young tutor's services,
and regretted his intention of leaving Blenheim, writing: 'I shall
never forget the care and attention you have ever shown to my poor
little boy in all his illnesses . . .'.[2]

After Coxe's departure, young William Mavor came up from Woodstock to teach the Palace children; and in 1776, Blandford left the cocoon of the schoolroom for the wider world of public school – Eton College, Windsor, where he was to remain until 1783. He seems to have been popular with his contemporaries there: at the beginning of the Michaelmas half, 1778, Dr Moore wrote to the Duchess: 'I hear with great pleasure the account the Eton boys give of him. Such accounts are always the least suspicious of any.'[3]

Dr Moore was, however, concerned about the self-imposed isolation of the folk at Blenheim. In 1778 he wrote to the Duke: 'I have seen with pain how much your Graces have both withdrawn yourselves from the world of late, and I have feared it would grow upon you . . .'. He added, perceptively: 'Your children are now growing up apace and they *must* mix with the world and how much better under your own eyes.'[4]

His injunctions then and later fell on deaf ears, and the enchanting group of lively children portrayed in Reynolds's great canvas were brought up not only sheltered from the rough tempests and hazards of life outside the encircling arms of family, but also without an example in their parents of the sense of public service, involvement and *noblesse oblige* which has ever been a characteristic of the British aristocracy.

Blandford was seventeen when he left Eton. His parents seem to have been in a quandary about his immediate programme – we learn from Dr Moore that a Grand Tour was discussed, but perhaps even then there were anxieties as to the wisdom of the giddy boy going abroad for so long a stretch: should he do so, Dr Moore opined he must be conducted by a 'man of Experience & decided Character'.[5] Moore's judgement of Blandford at this time is interesting: 'I own I think he has materials in him, that well attended to, will give your Graces satisfaction. It must not be forgotten that he is but Seventeen, & that his Duty & respect for your Graces are foundations on which much may be built.'[6]

In the event, George was sent to Paris for three months, accompanied by a tutor, a Mr Hinde. His cousin, George Herbert, commented to William Coxe (with whom he was to correspond for many years): 'What a man to send, a very good scholar, a very good University Tutor, but totally ignorant of any modern language except his own mother tongue, and as ignorant of the world. What strange people they [the Marlboroughs] are . . .'. He had obviously taken to his younger cousin, writing in the same letter: 'I like Lord Blandford vastly, he seems to possess so much of the man – and of the gentleman.'[7]

This tribute from a contemporary and equal is significant, and it is sad that we must follow the dimming of this bright image from the beautiful, sensitive-looking child Reynolds captured in 1778 and the manly youth, so seemingly ready and fit for the life and the great position which awaited him. It appears from contemporary sources[8] that the Duchess soon developed an antipathy for her eldest son; Lord Henry, some four years younger than Blandford, quickly gained parental approval and favour by his abilities and qualities, in contrast to his elder brother, whose mode of life and scrapes increasingly were to cause anxiety and despondence to his parents. Later – when Blandford's misdemeanours had put him for ever in parental bad books – their third son Francis, born in 1779, was after Henry's early death to become the repository of the Marlboroughs' frustrated hopes.

On his return from Paris, Blandford went in January 1784 to Christ Church, Oxford, where one hopes and assumes he enjoyed life, even if he did not distinguish himself academically. We do not hear of any nefarious doings while at the University, but *Jackson's Oxford Journal* printed an account of a balloon launching by the Marquess from a Mr Broderick's garden in St Giles in June 1784. Ballooning was greatly in fashion: in 1783 the first manned flight in a hot air balloon had taken place, the pioneers being the Montgolfier brothers, and the first Channel crossing by balloon would be made in 1785. The 'Machine' (as the newspaper describes it) launched by Blandford must have been very pretty, for it was 'stained with transparent sky colour, richly decorated'.[9] In 1786 Blandford was

14. 'The Old Manor House at Woodstock'. It is inscribed, 'Drawn and given to J. Malchair by the Marquis of Blandford. This is a very Early specimen of his lordship's performance in Drawing which nothing but my desire of knowing something about the stile of the Build. could have obtained from him.'

15. Bernini's fountain in its original position in the gardens made by the fourth Duke near the Grand Cascade, by Ferdinand Bauer.

16. *Overleaf*: Blenheim Palace: the Great Court and north front.

awarded an honorary MA – more a tribute to his noble lineage probably than to his scholastic attainments, since it was customary to give an honorary MA to gentleman-commoners.

The following year saw his coming-of-age, which was celebrated in great style:

> Last Tuesday being the Day on which the Marquis of Blandford came of age, the same was observed at Woodstock with every Demonstration of Joy. The Morning was ushered in with ringing of Bells, which continued incessantly through the Day. Convivial Associations were formed to dine at the different Inns in the Town, and in the Evening a splendid Entertainment was given by his Grace the Duke of Marlborough to the Corporation in their Council Chamber; and the Inhabitants were also plentifully regaled, and a Butt of Beer, with sufficient Quantity of Provisions ready dressed, distributed to each of the desmesne Towns. The Evening concluded with the utmost Harmony as well as convivial Festivity, and the Town of Woodstock was most brilliantly illuminated.[10]

Later that year Blandford was elected into the chamber and the borough of New Woodstock; he was a steward at Oxford Races, and began to take part in local life generally.

In 1790 the Duke presented his heir to the King for the first time, and in that same year Blandford entered Parliament, standing for the Oxfordshire seat held for the previous thirty years by his uncle, Lord Charles Spencer of Wheatfield, who made way (perhaps unwillingly) for his fledgling nephew. Six years later, however, Lord Charles was returned as the local member, Blandford eventually seeking another seat.

So far the bare chronological bones of our story indicate only that our young Marquess was following the established precedents for the heir to a great title. It would seem, however, that he was already the cause of dissatisfaction to his parents, for quite early on in his career George Blandford had shown signs of the extravagance which was

---

17. John, seventh Earl of Galloway, by Cosmo Alexander.

18. Anne Dashwood, seventh Countess of Galloway, with her daughter at the age of six, by Angelica Kauffmann, 1773.

to be an increasingly disastrous feature of his whole life. Many years later, Captain Gronow (1794–1865), a contemporary of Blandford's sons who spent a good deal of time with the family as a young man, was to write: 'Lord Blandford, afterwards fifth Duke of Marlborough, with many good and amiable qualities, was by far the most extravagant man I ever remember to have seen.'[11] (And the Captain must have seen a few in his time.) The Duke and Duchess, gravely disturbed by their eldest son's financial foolishness and irresponsibility, reacted as most parents in a similar situation do – they kept him on a tight rein as regards money. Gronow recorded that 'He lived in lodgings at Triphook's the bookseller in St James's Street, while his father and mother resided in great state at Marlborough House!'[12] But, predictably, far from practising economies, young Blandford resorted to moneylenders, who soon had him firmly in their grasp.

While his younger brother Henry's intelligence and diligence increasingly made him the preferred son, and marked him out for a distinguished career in diplomacy, Blandford was soon to show that he possessed gifts and interests of his own which, had they not been combined with traits of fecklessness and foolishness, might well have won him appreciation in his own and later generations as a patron of the arts and a man of cultivated and divers activities.

Blandford's propensity for gaiety and conviviality demonstrated itself at an early stage: in August 1790 it was reported that Oxford Town Hall had been enlarged at the young Marquess's expense to provide dancing room, and his father had weighed in with a gilt chandelier and chain.[13] And, aged barely twenty, Blandford had displayed his interest in rare books when in 1786 he bought the famous Bedford Missal for £698 – an early acquisition for a notable library he was to build up over the next forty years, putting him among the leading bibliophiles of his time.

He also had considerable musical talents which must have found outlets and encouragement at home in his youth, for singing and dancing were, as we know, an integral part of the theatrical activities at Blenheim. In 1789 Blandford spent several months on the continent (very possibly to evade the attentions of bailiffs); from Neuchâtel in early June he wrote a long, gossipy letter to his mother, describing how, in a place where he had no friends at all, he had found company and diversion with another Englishman – a captain in the militia who was a very good flute player: 'I am this instance come from playing quatuors [quartets] with him. We have played 10 hours today; on an average we play 6 hours every day . . .'.[14] Nor was he only a performer: the following year, the Marquess was to publish his own compositions for harpsichord, *XII Divertimenti per Cembalo*.

In this same letter, Blandford had expatiated on the kindness of other friends he had made abroad: 'He and Mme T. are really a second father and mother to me while I am separated from my . . . [word omitted] you and my dear Father. At Marseilles I was the spoilt child of his brother and sister and I am here not less of the same and know it . . .'. This letter casts a shaft of light on our hero at twenty-three: evidently he was at this period on tolerably good terms with his mother – a talented young man, companionable and warmly appreciative of simple family pleasures.

To Blandford's predilection for music and book-collecting must be added another accomplishment – painting. During his time at Oxford, J. B. Malchair (1731–1812), the water-colourist, had been leader of the band in the Music Room there; Blandford became a friend of Malchair, was influenced by him and worked in his style. The connection is easy to see, and although we have only two examples of the Marquess's work [see plate 14], he rates an entry in the *Dictionary of British Watercolour Artists up to 1920*.

✳◈✳◈✳

It was in 1790 that there burst on the world of society and fashion – to its infinite delight, and to the mortification of Blandford's family – *l'affaire* Gunning, or 'the Gunninghiad', as the saga was dubbed by Horace Walpole, whose letters chronicle the whole ridiculous scenario for our delectation.[15]

From the days of his youth the Marquess of Blandford had been regarded by the match-making mothers of society as a highly desirable 'catch'. Duchess Caroline also had her own plans for her son while he was still in his teens: her eye had lighted upon a banker's daughter, Sarah Child, rich, good and beautiful; but her scheme came to naught (Miss Child married the Earl of Westmorland). We do not know of any other matrimonial plans harboured by the

Duchess, but doubtless all candidates possessing the requisite qualities of wealth, birth and beauty (in that order) would have earned
the serious consideration of that haughty woman.

The 'catch-the-Marquess' stratagem that was to rivet London
society for a whole year, however, was devised and orchestrated by
a Mrs Susannah Gunning on behalf of her daughter Elizabeth –
although, according to Walpole, it had been the brainchild (if one
can so call it) of Gertrude, Duchess of Bedford, the ever disagreeable
and, by this time, senile mother of the Duchess of Marlborough.

The heroine of this scenario, Elizabeth, henceforth 'Gunnilda'
(as Walpole nicknamed her), was in her early twenties. The daughter
of Major General John Gunning and his wife Susannah, she was a
pretty girl, possessed of pleasing manners and an equable disposition.
John Gunning came of an old Irish family, the Gunnings of Castle
Coote, Co. Connaught. A successful soldier, he was chiefly known in
society as the younger brother of the beautiful Gunning sisters, who
had burst upon the social scene in 1750 when their parents came over
from Dublin to live in London, intent upon finding suitable husbands
for their three girls, Maria, Elizabeth and Kitty.

Maria and Elizabeth took London by storm, and for nigh on a
decade were the reigning beauties. When they first arrived, the
excitement caused by their loveliness and charm was such that they
were followed by crowds when they walked in the park – on one
such occasion, one of the sisters fainted and had to be taken home in
a chair. The two elder girls made brilliant matches, and Kitty a
satisfactory one. Maria married the Earl of Coventry in 1752, but
died of consumption eight years later. Elizabeth in the same year
married the Duke of Hamilton; he died in 1758, and a year later the
widowed Duchess married Colonel John Campbell, who was to
become the fifth Duke of Argyll; their eldest son, the Marquess of
Lorne, was one of the *dramatis personae* of 'the Gunninghiad'.

John Gunning was a mere boy of ten when his sisters married;
he grew to manhood with their praises and dazzling world advance-
ments ringing in his years. Educated at Westminster School, and
later gazetted as an ensign, he served for some time in Ireland, then
abroad during the Seven Years' War. As well as being a soldier, he
cultivated the superficial attributes of a gentleman's existence by
living beyond his means; he was also a debaucher and philanderer,

having made, upon his own reckoning, the conquest of two duchesses, fourteen countesses and four viscountesses (those of lower rank succumbing to his Irish charm being beyond the power of calculation). His father died in 1767, leaving an estate much encumbered by debt, and Elizabeth Argyll, greatly concerned for her brother, was instrumental in procuring for him a commission in the 49th Regiment of Foot. The following year, John Gunning married Susannah Minifie, the daughter of a Doctor of Divinity and a young woman of strong personality and undoubted talent as a romantic novelist. They had one child, Elizabeth, born in 1769.

After distinguishing himself in the War of American Independence, Gunning returned to England a Brigadier-General and was given command of the 65th Foot. His wife now decided that life in London was more suitable to the family of a 'General of the first Magnitude' (her words), and the Gunnings with their daughter Elizabeth removed themselves from Somerset to London, where they rented a house in St James's Place; they also leased a residence in Twickenham. Living in such style, Mrs and Miss Gunning soon were taking their part in London society, and Elizabeth became a *protégée* of the old Duchess of Bedford. Meanwhile, the General sought his company and amusements apart from his family and was not too much concerned with the activities of his wife and daughter.

Susannah Gunning's fertile imagination, which served her so well as a romantic novelist, now turned (with less happy results) to spinning a fantasy about her delightful and desirable daughter. Fired by the example of her sisters-in-law, who had – in Horace Walpole's words – been 'Countessed and double-Duchessed',[16] she nursed the most dazzling ambition for her own 'lambkin'. Two of the most desirable catches in London at this time were Gunnilda's first cousin, the 23-year-old Marquess of Lorne, and the heir to Blenheim, the Marquess of Blandford, aged twenty-four. Gunnilda had for some time nurtured affectionate feelings for her cousin (we do not know if they were reciprocated), and a match had been mooted, although the Duchess of Argyll seems to have been unaware of her niece's intentions; but Mrs Gunning was deemed to have preferred the idea of Blandford as a future son-in-law – no doubt either would have been acceptable.

During the summer of 1790 rumours circulated to the effect that

Gunnilda had been the recipient of many letters from Lord Blandford, and that he had proposed marriage to her. Horace Walpole at first discounted these tales as 'a foolish notion . . . an idea so improbable that even the luck of the Gunnings cannot make one believe it';[17] but on 2 August 1790 he was writing to his friend, Miss Mary Berry:

> Though I cannot yet believe it will be, there is certainly much more probability than I thought of another Gunning becoming a duchess . . . The Duchess of Gloucester says that Mrs Howe, who is apt to be well informed, does not believe it. My incredulity is still better founded, and hangs on the Duchess of Marlborough's wavering weathercock-hood, which always rests at forbidding the banns . . .

According to Horace Walpole, the Duchess had forbidden the marriage of Lord Blandford to Lady Caroline Waldegrave, and the marriage of one of her daughters to Lord Strathaven.[18] A week later, Walpole was writing to General Conway of the much-talked-of match: 'Lo! it took its rise solely in poor old Bedford's dotage, that still harps on conjunctions copulative, but now disavows it, as they say, on a remonstrance from her daughter [the Duchess of Marlborough].'[19]

For the greater part of this summer of 1790, Lord Blandford was out of town; letters from him were said to continue to arrive addressed to Gunnilda, but malicious tongues wagged, and rumours abounded that the letters were forgeries. By the autumn, Walpole was tiring of 'talking of the silly Miss and her match',[20] when his flagging interest was revived by the information that Miss Gunning, while at the house of his friends and correspondents, the Misses Agnes and Mary Berry, announced that she was to be married to Lord Blandford on 20 October.[21] However, the date came and went without the predicted marriage taking place, and Walpole wrote to Mary Berry on 8 November: 'The Marquisate is just where it was – to be and not to be . . .'.[22]

Meanwhile, the General was quoted in the newspapers as claiming descent from Charlemagne, in order to prove his daughter's worthiness for any match; this caused much ribaldry, and Walpole signed himself to Agnes Berry 'Yours etc., Eginhart, Secretary to Charlemagne and the Princess Gunnilda his daughter'.[23] The ludicrous statement proved to have been inserted by 'the Minifie' (Mrs Gunning), and when he learned of it the General replied with some dignity (and, one feels, unconscious wit) : 'It is true, I am well born, but I know no such family in Ireland as the Charlemagnes.'[24] A thoroughly good time was had by all – except, that is, the principals in this veritable *opéra bouffe*.

While this saga was unfolding, an event of deep sadness to many took place: Elizabeth, Duchess of Argyll, afflicted by the same malady of consumption that had killed her sister, Maria Coventry, died in London in December 1790 aged fifty-seven. Ever the generous and kindly champion of her family, she had taken her niece Elizabeth's part when malicious tongues wagged. Despite the Duke's grief, he continued to give his support and counsel to his wife's relations, and the Gunning family was often to be seen coming and going at Argyll House.

It afterwards emerged that Miss Gunnilda's elaborate design in counterfeiting letters from one Marquess was all part of a plan, concocted by both mother and daughter, to bring a declaration from the other lordling, the Marquess of Lorne; this artful subterfuge, however, was destined to failure. Early in 1791 General Gunning felt impelled, in the interests of his daughter's honour, to enquire of the young Marquess of Blandford as to what his intentions might be: Blandford strenuously denied having any intentions. On the letters being produced, he was forced to acknowledge that some of them had been written by him but denied that these expressed any affection, and roundly declared the others to be forgeries. Gunnilda, however, stuck to her story, insisting that she had received every encouragement from the Duke and Duchess of Marlborough. Her father thereupon caused her to write a 'narrative' of the whole affair, which he despatched by hand of his groom to Blenheim. Back, by the same messenger, came a letter, ostensibly from His Grace the Duke of Marlborough, in which the Duke averred that it had long been the wish of both himself and the Duchess to see their son married 'to some amiable woman', that they had been charmed by Miss Gunning, and that it was with

> infinite satisfaction we discovered Blandford's sentiments similar to our own . . . and, from the conduct of both

himself and his family, yourself and Miss Gunning had undoubtedly *every* right to look on a marriage as certain – indeed when I left town last summer, I regarded her as my future daughter, and I must say it is with sorrow I relinquish the idea. The actions of young men are not always to be accounted for; and it is with regret I acknowledge my son has been particular unaccountable in his . . .[25]

Delighted with the contents of this letter, General Gunning hastened round with it to Argyll House. But now some doubts set in; it all seemed too good to be true, the seals on the letter appeared to have been tampered with, and there were further suspicious discrepancies. A messenger was despatched to Lord Henry Spencer, the Marlborough's second son, begging him to repair to Argyll House, which he duly did. On inspecting the letter, he declared that the handwriting bore not the slightest resemblance to his father's hand. The whole ludicrous story was now revealed: Gunnilda had persuaded a cousin, Mrs Bowen, to prevail upon her husband, Captain Bowen, to copy the letter she (Gunnilda) had composed as from the Duke; she had then bribed her father's groom (who made a full confession) to deliver the forged missive; furthermore, Lord Blandford's already suspect letters were admitted to be fakes contrived by 'the Minifie' and Princess Gunnilda.

Upon the unfolding of this story, the General was, quite naturally, enraged: he had been duped from start to finish, and had been made the laughing stock of society. When the whole idiocy and enormity of the hoax was borne in on him, he summarily turned his wife and daughter out of their house in St James's Place. Gunnilda received sanctuary from the Duchess of Bedford, for not only was her father's door now shut to her, but she and her mother were *personae non grata* also at Argyll House. Walpole recounted how, faithful to her *protégée* and unabashed by the scandal, 'that crazy old Bedford exhibits Miss every morning on the Causeway in Hyde Park'.[26] Presently he reported: 'The Signora and her Infanta now *for privacy* are retired into St James's Street, next door Brooks's, whence it is supposed Miss will angle for unmarried marquises . . .'.[27]

Mrs Gunning, however, was not one to surrender without a fight: Horace Walpole, still unwearied, wrote to Mary Berry on 18 February 1791:

Here is a shocking (not a fatal) codicil to Gunnilda's story. But first I should tell you, that two days after the explosion, the Signora Madre took a postchaise-and-four, and drove to Blenheim; but, not finding the Duke and Duchess there, she inquired where the Marquis was, and pursued him to Sir H. Dashwood's;* finding him there, she began about her poor daughter – but he interrupted her, said there was an end put to all that, and desired to lead her to her chaise, which he insisted on doing, and did . . .[28]

He further told how the 'Signora Madre' had attempted to persuade Lord Blandford to get into her chaise, which he would on no account do for fear of being whisked off to Gretna Green and married by force! On being pressed by the lady to sign a paper saying that all was over between him and Gunnilda, he (Blandford) refused, saying: 'Madam, nothing was ever begun.'[29] For once our hero seems to have behaved with both sense and dignity.

But still the Gunning women persevered: in March 'Minifie' Gunning wrote and published a letter of over two hundred pages to her long-suffering brother-in-law, the Duke of Argyll. In Gunnilda's own narrative to the Marlboroughs, the 'ingenuous maid', Walpole recounted, had confessed that 'though she had not been able to resist so dazzling an offer, her heart was still her cousin's, the other Marquis.'[30] Now, after the fatal disclosures and the total discrediting of both mother and daughter, the undaunted pair apparently and incredibly still nurtured hopes of Lord Lorne. The 'Minifie's' epistle consisted of a passionate and verbose vindication of her 'glorious darling' and the 'unspottable innocence of that harmless lambkin':[31] the forgeries and deceptions, according to her, had been the work of the Bowens. The term 'minific' was subsequently coined to describe similar flights of hyperbole. At the end of March 1791, mother and daughter departed abruptly for France in order to avoid prosecution for libel by Captain Bowen, Walpole wryly remarking, '. . . in France there is not a marquis left to marry her.'[32] However, in July he reported that the dreadful pair were 'not only re-settled in St James's Street as boldly as ever, but constantly with old Bedford, who exults in having regained them . . .'.[33]

---

* Sir Henry Dashwood lived at Kirtlington Park, about six miles from Blenheim.

Society, gossip-writers and Grub Street continued for several months to circulate versions of this diverting affair, extracting the maximum fun, malice and scandal from it all. A cartoon was published called 'The New System of Gunning', showing 'Miss, astride a cannon . . . firing a volley of forged letters at the castle of Blenheim, and old Gertrude, emaciated and withered, and very like, lifting up her hoop to shelter injured innocence, as she calls her.'[34] Horace Walpole, who was greatly preoccupied by events in France where the Revolution was gathering its savage momentum, judged Gunnilda would soon be forgotten yet had to admit at the end of February 1791: 'Still she has been a great resource this winter.'[35]

Presently, a delightful ditty was published, and had everyone singing to the tune of 'The Cow with the Crumpled Horn':

This is the note that nobody wrote;
This is the groom that carried the note that nobody wrote;
This is Ma'am Gunning who was so very cunning to examine the groom that carried the note that nobody wrote.
This is Ma'am Bowen to whom it was owing, that Miss Minify Gunning was so very cunning to examine the groom that carried the note that nobody wrote.
These are the Marquises shy of the horn, who caused the maiden all-for-*Lorn*, to become on a sudden so tatter'd and torn, that Miss Minify Gunning was so very cunning to examine the groom, etc.
These are the two Dukes whose sharp rebukes made the two Marquises shy of the horn, and caused the maiden all-for-*Lorn*, etc.
This is the General somewhat too bold, whose head was so hot, though his heart was so cold, who proclaim'd himself single before it was meet, and his wife and his daughter turn'd into the street, to please the two Dukes, whose sharp rebukes, etc. etc. etc.[36]

After the summer of 1791, the female Gunnings disappeared from public view. Mrs Gunning died in 1800, while after all her high hopes Elizabeth married an Irishman, Captain James Plunkett, in 1803; she died in 1823. As for her father, the disreputable but unfortunate General John Gunning, the immediate result of all the publicity surrounding *l'affaire* was to alert his many creditors: his own lifestyle, combined with the extravagance of his wife and daughter, had dramatically increased his usual indebtedness, and he was faced with insolvency. He was rescued from this plight by James Duberly, a contractor and regimental clothier. Prosperous, decent and gentle-manly, and with a pretty, well-bred wife, Rebecca, Duberly had in the course of business transactions become a friend of the General's, who spent a good deal of time in the clothier's large and agreeable house in Soho Square. Horrified at his friend's predicament, Duberly hastened round to St James's Place and himself paid off all the creditors and, since the house and the servants had to be disposed of, invited John Gunning to stay at Soho Square. The reward Duberly was to receive for his generous action was the seduction of his wife by the General: he brought a case, and Gunning (who had by this time fled with Rebecca to Naples) was fined £5000.

One further event that was to be attributed to the Gunning saga was the sudden marriage of the Marquess of Blandford in the early autumn of 1791. Rumours had started to circulate early in September that Lord Blandford was about to be wed: Horace Walpole, of course, knew about them and on 11 September regaled Miss Mary Berry (who had been the chief recipient of the greater part of 'the Gunninghiad') with news of the 'sudden match patched up for Lord Blandford, with little more art than was employed by the fair Gunnilda. It is with Lady Susan Stewart, Lord Galloway's daughter, contrived by, and at the house of her relation and Lord Blandford's friend, Sir Henry Dashwood, and it is to be so instantly, that her Grace, his mother, will scarce have time to forbid the banns . . .'.[37] He was right; a few days later, on 15 September, George Blandford was married to Susan Stewart.

It was assumed, by the world at large, that this precipitate marriage was the direct result of the Gunning affair, and that the Marquess, having been unjustly implicated in the scandal, had been so alarmed by the lengths to which match-making mothers and their daughters were prepared to go that he had taken fright and was seeking sanctuary in the holy estate of matrimony. But the true reason for Blandford's sudden action lay in the fact that he had fallen passionately in love with a beautiful young married woman – Lady Mary Anne Sturt.

Lady Mary Anne Ashley Cooper was the daughter of the fourth Earl of Shaftesbury and his second wife, the Hon. Mary Bouverie. In 1788, when she was twenty, she had married Charles Sturt, a Member of Parliament for Dorset and the owner of a beautiful property, Crichel House, near Wimborne. Charles Sturt and Lord Blandford were friends – they had originally met at St Giles, the home of Lord and Lady Shaftesbury, only a few miles from Crichel. Invited by his friends, Blandford made frequent visits to Dorset and, within a year of the Sturts' marriage, he and Mary Anne had conceived a deep passion for each other: Charles Sturt always averred that this disturbing development was completely undetected by him. Realizing that the discovery of their love affair would bring ruin and disgrace – as in the long run it was destined to do – Blandford took the course which others before and since have tried: he married one woman in an attempt to obliterate the love he felt for another.

III

Susan

LORD BLANDFORD'S BRIDE, Lady Susan Stewart, was the third of the sixteen children of John, seventh Earl of Galloway, and his wife Anne. The Stewarts of Galloway are one of Scotland's most ancient families, descending from Scotland's High Stewards who were of Norman origin. Loyal supporters of the Stuart Kings, they owed their Barony in 1607 and the Earldom of Galloway in 1623 to James I and Charles I respectively. For over six hundred years Stewarts have inhabited that broad and gently undulating peninsula in south-west Scotland which lies between Wigtown Bay to the east and Luce Bay to the west. Today, to a traveller from the crowded south it seems remote – two hundred years ago it must have been as a world apart.

Although the Stewart family has lived for centuries in Wigtownshire, Galloway House, on the south-east side of the peninsula, has been the seat of the Earls of Galloway only since the middle of the eighteenth century; grey and imposing, the house (built by Susan's grandfather, Alexander, sixth Earl of Galloway between the years 1740–2) stands in splendid isolation on the edge of rolling pastoral countryside and within a few hundred yards of the sea. In our Susan Stewart's time it was less ponderous and gaunt in appearance than now, two massive wings having been added in the nineteenth century.

Although it was the sixth Earl who built the great mansion, it was his son John (1736–1806) who developed the park and woodlands which lie to the west and south-west of the house. Writing in 1801 to his factor, James Nish, he adjures him: 'Now Nish, 'tho you see I am an Economist about buying trees, yet I must beg you to be extravagant in beautifying about Galloway House, all my children are so partial to it that I want to make it as pretty as possible & soon tho' I shd. throw away a couple of hundred extraordinary.'[1] The plantations he made, added to by later generations, still survive to beautify and shelter the property.

In Scotland, as the great nobleman, landowner and Lord Lieutenant, the seventh Earl's days would have been agreeably filled with numerous ploys. He was evidently an enthusiast: an obituary notice described how 'his active mind and frame he never spared; he did nothing by halves.'[2] While he busily improved his own property and was a keen agriculturalist, he was awake to the needs of his country: he developed the nearby village and seaport of Garlieston, at one time directing his children's tutor, the Reverend Eliezir Williams, to investigate and to report to him on the dangerous state of the harbour and how it might be improved.

We do not know what was Lord Galloway's standing in the county, but at some stage he fell foul of the spleen and sharp pen of Scotland's great poet, Robert Burns (1759–96), whose antipathy probably was based more on political prejudice than personal knowledge, for the Earl refused to receive the radical poet at Galloway House; peer and ploughman also clashed in local politics in 1793–5, when Galloway successfully supported Gordon of Balmashie against Burns's *protégé* candidate in the contest for the Stewartry of Kirkcudbrightshire. Burns gave vent to his ire in verse on viewing 'the Beautiful Seat of Lord Galloway' from across Wigtown Bay:

> What dost thou in that mansion fair?
>   Flit, Galloway, and find
> Some narrow, dirty, dungeon cave,
>   The picture of thy mind!

And on another occasion:

> No Stewart art thou, Galloway,
>   The Stewarts all were brave;
> Besides, the Stewarts were but fools,
>   Not one of them a knave.

And when the poet heard (or imagined) that the noble object of his scorn might seek to visit some retribution upon him:

To the Same,
On the author being threatened with his resentment

> Spare me thy vengeance, Galloway,
>   In quiet let me live:
> I ask no kindness at thy hand,
>   For thou has none to give.

Many people thought that 'Robbie' had become rather over-excited, and Lord Galloway, far from seeking to revenge himself, preferred to rise above these vicious attacks and was reported as saying, 'it would not become him when his good old master the King despised and disregarded the paltry attacks of a Peter Pindar [the English satirist] to feel himself hurt by those of a licentious, rhyming ploughman.'[3]

But the overall impression we receive of Lord Galloway remains that of an unlikeable personality of inferior abilities. His father, the sixth Earl, renowned for his political intriguing and for his Jacobite sympathies, had doted on his son and heir, a fact remarked upon by James Boswell, who in 1762 wrote of him: 'Lord Garlies is a little man with a great flow of animal spirits. He has been indulged and even idolised by Lord Galloway which has given him a petulant forwardness that cannot fail to disgust people of sense and delicacy. He is also got into the political tract but as his parts are but inferior he will probably never equal his father.'[4]

Boswell's severe appraisal of Lord Garlies would seem to have been only just. During the forty years or so of his involvement in the English political scene he became known as a self-seeking opportunist who displayed an almost fanatical zeal in seeking to promote his family interests.

As Viscount Garlies, he sat successively from 1761 for two English seats. After his father's death in 1773, the seventh Earl became a representative Scottish peer; in 1775 he was created a Knight of the Thistle. Politically, Galloway was a strong Tory, attaching himself to the grouping round the Duke of Bedford, Earl Gower and Lord Grenville; his activities seem to have been confined to lobbying those with power for place or preferment. He held various minor government offices, and from 1784 was a Lord of the Bedchamber to George III. But his greatest wish was to be given an English peerage, and as Lord Garlies in 1766 he had solicited the influence of both the Duke of Bedford and the Duke of Marlborough in procuring for him this title: 'It is my *omnium*, the only thing in life I wish for,'[5] he wrote to Bedford. It was not until 1796 that Galloway gained his '*omnium*', and was created Baron Stewart of Garlies, by which time his daughter Susan had been married for several years to Marlborough's heir.

Lord Galloway married twice: his first wife, a daughter of the Earl of Warwick, died within a year of their marriage; a year later, in 1764, Lord Garlies (as he then was) married Anne, daughter of Sir James Dashwood Bt of Kirtlington Park in Oxfordshire. This second marriage was to be long and fruitful, and if we have retained a disagreeable impression of the Earl as a public personality, he had the reputation at least of being an exemplary husband and father. Of the sixteen children Anne Galloway bore her husband – eight sons and eight daughters – fourteen survived to adulthood. Of this large family, our heroine, Susan, the third child, was born on 11 April 1767.

The Galloways divided their time between Wigtownshire and London, where they had a house, No. 19 Charles Street, leading off St James's Square. (The eighteenth-century house in what is now Charles II Street was demolished in 1912.) In 1775 Lord Galloway obtained a renewal of the Crown lease of his London house and acquired that of the house next door, and on this combined site he built a new residence, designed by John Johnson. Apart from the many interests and obligations of his political and court life which required his presence in London, the Earl was a keen opera-goer and was, we are told, 'generally to be found, when in town, in the pit, close to the orchestra, loud in applause of any favourite performer.'[6]

The building operations of both the sixth and seventh Earls of Galloway – of the father who built the new house in Scotland, and of the son who rebuilt the family's town residence – combined with other unproductive investments, and the seventh Earl's lavish

19. George, Marquess of Blandford aged fifteen, by John Downman, 1781.
20. *Overleaf*: Galloway House, Garlieston, from a painting on a snuffbox by George, Marquess of Blandford.
21. St James's Street, 1792. On the left is Boodles', on the right Brooks's, now as then fashionable men's clubs and largely unchanged in aspect.

SYMPTOMS of AFFECTION or a Specimen of MARTIAL PROWESS

The Seige of BLENHEIM—
—or the new system of GUNNING, discoverd

London life and activities, resulted over a period of time in the
selling off of many of their Wigtownshire lands, and in the consequent diminution of the family's fortunes, which never recovered.[7]

Although we do not know whether Susan was born in Scotland
or in England, certainly the greater part of the Stewart children's
childhood and youth was passed in Wigtownshire, their education
being taken care of by tutors. It is through the memoir published by
the son of one of these tutors – the Reverend Eliezir Williams (1754–
1820) – that we get glimpses of the Galloways at this time. Williams
was their tutor from 1783 for about twelve or thirteen years; his
connection with the family had come about in 1780, when George,
Lord Garlies, then a lad of twelve, went as a midshipman in HMS
Cambridge, the ship being then under the command of his uncle,
Admiral Keith Stewart. Eliezir Williams performed a dual task,
being at once ship's chaplain and tutor to the young nobleman. The
family must have formed a liking and a good opinion of him, for a
few years later he relinquished his chaplaincy to take charge of the
education of Garlies' brothers and sisters at Galloway House. A
large and lively troupe he must have found them all, and so close
in age as to be at first confusing: indeed Garlies suggested to Williams
that it would be a good idea to have 'a label affixed to each one to
prevent mistakes'.[8]

Some of the Stewart boys were educated at home up to university age. George, the heir, as we have seen, rather unusually for an
elder son had followed his uncle's footsteps by entering the navy,
where he made a gallant and distinguished career for himself; as a
Captain at the taking of Guadeloupe in 1794 he was severely wound-
ed in the face, and Mr Pitt remarked: 'One would almost lose a

22. *Previous page*: Major General Gunning. by Catherine Read.

23. Elizabeth Gunning, Duchess of Hamilton and Argyll, by Francois-Hubert
Drouais, 1763.

24. Catherine (Kitty) Gunning, by Francis Cotes.

25. Maria Gunning, Countess of Coventry, by Francis Cotes.

26. *Opposite*: 'Symptoms of Affection, or A Specimen of Marital Prowess', by
Isaac Cruikshank, 1791. General Gunning puts his wife and daughter into the
street.

27. 'The Siege of Blenheim, or The New System of Gunning Discovered' by
James Gillray, 1791.

Nose to have gained such honour as Lord Garlies has acquired.'[9] William, the next in age, became a soldier, joining the army as an ensign in 1786, at the age of twelve. After a long, brilliant and brave military career, he became a Lieutenant-General in 1813; he was a close friend of Lord Nelson, and was instrumental in founding the Rifle Brigade.

The third of the surviving sons, Charles, went to Oxford straight from Galloway House in 1792, aged seventeen; he was later to go into Holy Orders and, after serving for many years in North America, in 1825 became Bishop of Quebec. Of Montgomery, born in 1780, we know little but the two youngest brothers, Edward and James, were the only Stewarts in this generation recorded as going to public school in England: they both started at Charterhouse in 1796, the same year which saw Williams' departure from his post as tutor to the family.

It is evident that Susan came of a lively and gallant stock. She and her sisters must have had a very good education, sharing as they did lessons with their brothers, and one can imagine a happy, carefree childhood in Scotland, by the sea, with so many companions for games and sports. Susan seems to have been quite athletic: her brother William (the soldier), writing to their tutor from Netherby in Yorkshire where he and Susan were staying with their elder married sister, Lady Catherine Graham, sends a message: 'Susan, also with her kind remembrance, will thank you to desire Daniel to order Grant, the bow and arrow maker, to send the arrows, enclosed in a tin quiver, to Galloway House.'[10] Brought up so much in the countryside, the young Stewarts were a hardy, healthy lot, and the keen Scottish seaside air must have contributed to the fact that so many of them survived the perils of childhood illnesses.

A delightful glimpse of life at Galloway House is contained in a letter written by Susan's brother George, when eighth Earl, to his brother-in-law, the Hon. Arthur Paget, whose sister, Lady Jane Paget, he had married in 1797. The date of the letter is 18 September 1811, and the seventh Earl had been dead some five years, so that a younger generation were now installed in the family home; it was thirty-odd years since George and Susan had been youngsters there, but the ploys and pleasures described in this letter would scarcely have changed. George Galloway wrote:

I much regret you could not with Augusta [Paget's wife]
visit us this Autumn and stay thro' the Winter, this is an
admirable Winter Residence, altho' the Waves roar and
break into our Garden, we are perfectly sheltered notwithstanding and always dry, and bathing in a Machine
on Sands or diving off Rocks every day. My children are
not the same since their residence here, being so improved
in Health. Now what have you to do so material that need
prevent you coming Bag and Baggage Here for the Winter,
and before which sets in we will if you please (partie
quarrée*) take a trip to Inverary; afterwards growl and
find fault over a good Sea Coal fire with the Newspapers
at all parties, a grand privilege I conceive, and applicable
to Britain alone. I have a Billiard Table, an old Library,
a little game of all sorts, and much wild scenery to employ
both time and Imagination, and nobody to interrupt us
or to annoy; and Woodcocks are coming. Now, my dear
fellow, tho' the distance alarms, a long residence thro' the
Winter compensates the fatigue and trouble, and when the
Sun returns we will both Families together break forth
from our Retreat, and enter the World again, for this
retired Corner is really a Retreat, tho' all chearful and
gay within itself.

October is the best month in the year to travel. How
Jane would enjoy the idea of our united Families for one
comfortable winter; as you may suppose here are plenty
of Rooms etc. calling for Inhabitants and indeed society is
all that we require; think upon all this before you say No . . .

Galloway[11]

What a lovely invitation! And what a pleasant picture it paints
of a winter's programme – one way and another there would not
have been many dull or idle days. We wonder if this delightful
suggestion was ever taken up.

But if the young and growing Stewarts of the generation with
which we are concerned, who were 'so partial' to Galloway House,
spent the greater part of their time there, we need not suppose them
to have been mere country bumpkins. On their visits to London
they lived in the handsome new house built by their father in fashion-

---

* *partie carrée*, a pleasure party consisting of two gentlemen and two ladies.

able St James's; the seventh Earl was a man of varied interests, a representative Scottish peer and a member of the Royal Household, so as they grew up the children would have heard public affairs and events discussed. Very probably, also, their father would have shared his musical tastes with his children; and someone at some time must have taught Susan how to draw and paint flowers, for she was to become an accomplished artist in this genre.

The family had relations in England – Lady Galloway was one of the three daughters of Sir James Dashwood, second Baronet (1715–79), and his wife Elizabeth Spencer of Rendlesham in Suffolk. Originally from Dorset and Somerset, Sir James in the 1740s built a magnificent Palladian mansion standing on high ground east of the Cherwell in Oxfordshire – Kirtlington Park. With the exception of Blenheim Palace (only a few miles away), Kirtlington was held to be the finest habitation in the county, Horace Walpole remarking wryly in 1753: 'I passed by Sir James Dashwood's, a vast new house situated so high that it seems to stand for the county as well as himself.'[12]

In 1752, Sir James signed a contract with Lancelot Brown for the landscaping of the grounds and parkland at Kirtlington; Brown's work there lasted about four years and cost his patron nearly £1000. One wonders if the fine 'improvements' at his neighbour's property may have fired the imagination and spirit of emulation of the young Duke of Marlborough, who succeeded in 1758, and encouraged him also to call in the great Capability a few years later for Langley Park and Blenheim.

Sir James had three daughters, two of whom made noble marriages: Elizabeth, the eldest, marrying the fourth Duke of Manchester, and Anne marrying Lord Garlies, later seventh Earl of Galloway; Catherine married a Mr Lucius Knightly of Fawsley. Sir James must have been very rich, for as well as building such a handsome house, his three daughters were well endowed on marriage. It was not only fortunate for the girls that their father was so wealthy – his heir, Henry Watkin Dashwood, was a big spender, and the last years of Sir James's life were clouded by his son's extravagances: in 1775, when Henry was thirty, his father paid his debts to the tune of £25,000, and such was the continuing drain of debt that some of the rooms at Kirtlington House could not be completed.

Blenheim and Kirtlington being so near each other, it was natural for the two families to be on friendly terms. But although Henry Watkin Dashwood, who succeeded to the baronetcy in 1779, was a near-contemporary of the fourth Duke of Marlborough, the friendship in this generation seems to have been between Sir Henry and Blandford, twenty-one years his junior, rather than with his father – who in any case would have found little in common with this spendthrift baronet. Blandford perhaps sought refuge from parental supervision and criticism with the Dashwoods (a large family, like the Spencers); and Sir Henry's extravagant ways and the inconvenience of his own indebtedness may have made him a sympathetic friend to his younger neighbour – and perhaps an unfortunate example. At any rate, it was at Kirtlington House that Blandford took refuge at the height of the Gunning fiasco, and to where the 'Signora Madre' Gunning pursued him with her vain protestations. It was here also that we learn from Horace Walpole that the match between George Blandford and Susan Stewart was 'patched up' in the autumn of 1791.

Although the marriage itself was evidently arranged in haste, it is more than likely that Blandford and his bride already knew each other. Lady Susan Stewart was Sir Henry Dashwood's niece, and nothing would have been more natural than for her to have visited her English relations in Oxfordshire from time to time, and so to have met the young Spencers from Blenheim.

It will come as no surprise to the reader to learn that the match was not to the liking of the Marlboroughs. Duchess Caroline in particular was displeased: perhaps it was the haste with which the marriage was decided upon and planned, without their consultation; perhaps the Duke and Duchess did not know Lady Susan, and although she was well-born, she was almost certainly not rich. However, his parents should have counted their blessings: given their son's volatility, he might well have made a disastrous misalliance; and had they known (which is improbable) of his recent passionate entanglement with a married woman, with all its potential for public scandal, their attitude might well have been very different. That ever sensible adviser Dr Moore, now Archbishop of Canterbury, weighed in as peace-maker; he was glad (and no doubt felt the Marlboroughs should have been so too) that Lord Blandford had married a girl of rank and good connections; he urged the Duke and Duchess to receive the young couple as soon as possible and to give them 'every mark of your love and forgiveness'.[13] They certainly did not immediately follow this sensible, humane advice.

We have yet another source of information on the Marlboroughs' affairs at this time in the correspondence between Lord Auckland and Lord Henry Spencer, who had adopted diplomacy as his career. On his appointment as Ambassador to The Hague, Auckland had taken Lord Henry with him as a member of his staff; but at this date, soon after Blandford's marriage to Susan Stewart, he was back in England and staying at Lambeth Palace. Writing to Henry Spencer in The Hague, the Ambassador regaled him with the family gossip, gleaned after a visit the Archbishop had paid to Blenheim:

> Do you know that previous to the marriage Lord Galloway went to Blenheim: 'God help me, my lady duchess, do intercede with my lord duke to make the young people happy; a word from you would do everything, you have such influence.' – 'What do you mean?' – 'Ay, God help me! it ought to be so; happily your grace governs the duke, as my lady governs me, and as my daughter will govern Lord Blandford.' This is a small part of a long dialogue which I have heard reported, and the rest was equally good though ineffectual.[14]

Readers will not be surprised that this warmhearted, if somewhat eccentric intervention on behalf of the young people was to no avail.

His parents' disapproval notwithstanding, George Blandford and Susan Stewart were married at her parents' house in Charles Street by Special Licence on 15 September 1791. The Duke and Duchess of Marlborough were not present; they were at Blenheim, where they had been visited by Archbishop Moore a few days earlier – perhaps this good and kindly friend of the family had endeavoured to soften their stagnant hearts and to persuade them to attend the wedding. At any rate, Dr Moore returned to London on the 14th and sealed the Special Licence;[15] the witnesses signing the register were Lord and Lady Galloway, the bride's parents.

Because of the short time available for more elaborate arrangements, and the fact that the marriage was under a cloud of disapproval emanating from Blenheim, the ceremony was a quiet affair.

In any case, weddings at that time were not, as now, occasions for great festivities or entertainments to which many people were bidden; even royal weddings were conducted in private, and marriages frequently took place, as this one did, in the home of the bride.

Immediately after the ceremony, the Marquess and Marchioness of Blandford set off for Kimbolton Castle in Huntingdonshire, one of the homes of the fifth Duke of Manchester (Susan's first cousin on her mother's side), which the Dowager Duchess had put at the young couple's disposal and which was to be their home for the first year of their marriage. It would seem that Susan's family rallied round to help, in marked contrast to the unbending attitude of the Marlboroughs; it must have been sadly mortifying for Blandford.

The representations made by Lord Galloway to the Duchess of Marlborough before the marriage had fallen on deaf ears, and it must have been the mark and measure of the Duke's disapproval that he did not make available, or otherwise provide for, a home for his heir on his marriage; furthermore, the allowance he had made to Blandford when he left Oxford (which anyway had proved totally inadequate even for his bachelor needs) was not increased. All this interesting information we glean from the newspapers of the day – then, as now, keenly concerned in people's private affairs and financial arrangements.

Not only was the Marlboroughs' attitude to the newly-weds a matter of comment in the press – other members of their family and friends thought the Duke and Duchess's continuing disapproval both ridiculous and embarrassing. On 20 March 1792, Lord Auckland, again writing to Lord Henry in The Hague, ends a long letter: 'We have not seen the duke and duchess, but we mean soon to attack them violently for a visit. I understand that they have seen your brother, but have not seen his lady, which I think odd.'[16]

So evidently did Lady Pembroke, Blandford's much loved and tactful Aunt Elizabeth, who intervened behind the scenes to good effect, so that before the Blandfords made their obeisances to the Queen at the Drawing Room on 25 March, some sort of reconciliation had been contrived. Lord and Lady Blandford, together with his sister Caroline and her husband, Lord Clifden, whom she had recently married, were all presented to the Queen by the Duke and

Duchess of Marlborough. A few days later, on 30 March, *The Times* carried a report of a 'splendid Ball and supper' given by the Queen at Buckingham House; among those listed were the Duke and Duchess of Marlborough and the Marquess and Marchioness of Blandford.

But this reconciliation between the Marlboroughs and their son and daughter-in-law was of short duration, and by the following year the Duke was barely on speaking terms with Blandford. We get a glimpse of the tensions within the family in a letter from Lord Henry Spencer to Lord Auckland, written on 17 August 1793 from Copenhagen, where he was now *en poste*:

> I learn from my sister Elizabeth that my father is to leave Brightelmstone [Brighton] as soon as the Oxford Militia arrives there. He will hardly go to Blenheim because my brother is to be the steward of the Oxford races. It is a sad inconvenience in England that people can go to no place without meeting relations and friends. I am determined not to add to the embarrassment, and shall keep out of the way till I am sure that my presence and that of the rest of us will be perfectly agreeable.[17]

It is curious that race meetings seem to have provided occasions when the family's propensity for 'being difficult' was to the fore: two years earlier, Mrs Lybbe Powys, referring in her diary to the Oxford Races, had commented: 'The Duke and Duchess of Marlborough would not (as usual) attend the diversion, but endeavour'd to keep company from going; but, to the universal satisfaction, the balls were never so brilliant. How strange that those parents seem ever to act contrary to most others, by giving dissatisfaction instead of pleasure to their children.'[18]

George and Susan's first real home was Culham Court, near Henley, which they rented; some three years later they moved to another leased house – Bill Hill, near Wokingham in Berkshire. We have few details of these houses, and they lived in each for so brief a time that they could hardly have impressed upon either their tastes or personalities; nor do we find any accounts of their lives in these early years of their marriage. We can, however, follow up a few clues and venture our own deductions. The first eight years saw the quickly succeeding births of their six children. Their first child, Susan Caroline, was born in 1792 but survived only a few months, which must have been a grief for the young couple; but the following year saw the birth of a son and heir, George, who until his grandfather's death would bear the courtesy title of Earl of Sunderland. Another son, Charles, was born in 1794; Henry in 1796; John in 1797; and lastly, their second and only surviving daughter, Caroline Susan, was born in 1798. All these five children were to thrive and attain maturity, and one can imagine that they must have made a cheerful team, so close in age as they were.

It was during these years of childbearing that Susan Blandford produced the greater number of the enchanting watercolour paintings of flowers and plants which some two hundred years later her descendant, the eleventh Duke of Marlborough, was to find in a folder in the Long Library at Blenheim, all meticulously signed, labelled and dated – one hundred paintings in all, the first dated 1794, the last one 1804. Susan must certainly have had lessons from a high-class teacher to have acquired the skill to execute such accomplished studies; but, as with so many facets of her life, we are left guessing as to when, where and from whom she received the tuition which developed a natural talent to so marked a degree. Another mystery remains: the only paintings we know of are these, accidentally discovered at Blenheim; yet it is difficult to believe that Susan suddenly stopped painting for ever in the summer of 1804. This collection forms almost the only tangible evidence we have of our heroine, and perhaps these paintings are the silent but vivid witnesses to the happier phase of her married life, before the constant and public infidelities of her husband and his catastrophic money troubles became not only intolerable, but the cause of a deep and unbridgeable gulf between them.

Of George Blandford we know a great deal, both from his own pen and from the (mostly scornful) observations of his contemporaries; but Susan remains a shadowy, mute figure. Attempts to trace correspondence with family or friends, or any evidence that she kept a journal, have proved largely fruitless: we have some personal accounts, but the very few letters which have survived are about housekeeping matters and children's school bills. In writing

of Susan Blandford, therefore, one can only attempt a portrait
sketch, drawn from oblique references and sidelights cast here and
there in other people's diaries and letters. Her own relations, and
her husband's family, often had cause to pity her lot – they also,
evidently, liked and esteemed her. Nevertheless it is from such
tenuous shreds of evidence that we receive a quite positive impression of her character: Susan comes through to us as a woman of
straightforward niceness; of an agreeable nature and an understanding heart; of a character possessing in its make-up a remarkable
lack of vindictiveness (which was perhaps fortunate) and the
capacity to forgive or overlook the faults and misdeeds of those she
loved – this most particularly was to prove true of her relationship
with her eldest son. Running through her personality was a streak
of firmness: her son-in-law, David Pennant, who loved her, wrote
that her 'mind is naturally a very strong one',[19] and, as our tale
unfolds, we shall see that Susan was a woman capable of resolute,
independent action.

Although we know George Blandford married Susan Stewart
for expediency's sake, it is unlikely, given his romantic nature, that
he would have married someone who repelled him. For Susan's
part, what could have been more probable than that she fell in love
with the dashing young marquess she met at her Uncle and Aunt
Dashwood's house at Kirtlington? But to leave the realm of con-
jecture – with the evidence we have, it seems justifiable to think
that as they set out together, the young Blandfords had as good a
chance as many for reasonable happiness. With all his faults, George
Blandford was neither a bad man, nor a cold one: indeed his senti-
mentality was possibly one of his more endearing – if irritating –
characteristics. Nor would he have been a dull companion. His
enthusiasms must have been positively infectious: his love of music
and music-making may well have appealed to the daughter of so
ardent an opera-goer as Lord Galloway; as a well-educated girl,
she may have been interested in her husband's activities as a biblio-
phile; and since, very soon after their marriage, Blandford started
out on his career as a botanist and plant collector, Susan's artistic
appreciation of plants and flowers would have complemented his
veritable passion for them, and his own talents as an artist would
have been an added bond.

For all these reasons (and not denying this author's innate optimism), we can allow ourselves to believe that these early years together may have been, for George and Susan, quite happy ones, their relationship cemented by physical attraction, by their growing brood of children, and by agreeable mutual interests and occupations.

IV

Gardeners and Gardening

> In Xanadu did Kubla Khan
> A stately pleasure-dome decree . . .
> (*Samuel Taylor Coleridge, 'Kubla Khan'*)

A S QUITE A YOUNG MAN Blandford had started to collect the rare books which over some thirty years would grow to form an an impressive library; early on, too, his love of music and his undeniable talent both for playing instruments and composing was a constant pleasure and a prominent feature in his life. We do not know if gardening and botany appealed to him before his marriage, but the moment he had an establishment of his own – albeit only a rented one – he became a rabid plant collector; as soon as he acquired a property with the prospect of a long tenure, he also showed that he was a garden-maker on an imaginative and extravagant scale.

Capability Brown had been at work on his great 'improvements' at Blenheim already for two years when George Spencer, Marquess of Blandford, the heir to that wide domain, was born in 1766. But perhaps, even as a child, George may have been conscious of some of the works wrought by 'magician Brown'. A young boy would have enjoyed the laborious scooping out and then slow filling of the great lake, whose shining expanse was to become, and remain, one of the splendours of Blenheim. As a boy of eight, he may have watched the installation of the famous Bernini fountain[1] in a clearing in part of the new gardens made by his father, not far from where the newly enlarged lake tumbled over Brown's Grand Cascade. The fountain, said to be the last work of Bernini, was a copy of the one he had made for the Piazza Navona in Rome; it was presented to the first Duke of Marlborough by the Spanish Ambassador at the Papal Court, but neither the Great Duke nor his immediate successors could find a suitable place for it (it wasn't really big enough!), and it lay forgotten until his great-grandson, the fourth Duke (under the aegis of Sir William Chambers) found this romantic emplacement for it.

In the 1770s and 80s, as Blandford grew from boyhood to manhood, he probably toured with his parents the plantations created by Brown. Both the 'improvers' and their patrons, in those years when the great 'landskip'[2] gardens were in the making, must have had long-distance vision indeed for the famous 'clumps and belts' were then hosts of skinny saplings. Maybe the young man's own imagination and ambition were stirred: perhaps he glimpsed his own visionary 'landskip', and the day when he would reign at Blenheim and make his own contribution to the noble scene. When the son's tastes and talents were given rein, however, they would be different from his father's – for within the passing of a generation the concept of the garden and landscape scene was to undergo a marked change.

William Kent (1684–1748), with his near-contemporary and friend, the poet Alexander Pope (1688–1744), had been the chief pioneers and exponents of the new 'Natural Style', which seized the imagination of the great landowners and the cultivated world. Capability Brown was Kent's direct successor, and over the greater part of the eighteenth century these men and their enlightened followers and patrons imprinted on the English countryside a parkland character which the passing of two hundred years, an industrial and a social revolution, and ever changing methods in agriculture and the construction of motorways have not completely obliterated.

Capability and his train of 'improvers' were thorough-going (some people said ruthless) in seeking to impose their picture of an Elysium upon the English countryside. As at Blenheim in the 1770s, existing gardens and terraces near the house were swept away; and up and down the country, lawns and pasture rolled like a green sea up to the walls of the houses themselves. Deer, cattle and sheep (considered desirable ornaments as part of the 'landskip', they were also invaluable mowing machines) were kept at a convenient distance by a new device – the sunken fence or ha-ha.* Nor were already established features the only 'encumbrances' to be removed in the cause of 'improvement': whole hills and even villages deemed as interruptions to the fair prospect were carried off regardless. The reader will remember that at Blenheim, pleasant High Lodge was demolished and rebuilt in a Gothick style to serve the context of Capability's newly planned prospect from the park.

The 'improvers' and their school of thought had their opponents and detractors, and the controversy waxed fiercely among the *cognoscenti* – property owners, architects, gardeners, poets, artists, parsons and philosophers joining in the fray. Today these contemporary controversies have lost their edge; a later generation can surely feel only admiration and gratitude for Capability Brown's work: he handed down a legacy of form and beauty we strive to preserve as best we can, in times when harmony and grace in our environment have become rare and precious possessions.

Even during the years of Capability's greatest fame, new ideas on garden design were germinating. There were those who felt that the abrupt change from the sophistication of a mansion to rolling parkland with clumps and belts of trees was too sudden, and that more consideration should be paid to the immediate surroundings and setting of the house, in order to arrive at a graceful transition. Another consideration also now arose: as the eighteenth century advanced, new species of trees, shrubs and plants were being imported into this country in increasing numbers by the plant collectors and explorers ranging throughout the world, and during the first thirty years of the nineteenth century the growing trickle of new plant introductions swelled to floodtide. Plant collecting became all the rage – but where in Capability Brown's rolling expanses were these exotic discoveries to be exhibited? Surely not tucked away behind the walls of the kitchen garden!

---

* The ha-ha originated on the continent, but was introduced into England by Charles Bridgeman (d. 1738), gardener to Queen Caroline, and was used extensively by Kent and Brown.

As Brown had succeeded Kent as the Master, so in his turn was Humphry Repton (1752–1818) to continue the story of landscape and garden design, changing it to meet the needs and tastes of a new generation of patrons and gardeners. Repton was working at a time when new plants of every kind were flooding into England and, no longer confined to botanical institutions or an elitist few, were becoming available to an increasingly voracious number of collectors. Among these were not only the owners of the great domains, but also the *nouveaux riches* of the industrial revolution, who sought to surround their spacious suburban villa residences with elegant gardens filled with exotics. Humphry Repton introduced shrubberies, and was the first to use the term 'arboretum' to describe an area reserved for a special collection of trees. The *maestro* of the 'Picturesque' school of gardening, Repton's constant preoccupation to provide a harmonious transition from house to park, or to furnish less grand gardens artistically, coincided with the need to accommodate new varieties of plants, shrubs and trees. Terraces, so often swept away by earlier 'improvers', came into fashion once more as part of the harmonious linking of the artificial with the natural; fences of elegant design often now replaced the ha-ha to divide garden from park. And, looking further back, Repton found inspiration for what he called his 'assemblage of gardens'[3] in the designs of Tudor and Jacobean times, and from George London (d. 1713), nurseryman and William and Mary's Superintendent of the Gardens at Hampton Court. Repton reintroduced flower beds and made fashionable specialized gardens devoted to one group of plants such as roses or American plants (for which specially designed peat beds were constructed). These ideas are, of course, still very much in vogue today, living on in a modern idiom with one-colour or one-season borders or gardens, to add to the almost endless variations on the theme.

Of the three men of genius – Kent, Brown and Repton – who dominated the English landscape movement for nigh on a century, Humphry Repton is the one who has left us the fullest records of his ideas and work. His talent as an accomplished artist made it easy for him to demonstrate his views, and to leave visual records of his designs. Repton's 'Red Books' are famous, wherein his plans for each commission were minutely set down and delightfully illustrated, with 'flaps' which when raised gave the 'before and after' effect for his patrons to see. He also wrote about his theories on gardening and landscaping in a series of books and pamphlets: his first major publication was *Sketches & Hints on Landscape Gardens*, which appeared in 1795, his style and technique thus becoming known to a wide and eager audience. His professional career also coincided with a great increase in the number of magazines and pamphlets published on every manner of subject, including gardening and botany, for one of such magazines, William Peacock's *The Polite Repository, or Almanack*, Repton supplied many illustrations. This and other publications spread the knowledge of botanical acquisitions and developments in gardening design and horticultural practice.

The Marquess of Blandford started his career as a gardener and plant collector in the 1790s, when Humphry Repton was already the major influence on landscaping and gardening styles. Although there is no record of Repton having worked for him, we will see that Blandford was very much influenced by the fashions of his day, and his gardens abounded in Reptonian touches; but his own brain was teeming with ideas and fancies, his enthusiasm and energy were boundless and – of course – money was no object.

From the moment he married in 1791, Blandford must have been on the look-out for a country property which would both give him scope to indulge his growing obsession for gardening, and also provide for himself and his family a long-term home base; his father was in his early fifties, and there was every likelihood that Blandford had many years to go before entering upon his ducal inheritance. Meanwhile, living in rented properties, he gardened as best he might; in particular, whether at Culham Court or Bill Hill, he could concentrate on collecting the novelties and rarities in plants which so fascinated him, while ever keeping his eyes open for the right property where he could give full rein to his enthusiasms.

It is during these interim years that we come upon an illuminating

---

28. *Opposite*: George, Marquess of Blandford, later fifth Duke of Marlborough, by Richard Cosway.

29. *Overleaf*: Whiteknights from the north, 1791.

30. The Hot-House Aquarium. Engraving by George Tod, 1823.

GEORGE (4TH D...

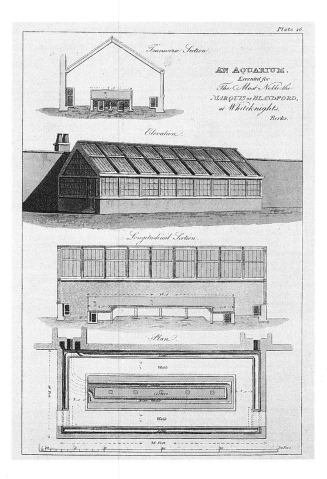

Plate 16.

Transverse Section.

AN AQUARIUM.
Executed for
The Most Noble the
MARQUIS of BLANDFORD,
at Whiteknights.
Berks.

Elevation.

Longitudinal Section.

Plan.

Walk

Cistern

Walk

Pub. by S. Curtis W. Aworth, Aug. 1, 1819.

Susan Duchess of Marlborough

and enjoyable exchange of letters between Lord Blandford, Sir Joseph Banks (1743–1820), the 'Grand Panjandrum' of Kew Gardens, and William Townsend Aiton (1768–1843), the Superintendent there. Originally the gardens of Kew House, which had been leased in 1730 by Frederick, Prince of Wales (son of George II), extended to only nine acres. The Prince had employed William Kent to redesign the grounds, and when he died in 1751 his widow, the Dowager Princess Augusta of Saxe-Gotha, continued to further develop her husband's work, employing at various times both Sir William Chambers and Capability Brown. She had for her adviser John Stuart, third Earl of Bute, who had been in the Prince's entourage and who was himself an amateur botanist of repute. Between them, Princess and peer made Kew the largest botanic garden in England, whose standing was internationally respected. When George III succeeded his grandfather in 1760 he enthusiastically supported his mother's activities there, and after her death in 1772 he bought Kew House and Gardens outright, linking the property to the grounds of adjoining Richmond House.

After Princess Augusta's death, Lord Bute's connection with the Gardens ceased, and Sir Joseph Banks became the presiding power at Kew for the next fifty years. Banks was a commanding figure in the realms of natural history and botany: he had become President of the Royal Society at the age of thirty-five; he had accompanied Captain Cook on his voyage to Australia and New Zealand in the *Endeavour* in 1769. Under his aegis Kew continued to wax both in size and in repute, and for the greater part of his time there Banks was assisted by the knowledgeable and remarkable W. T. Aiton, who succeeded his father as Superintendent in 1793.

The prestige of Kew Gardens, with its ever-growing collection of exotic plants, was a source of interest to all plant collectors and botanists, and a cause of envy to those who, like Blandford, were of

---

31. *Previous page*: *Blandfordia nobilis*, Showy Blandford, from Curtis's *Botanical Magazine*, 1817–18. 'This plant was first named by Sir James Edward Smith in honour of the Marquis of Blandford, now Duke of Marlborough; the one before assigned to His Grace by Mr Andrews in the *Botanists' Repository* being the Galax of Linnaeus.'

32. *Opposite*: Susan, Marchioness of Blandford, later fifth Duchess of Marlborough, by George Perfect Harding.

an acquisitive nature. In the archives of the Royal Botanic Gardens at Kew there is, in what strongly resembles Aiton's handwriting, a list headed: 'Sent the following Plants to the Marquis of Blandford, August 1796'.[4] Following the list of six or seven plants is the plaintive note: 'But Lord Blandford never added any plant to the Royal Collection'! A few months later we find the following letter from Aiton to the Marquess, couched in a somewhat vehement tone:

> My Lord,
> As His Majestys Collection of *Stapelia* brought by Mr Masson* two years ago, into England & now in the Gardens of Kew, were procured with many difficulties & considerable Expenses, I really cannot hold myself answerable in my charge as Gardener to His Majesty, to divide them with your Lordship, in the manner you have requested of me to do. I will not therefore venture on any thing of the kind without the full approbation of Sir Joseph Banks, or that I have His Majestys pleasure of of Commands for that purpose.
> The old plant of *Fuchsia*, I fear will not live very long, & as I have only two little plants of it likely to thrive in the Royal Gardens as succession, I beg your Lordship will receive this as my Apology for not forwarding it by your Gardiner.
>
> I have the honor to be my Lord
> Your Lordships most obedt. Hum Serv*.
> W. T. Aiton.[5]

Some sixteen months later, on 1 December 1797, Blandford wrote from Bill Hill an immensely long screed to Banks, complaining vociferously of his treatment at the hands of the Superintendent.[6] He starts by reminding Sir Joseph of 'the many kind things the King said both to Ld. Galloway [a Lord-in-waiting] and you about my partaking of the remnants of his Majesty's garden at Kew . . .', and goes on to remind Banks how, when they had walked together over the Gardens, he (Sir Joseph) had 'desired that I might have a few plants to carry home with me': Blandford had never imagined that 'his Majesty's bounty was meant to stop there'. The previous

---

* Francis Masson (1741–1805). An under-gardener at Kew, he was the first collector to be sent by Banks overseas, to the Cape in 1772.

summer, he continued, he had visited Kew with Lady Blandford and his sister; upon asking Mr Aiton for some plants, he had received the reply that 'the King was not very fond of parting with his Plants'. On the Marquess's reminding him of what the King had said, Aiton had (no doubt reluctantly) relented, and had given him a few. The tale of complaint continued: Blandford had fixed his eye on a plant, a *Houstonia coccinea* (*Bouvardia ternata*); he had counted that there were eleven or twelve such plants, so there should have been no problem; again Aiton had at first refused, but eventually said he would send it with the rest of the plants promised. In due course these had arrived, 'but no *Houstonia* – I wrote repeatedly for it, conceiving it a mistake, but no answer came . . .'. A year later, the long-promised *Houstonia* had arrived – but meanwhile he had procured it from a nurseryman! Now for the final outrage: this year (1797) Blandford himself had not been able to visit Kew, but he had sent his gardener, who was desirous of seeing the famous gardens. At this point in the letter he mentions, in a slightly throwaway fashion, that his gardener combined this excursion with one to take plants (some two hundred species) for shipment to the Botanic Garden in Jamaica. The gardener had duly called in at Kew bearing a note for Mr Aiton requesting 'a few *cuttings* of some of the *Stapelias* which were imported last year, & which are very easy of propagation . . . I have got 15 sorts of them from different Nurserymen'. Blandford adds meaningfully (brackets and emphasis are his): '(I need not tell *you* from whom they *must* have come . . .)'. He concludes that either he or Mr Aiton must have misunderstood the King's wishes, and asks Sir Joseph: 'Should you see no impropriety in my being allotted some [stapelias] I must impose further on your goodness to order Mr Aiton to send them.' Within his own letter he encloses the note from Aiton which had triggered off his complaints.

A few days later Sir Joseph Banks indited a long and courteous, but quite stiff, reply: the King's orders had been quite clear – 'Your Lordship should have such plants as you wanted, & could properly be spared.' It was, Sir Joseph said, upon the interpretation of the word 'properly' 'that your Lordship & me can possibly differ'. Two considerations existed – the scarceness of any plant in question and the necessity to preserve the superiority of the royal collection at Kew Gardens: of these considerations Banks politely but firmly writes he must be the sole judge. He stands by his Superintendent, stating finally (and we detect a note of irritation):

> Probably your Lordship will be satisfied by this that Mr Aiton could not with propriety suffer your Lordship's Gardener to take cuttings from the Stapelias at his discretion: indeed I have never encouraged the admission of Gentlemen's Gardiners to cut for themselves: I have generally found those gentlemen little thankful for what they get, & very clamorous for what is refused them. [7]

This eminently reasonable letter did not, however, close the incident. On the contrary, the very next day, 5 December, another long letter wings from an even more indignant Marquess to the distinguished and, one assumes, busy Sir Joseph: Lord Blandford and his gardener have been grossly misrepresented to Banks in the matter of the stapelias: he had never intended or asked that his gardener should take the cuttings himself; he (Blandford) had only requested a few cuttings of 'any of the large flowering Stapelias he could spare or *any thing else* he could spare . . .'. He continues to work up a fine head of steam of righteous indignation against the peccant Aiton – finally: 'Had I really made the request he insinuates that I made, or my Gardener been such a ninny as to ask to have the cutting up of one of the plants at Kew, we should well deserve to have the Kew Gardens shut against us.' [8]

The same thought may well have crossed Sir Joseph's mind; but the Marquess was not only a nobleman – his father the Duke was also the valued friend of the King. Blandford ends his long complaint by apologizing profusely (indeed, I should hope so) for giving Sir Joseph so much trouble about a few cuttings: Lady Blandford sends her best remembrance to Lady and Miss Banks, and they both hope for a visit from the Banks family to Whiteknights in the spring.

What a gale in a greenhouse!

✳✧✳✧✳

It was while the young Blandfords were living at Bill Hill that an important property – Whiteknights, close to Reading – came on the market: it seemed to offer everything they were seeking. Despite the Duke of Marlborough's deep dissatisfaction with his son and heir he was evidently now prepared to help him establish a suitable home, and Whiteknights was bought by the family trustees for this purpose in 1798, Blandford leasing the place from his father.[9]

The history of the ancient manor of Erleigh (or Earley) Whiteknights is well recorded from the twelfth century, and from 1606 Whiteknights, as it came to be called (White Knights and White-Knights were other contemporary forms of the name), remained in the ownership of one family – the Englefields – for over 170 years.[10]

The Englefields were staunch Roman Catholics, and had suffered the pains and liabilities to which members of that faith were subjected until 1829, when the Catholic Emancipation Act was passed. In 1783, the seventh (and last) Baronet, Sir Henry Charles Englefield, had become so 'disgusted at the offensive prejudices of the neighbouring gentry'[11] that he had broken his family's long connection with Whiteknights and had sold the property to one William Byam Martin, who, fifteen years later, sold the place to the Marlborough family.[12]

Although the lives of succeeding generations of Englefields are well recorded, little is known of the style and size of the house (or houses) which preceded the mansion in existence when the property changed hands in 1798. An engraving made in 1776 by Governor Pownall (so called because he had been a Governor of Massachusetts),[13] a friend of the sixth Baronet, shows a square, unpretentious, white stuccoed house, probably dating from the second half of the eighteenth century, set in wooded parkland by a stretch of water.

During the early eighteenth century Whiteknights had acquired a certain literary lustre, for the then owner, Anthony Englefield, was a great admirer of poets and received such visitors as the Restoration dramatist William Wycherley (1640–1716) and John Gay (1685–1732), the author of *The Beggar's Opera*; while living not far away at Binfield was young Alexander Pope, whose friendship with the Englefield family was to last through two generations.

Some time in the middle years of the century Whiteknights was laid out in the fashionable manner of a *'ferme ornée'* and earned a reputation among the landscape gardening *cognoscenti*. The literary-minded Englefields had been succeeded by an outdoor generation, influenced by the vision of England as an Elysian or Arcadian scene.

The former concept, poetically inspired by Alexander Pope and created by William Kent, was further developed over an even wider canvas by Capability Brown. Meanwhile Arcady, with nymphs and shepherdesses for its *corps de ballet* rather than the god-like dwellers of Elysium, was first conjured up at Woburn Farm in the Thames valley by Philip Southcote (1697 or 8–1758), who created his visionary countryside by laying out his gardens and farmland complete with a ruined chapel, seats, bridges and alcoves to achieve the *'ferme ornée'* effect. Arcady also had its bard and publicist in the pastoral poet William Shenstone (1714–63): influenced by Southcote, he too created his ideal 'landskip' at The Leasowes, near Birmingham. The Arcadians soon had many emulators.

In 1753 Horace Walpole paid a visit to Whiteknights. Writing to John Chute on 4 August, he commented: 'I went to see Sir H. Englefield's, which [others] prefer, but I think very undeservedly, to Mr Southcote's. It is not above a quarter as extensive, and wants the river. There is a pretty view of Reading seen under a rude arch, and the water is well disposed. The buildings are very insignificant, and the house far from good . . .'.[14]

We must defer to Mr Walpole's judgement, for he was a man of taste and knowledge, deeply interested in gardening and land-scaping, and the author of a famous essay, 'Modern Gardening'. At the time of his visit to Whiteknights he had already acquired Strawberry Hill, near Twickenham, where he was constructing a Gothick fantasy and laying out a garden. But to twentieth-century eyes, the plain stuccoed house in its agreeable pastoral setting which that great arbiter of taste found so lacking looks pleasant and dignified enough. It would be interesting to know Walpole's reaction to the assorted styles of architecture of the edifices which now encumber the site, albeit they shelter a seat of progressive learning and science – Reading University.

✳◈✳◈✳

When George, Marquess of Blandford, and his wife Susan came to live at Whiteknights at the turn of the century, they were in their thirties and had been married for nearly ten years. Of their five children, so closely grouped together in age, George, Earl of Sunderland, the heir, was nearly seven years old; Charles nearly six; Henry, four and John, three; while the only surviving girl, baby Caroline, was scarcely two years old.

Blandford no doubt began his campaign of 'improvements' as soon as the ink was dry on the contracts, and started to move his already considerable botanical collection from Bill Hill to White-knights as soon as flowerbeds were ready to receive the plants, and glasshouses available to protect the more delicate species. In a letter from Bill Hill dated 9 August 1798 to the famous botanist, J. E. (later Sir James) Smith (1759–1828), Blandford tells him: 'I have just had notice of between 200 and 300 plants having left Jamaica from Dr Dancer; a great many new genera. I shall be very happy to show them to you, as well as all my others, when I am settled at White Knights.'[15]

Dr Thomas Dancer (1755?–1811), originally a physician prac-tising in Jamaica, had acquired the title and role of the 'Island Botanist', through his great knowledge of the native plant species. He was closely connected with the Botanic Garden in Jamaica, and was in frequent correspondence with Sir Joseph Banks and others, exchanging plants and seeds with them. We know already that Blandford had despatched a large consignment of plants the previous December, destined for Jamaica: probably the collection we hear of now was the handsome *quid pro quo*. It would be interesting to know how many of these plants making the long journey between England and the West Indies survived; until the invention of the Wardian Case in 1839, despite every possible care being lavished upon them (often at the expense of the comfort of passengers and crew), an enormous proportion of plants and seeds in transit perished before, or soon after, arrival at their destinations.

There is a profound saying: 'Live – as if you would die tomorrow; garden – as if you would live a hundred years.' Blandford most certainly followed the second part of that precept: a born optimist, he obviously regarded Whiteknights as a long-term proposition; there would be no need to abandon the place even when he suc-ceeded to the dukedom, and in time it would become another jewel in the heritage – and one of his own fashioning. Fortunately for him, he neither foresaw (and certainly did not guard against) the financial ruin which would engulf him in less than twenty years.

Only the faintest vestiges remain at Whiteknights of the prolific plantings upon which now, at the turn of his century, Lord Blandford embarked; but happily for us, the whole of the amazing creation which he called into being within the span of two decades survives and has been preserved for our delighted eyes in a book entitled:

A
Descriptive Account
of the

Mansion and Gardens
of
White-Knights

a Seat of

His Grace the Duke of Marlborough

by Mrs Hofland
illustrated with engravings from
pictures taken on the spot by T. C. Hofland

This handsome folio volume was commissioned by Lord Blandford in 1816, and published three years later. It describes in copious detail and in flowery and felicitous terms the mansion and gardens at Whiteknights. The writer and illustrator, Barbara and Thomas Hofland, were a remarkable couple.[16] But whereas their artistic and literary skills were complementary, Barbara Hofland would seem to have outshone her husband both in strength of character and in spirit.

Thomas Christopher Hofland had been born in 1777 into a prosperous Yorkshire manufacturing family with interests in cotton-making machinery, and had been brought up to gentlemanly pursuits. But in 1796, when the family fortunes failed and his parents retired to Kew, he sold his horse and gun and bought three months' drawing lessons; he quickly achieved a measure of success as a land-

33. Lancelot 'Capability' Brown, by Nathaniel Dance.
34. Humphry Repton, after a miniature by Samuel Shelley.
35. William Kent, by Bartholomew Dandridge.
36. Sir Joseph Banks, by Thomas Phillips, 1810.

July 13th 1799

scape artist, exhibiting at the Royal Academy in 1798. Under the threat of a Napoleonic invasion he enlisted in a volunteer regiment and quite by chance caught the eye of George III, who, hearing of the young man's artistic talents, found employment for him drawing botanical studies for Kew Gardens. Hofland later turned to teaching art, and was working in Doncaster when, in 1808, he met his future wife, then Barbara Hoole.

Barbara had had a very different upbringing: she was born in 1770, the daughter of Robert Wreaks, an ironmonger in Sheffield, who had died when she was three years old, and she had been raised by a maiden aunt. Her literary talent became apparent quite early, and some of her poems were published in the Sheffield weekly paper. By this time she was running her own milliner's shop and, at the age of twenty-six, she married a local merchant, Thomas Hoole. A daughter died in infancy and then, only three years after their marriage, Thomas died, leaving his wife with a three-year-old son. Barbara was grief-stricken, but resilient: she opened her own school in High Harrogate in order to keep herself and to provide for the education of her son, and, as well as publishing more poetry, she now began writing books for children, which were an immediate success. It was at this period that she met and fell in love with Thomas Hofland, seven years her junior. They were married in 1810, and the following year moved to London.

By this date Barbara Hofland had become an established author, her stories and plays for children being published abroad and translated into many languages. Personal charm as well as literary fame gained her access to the literary and artistic world, where she soon made many friends. In particular she formed a close and lasting friendship with the novelist and dramatist Mary Russell Mitford (1787–1855), famous to us as the author of *Our Village*, and an inveterate and sparkling letter-writer. In one of many letters to her friend the banker, politician and amateur artist Sir William Elford (1749–1837), Miss Mitford wrote that Mr Hofland was an artist

---

37. W. T. Aiton, by L. Poyot, 1829.

38. Horace Walpole, fourth Earl of Orford, by George Dance, 1793.

39. J. C. Loudon, from the frontispiece to his *Self-Instruction for Young Gardeners*, 1845.

'whom I admire very much (am I right?), and his wife, whom, as a woman and authoress, I equally love and admire. (Pray, if you wish to "cry quarts", read her children's books – her "Good Grandmother" and her "Son of a Genius".)'[17] In another letter, Miss Mitford gives us an engaging pen portrait of 'this very acute clever and imaginative woman. I don't know anything more entertaining than the contrast between her strong Yorkshire dialect, which has a twang like Cheshire cheese, and the elegant ornamented diction in which she clothes her original and fanciful conceptions.'[18]

Although Hofland was busy with various commissions, and exhibited his work in the Leeds Academy and the Royal Academy, his income was irregular and precarious. He also spent much time fishing: he was a keen angler, and later was to write a book on the subject, *The Angler's Manual*, published in 1839; he also had the enjoyable distinction of having a fly named after him – 'Hofland's Fancy'. But Thomas suffered from bouts of grave ill-health which, as well as interrupting his work, made him temperamental and difficult to live with. The combination of bad health and the chancy nature of an artist's life, together with his addiction to fishing, resulted in the burden of earning regular money falling largely on Barbara and her popular pen.

But although Barbara was gifted and surrounded by friends, her life was ever beset with sorrow and difficulty. The Hoflands had no children between them, but in 1816 Thomas fathered an illegitimate son, Thomas Richard, whom Barbara, with her warm and loving disposition, cherished and reared as her own. It was in this same year that the Hoflands moved from inner London to the then still countrified district of Twickenham, and it was in 1816 also that they received the commission from the Marquess of Blandford. They set about their task with a will, and in three years this remarkable husband-and-wife team produced a handsome illustrated volume, describing in vivid words and delightful paintings the enchanted realm that was Whiteknights.

V

A Guided Tour

So twice five miles of fertile ground
With walls and towers were girdled round;
And there were gardens bright with sinuous rills
Where blossom'd many an incense-bearing tree;
And here were forests ancient as the hills,
Enfolding sunny spots of greenery.
(*Samuel Taylor Coleridge, 'Kubla Khan'*)

IN ORDER THAT MY READERS may without further delay enjoy an extensive tour of Whiteknights in the company of such an excellent guide as Mrs Hofland, the author – invoking the magic of poetic licence – is advancing our story in time, so that we can fully appreciate the genuine and astonishing achievement masterminded by Lord Blandford, the creation of which probably gave him greater happiness and satisfaction than his noble heritage and possessions.

Let us therefore imagine that it is a fine day in early summer 1816, and, approaching Whiteknights from the direction of London, we join our guide, Mrs Hofland, at the three-arched gateway through which we enter the park.* As we proceed, we are at once struck by the number and beauty of the old established trees; the Englefield family had planted and enriched their estate, so Lord Blandford found a fine setting to give background and substance to

---

* Throughout this account of Whiteknights gardens the original spellings in the Hofland book have been retained, both in the quotations and in plant names; where appropriate, modern plant names have been added in brackets.

the plans and plantings he was to carry out in his time at White-knights. Soon after entering the park we see on our right the ruins of an ancient chapel, the façade of which has been rebuilt in the fashionable style of 'ornamented' Gothick; at the same time we come into view of 'a most noble piece of water (which in this place assumes the form of a river)',[1] beyond which we see the house, which Mrs Hofland describes as 'a handsome modern structure'. We shall hope to visit the mansion another time; today all the daylight hours and all our energies will be consumed by our walk round the extensive gardens and woods. And, first of all, Mrs Hofland conducts us to the Botanic Gardens, across the lawn at no great distance from the house.

The path which leads us to the Botanic Gardens is surrounded by stately trees: cedars of Lebanon, stone pines, tulip trees and scarlet thorns. We now find ourselves at once in a world of fantasy and exoticism, for the inside of the entrance 'is adorned by three Oriental arches surmounted with crescents' over which 'the Jessamine and Corchorus [*Kerria japonica* 'Pleniflora'] grow luxuriantly'. These arches remind us of the fanciful flights into oriental motifs at Sezincote in Gloucestershire, and at that most lavish and fantastical 'pleasure dome' of all – the Prince Regent's Pavilion at Brighton, for which Humphry Repton also designed Indianesque features.

The Gardens in which we now find ourselves are oblong in form and are sub-divided into 'squares, circles, lawns and groves, with the most agreeable variety to the eye'. Our attention is at once drawn to 'one broad Border, or Belt, which surrounds the whole grounds, and [which] is entirely devoted to American plants'.

We next cross a lawn upon which are 'baskets of exotic flowers', such as begonias and scarlet sage: these 'baskets', usually circular and constructed of wood or cast-iron in the height of the present gardening fashion, form a raised rim to simulate basketwork, within which flowers are planted, making a most charming effect.[2]

We now reach the first of many seats that are scattered throughout the gardens, offering resting places and viewpoints from which visitors may contemplate various features and prospects. As we proceed, we will be amazed by the variety of design and form these seats and bowers will afford. This first one – the Open Hexagon Seat – is a 'Pavilion of Lattice-work painted green' over which grow

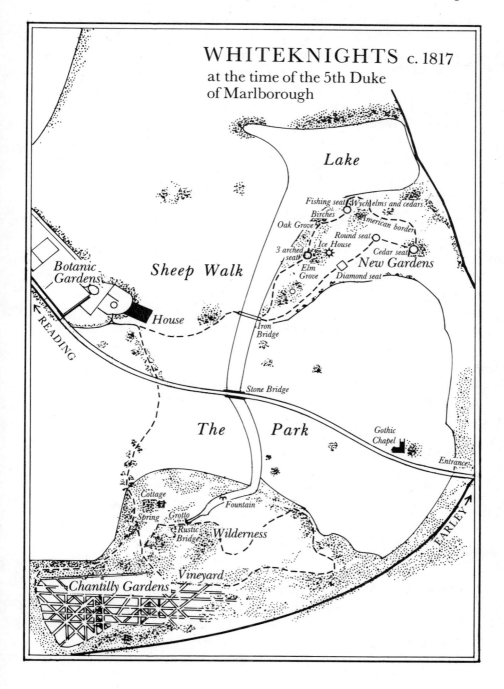

WHITEKNIGHTS c. 1817
at the time of the 5th Duke
of Marlborough

Lake

Fishing seat Wych elms and cedars
Birches
Oak Grove   American border
                Round seat
            Ice House
3 arched   Cedar seat
seat   New Gardens
        Elm   Diamond seat
        Grove

Botanic
Gardens

Sheep Walk

House

Iron
Bridge

READING

Stone Bridge

The   Park

Gothic
Chapel

Entrance

EARLEY

Cottage
Spring   Grotto   Fountain
    Rustic
    Bridge   Wilderness

Vineyard
Chantilly Gardens

creepers, and round which are placed baskets of the rarest greenhouse plants. Close by are planted *Magnolia glauca* (*Magnolia virginiana*), the 'Moutang or Piony tree [*Paeonia suffruticosa*], the *Erica multiflora* [*Erica ?vagens*] in both its colours, and the scarlet Azalea . . .'.

Next we come upon two bowers in contrasting styles: a Rustic Bower (covered with honeysuckle and jessamine) and a Gothick Bower. Between these, we glimpse a part of the encircling American Border which contains some notable trees and plants including 'the first *Magnolia Auriculata* [*Magnolia Fraseri*] ever imported, . . . *Juniperus Oxycedrus, Ailanthus Glandulosa* [*Ailanthus altissima*], *Nyssa Denticulata* [*Nyssa aquatica*], and other American plants, remarkable for their beauty or valuable from their scarcity.'

Through the Orange Grove, where a 'noble hedge' of laurel affords a backdrop to orange trees grown in tubs, we approach the Temple of Pomona. The Temple turns out to be a 'superb Greenhouse of an oblong form' in which circular beds and a central hexagonal bed 'for the reception of rare plants' are surrounded by trellised arches twined with creeping plants. Here too there are garden chairs, and two recesses painted to resemble *verd antique* (an ornamental variety of marble) in which are placed sofas; in the centre, 'enshrined by the Catalonian Jessamine and white Camellia, appears the presiding Goddess of the place . . .'. This Temple greenhouse is devoted to the display of rare and tender plants which include *Arbutus latifolia* and *longifolia* (*Arbutus ?andrachnoides*), *Bignonia grandiflora* (*Campsis grandiflora*), and *Thea bohea* (*Camellia sinensis*). It would be tempting to recline on the sofas so thoughtfully placed, and enjoy the rarities displayed, but we must continue our tour. Leaving the Temple, we find ourselves in The Square, on all sides of which are stages for plants from all over the world: 'most curious and valuable productions peculiar to China, Botany Bay, and the Cape of Good Hope; with a compartment allotted for the whole tribe of *Erica*.'

After walking through a Terrace Garden we visit the first of six more greenhouses, each dedicated to different collections of plants. The Marquess has been among those private proprietors who have recently taken advantage of the new advances in the construction of glass and wooden greenhouses, with heat supplied through furnaces and flues. And he is in the van of modern design in the erection of two aquatic houses: the Hothouse Aquarium and the Greenhouse Aquarium.[3] Outside, the Greenhouse Aquarium is 'incrustated by beautiful rock-work, and the walls are latticed some feet from the ground, for the advantage of creeping plants . . .'. Within, there is an immense lead-lined cistern, twenty-six feet long by seven feet wide, heated by flues beneath it.[4]

The Conservatory also is worthy of special mention: sixty-six feet long and twenty feet wide, it is a ravishing sight, for the 'most rare and exquisitely beautiful exotics' are all displayed in 'jars, vases and bowls, of scarce, costly, and elegant china' which (as our guide, Mrs Hofland, improvingly remarks), since it 'fascinates without injury, may be indulged without regret'.

But we cannot linger any longer in the magnificent greenhouses, for we still have much to see. We now cross a velvet lawn with more baskets brimming with flowers and vases full of plants and enwreathed with vines, and a new feature – fine china barrel seats placed upon the grass. We come to an 'elegant inclosure' formed by a hexagonal treillage with six open doorways and a circular lawn inside, in the middle of which is a 'beautiful and singular' fountain executed from a design by Lady Diana Beauclerk, the Marquess's artistic and enchanting aunt.

The fountain itself is fantastic: dolphins support a shell from which water falls into the basin below; underneath more dolphins, and shells from which three lizards are drinking; the base is decorated in 'the most picturesque manner' with, among other things, petrified fungi, white and purple fluor spar, blue John, spiral shells, rose-tinted conches and nautili; in the cracks, creeping mosses are like 'vegetable emeralds' – it is indeed a ravishing sight.

We see as we continue our walk how the visitor is led from one pleasure or surprise to another, in this veritable 'assemblage' of gardens within a garden: we have passed the Terrace Garden and remarked on The Square, but there remain several more enclosures, each different and delightful in their effect. One unusual feature we admire is the manner in which Lord Blandford has ordained the placing of the hardy herbaceous plants: they are planted in compartments which are eighteen inches lower than the surrounding turf, thus giving the viewer a new impression of their character and beauty.[5]

Soon we come upon a plantation of dahlias, 'in which every possible variety of this new and beautiful plant are seen in their highest splendour.'* In the Linnaean Garden – a veritable 'scientific museum' where plants are arranged in their botanical families, we find a Chinese Temple, the roof of which is canopied and painted in two greens; twining up the arches which support the roof are several varieties of clematis. Here we are reminded of the musical tastes and talents of the Marquess, for within the Temple there are set seats and stands for music. Nearby is the 'prodigious nursery' of young geraniums (a plant to be found in great profusion in these gardens) and the Japan Garden, a smaller enclosure filled with Japanese and American plants.

One of the most fascinating collections of plants we saw on our tour was in the Striped Garden, which we entered after leaving the hexagonal treillage surrounding the fantastic fountain: here, as its name denotes, the trees and plants are nearly all striped or variegated, giving a most unusual and amusing effect. As we have passed from one garden to another we have seen clumps and circles of rhododendrons intermixed with azaleas and magnolias in variety, all rare species at the time of their planting. But, in retrospect, assuredly the most remarkable sight of all was the Magnolia Wall: 20 feet high and 140 feet long, it is unquestionably unique, for the whole of this wall is completely covered with *Magnolia grandiflora*: 'the flowers are of spotless pearly white, and when fully expanded, from ten to twelve inches in diameter: their fragrance excels even their beauty . . .'

We have now completed our tour of the Botanic Gardens, but much remains to be seen, for the area of these Gardens, although extensive, did not provide sufficient scope for the schemes emanating

* The dahlia was introduced from Mexico into Europe in 1789, and into England by the Marchioness of Bute; these plants however soon died out, but Lady Holland reintroduced dahlias successfully in 1804. (John Fisher, *The Origins of Garden Plants*, Constable, 1982.)

40. Watercolour of *Pelargonium pettatum lateripes*, by Susan, Marchioness of Blandford, 1795
41. *Overleaf*: Whiteknights: a lady reading in the gardens with a view of the east and north fronts of the house, by Thomas Hofland, 1817.

Geranium laterip.
August 1795.

S. Blandford.

Rosa semperflorens —
July 1795 —

S. Blandford.

Cyclamen Persicum Feb 25 98.

S. Blandford.

Convolvulus Major —
Nov 20 1795.

S. Blandford.

Glycine coccinea B.B.
April & June 1795. —

from the vivid and active imagination of our noble Marquess, nor afford space enough to accommodate his ever-increasing collection of plants. Accordingly, Lord Blandford has taken in further acres of his property to form the New Gardens, and a further area for planting designated as the Woods, or Wilderness. In all now, the woods, park and gardens embrace some 280 acres.

✳❖✳❖✳

Still accompanied by Mrs Hofland, and traversing the lawn which encircles the house, and part of the sheep-walk, we enter the New Gardens by crossing the Iron Bridge over that part of the lake which gives the appearance of a river. Our attention is drawn to this light, elegant and beautiful construction, which has a span of 110 feet, and we are told that it is 'formed on the most new and approved principles, the plates of iron collapsing over each other'.

Beyond this bridge we find ourselves in the New Gardens, a large area bounded on one side by the curving shore of the lake, which now broadens out into a noble expanse of water where many long-established and beautiful groups of native trees abound, forming a canopy and a framework for the new plantings made by Lord Blandford. In these New Gardens, the plan upon which the Botanic Gardens was ordered is completely changed: in the former was a succession of gardens within a greater garden, each with a varied theme; here we enjoy a woodland walk, where all lines are sinuous and free. The pathways twist and turn and lead us in an agreeable progression through groves of elms, wych elms, red cedars, and oaks. Mrs Hofland points out to us the numerous varieties and how, planted in and among the more stately and ancient trees, we find 'the gay Ash and pensile Birch' mingling with 'dark Larches and changing Chestnuts . . . shining Laurels, and unbending Hollies . . .'. Here too is an American border with a variety of shrubs and flowers from that vast continent.

As we proceed on our walk we find arbours and seats (a feature we remarked upon in the Botanic Gardens) – but no longer see the fantastic, exotic and oriental touches we admired there: although

---

42. Watercolours by Susan, Marchioness of Blandford, 1795. (*Clockwise from top left*): *Rosa chinensis 'semperflorens'*, *Cyclamen persicum*, *Ipomoea purpurea*, *Kennedia coccinea*. This is their modern nomenclature.

the construction of the seats we now come upon is elaborate and intricate, a pure rusticity prevails in their design, which we find perfectly suited to the different spirit of this part of the grounds. Farther on we shall see in turn the Diamond Seat (a Rustic Temple); the Cedar Seat; the Fishing Seat; and the Three-Arched Seat – this last, Mrs Hofland informs us, is 'generally considered the most elegantly conceived of all these sweetly fanciful Bowers, which owe their singular beauty and appropriate construction solely to the superior taste and ingenuity' of Lord Blandford.

As we wander on our way, clearings in the groves or the dis-position of the arbours and seats invite us to pause, and, turning round, we see delightful vistas of the park beyond these Gardens and different views of the house, a particularly pleasing one being from the vicinity of the Diamond Seat, which we come to soon after entering the New Gardens; from here the house is seen to great advantage, and 'the lawn which more immediately surrounds the place is ornamented by beautiful flowering shrubs, in which the Rhododendrons are particularly gay and luxuriant.'

When we emerge from the Cedar Walk we get a delightful view of the lake and realize for the first time 'its extent, magnificence, and beauty', and Mrs Hofland remarks how much the scene resembles Lake Windermere in that part which is near to Ambleside. The shoreline is beautified by plantations of weeping willows, backed by soaring poplars.

We return towards the house along the lakeside and, crossing over the Iron Bridge once more, look back over the plantations and groves we have just visited with so much pleasure.

✳❖✳❖✳

In a south-easterly direction across the park from the house lie yet more extensive pleasure grounds, known as the Woods, or Wilder-ness, and it is to these that Mrs Hofland now conducts us. As we go she explains that, until a few years since, these acres we are about to visit were 'literally what their name implies'. Now (as if by some magic wand) they have been transformed, and are embellished by 'beautiful walks, velvet lawns, exotic plantations, flowery arcades and gay pavillions'.

Once again, the character of these gardens is different from that of either the Botanic Gardens or the New Gardens: although certain features and some varieties of plants and trees may be repeated, it is nearly always in a different idiom or context. In contrast to the New Gardens, the effect of beauty achieved here is more contrived, and in parts a geometric plan has been imposed: in many ways we see resemblances to the ever-changing themes of the Botanic Gardens, while the seats and arbours which have been such a feature through-out our tour again provide an exotic and fanciful effect, recalling those we first admired in the Botanic Gardens.

The Woods are entered through a curious fence constructed with large stones brought from the Marlborough estates in Wilt-shire, and named 'grey wethers' after their resemblance to the sheep which graze on the downs there. Once inside this barrier, we are led by a broad and winding path through a plantation of young forest trees, which are intermixed with arbutus, flowering ash, ever-green oak, snowy mespilus and red-berried elder. Once again, as in the New Gardens, the newer plantings are sheltered and framed by mature forest trees.

That beautiful American tree the catalpa here forms a walk partly encircling an amphitheatre, whose focus is a Greek Antique Vase. Close by we come upon the first of the elaborate and beautiful arbours which also adorn these gardens: named simply the Seat, it is the largest and, Mrs Hofland considers, 'the most beautiful in all the pleasure grounds of White Knights'. The Seat, although constructed of hazel, birch and yew, does not give an overall 'rustic' effect, but rather an elaborate or sophisticated one: the central supporting pillars form Gothick arches, and the wings of the arbour are framed with trellis-work; the roof is thatched with straw, and the canopied interior lined with rushes.

From this Seat we have immediate access to an altogether new and wonderful feature, the Laburnum Bower: 'This immense Treillage is a beautiful Arcade twelve hundred feet in length'; it is formed of rustic lattice-work, covered with branches of laburnum. It must indeed be a sight to gasp at when in the golden glory of its blossoming. Along this arcade or tunnel are placed at intervals little rustic seats, opposite which openings have been cut to give views of the grounds and surrounding countryside. At the farther end of the Bower, the trellis widens out into a hexagon in which are placed seats and stands for music; we recall that in the Chinese Temple in the Botanic Gardens there are similar arrangements for music-making, but here, in this 'Rustic Orchestra', there is room to accommodate the Marquess's complete band!

Next we enter the Chantilly Gardens, devised in a geometric pattern in the French fashion, after the manner of the gardens at the Château de Chantilly. Here green paths intersect each other at right angles and diagonally, often six or so paths converging at the 'foot of a towering Elm or gigantic Oak'. The alleys thus formed are full of musk roses, yet more tulip trees and many native and exotic flowering plants.

Another feature in these gardens is the Vineyard, to which we soon come: this is oblong in shape, and surrounded by a thick laurel hedge. The vines are kept low, as in a true vineyard and, we are told, are very productive.

As we continue our walk we admire the velvet green of inter-vening lawns which are beautified by 'baskets' (similar to those we saw in the Botanic Gardens) 'inclosing the most brilliant flowers, whose gay tints mingle with the soft greens, and form the most delightful contrasts'.

One of the seats which pleases us greatly is the 'Pavillion', which is to be found in the middle of the near-circular Juniper Lawn, almost encircled by yet another American border full of azaleas, white cedars, fern-leaved beeches and many specimens of *Magnolia glauca* (*Magnolia virginiana*) 'which sheds unrivalled perfume from innumerable flowers that shine like stars . . .'.

The Pavillion is an elegant, octagonal summer-house formed of wood in shaded greens; its projecting roof is supported by light pillars enclosed by lattice-work, in which are entwined *Corchorus japonica* (kerria) and *Atragene austriaca* (*Clematis alpina*). From the four latticed windows, which are also entrances to the Pavillion, there are varied and enchanting views: through one we have a fine view of the house backed by trees, with the stone bridge and part of the lake in the foreground; from another we have a 'sweet peep' of the distant Grotto (to which we shall presently come); and yet another opens on a fine perspective of the adjoining park. The roof of this enchanting construction has a dome finished by a gilded urn, giving a charmingly exotic effect, and we agree with Mrs Hofland that 'its general appearance is gay and splendid'.

Proceeding through a brilliantly planted flower garden, we reach the termination of the lake in its river-like form, over which is a Rustic Bridge made entirely from the roots and branches of trees in their natural state, around which ivy is entwined, the whole making a most picturesque effect.

Two fountains mark the approach to the Grotto, which has the appearance of a rocky cavern. Within, a magical effect has been contrived: from the rocky roof descend branches of coral; seaweeds are mixed with ferns; pink, black and white conches abound, and masses of glittering violet spar, white 'chrystals', ores and nautili; clams and large shells decorate the entrance.

We now are nearly at the end of our delightful promenade and have arrived at a most peaceful and inspiring scene: we are in part of the original woods, and come to this beautiful circular glade 'shaded by Ash, Chestnut, Oak and Hazel trees, the rich foliage of which is fed by and reflected in an irregularly formed and pellucid water' known as the Spring. In the heart of the glade, and viewed across the water, is a charming Cottage which completes this Arcadian scene, at once harmonious, simple and reposeful. We find the Cottage has been delightfully fitted up as tea-rooms, the windows ornamented by coloured glass and in the main room china ornaments placed on fanciful brackets. The table in the middle is laden with finest fruits – also in porcelain! – completing an effect that is both decorative and picturesque.

On leaving with reluctant steps this delightful spot, we wend our way once more into the park, and here take leave of Mrs Hofland, our excellent and gifted guide, hoping that others like ourselves may have the good fortune to be conducted by her through these varied and beautiful woods and gardens.

VI

Mary Anne

THE BLANDFORDS had not been long at Whiteknights when a scandal erupted in their midst, accompanied by all the pains and mortifications of widespread publicity. We know from his own admission that when George Blandford sought refuge in marriage with Susan Stewart so precipitately in the autumn of 1791, it was not, as society believed (in the wake of *l'affaire* Gunning), to escape the machinations of match-making mothers (and daughters), but an attempt to blot out the passion he had conceived some two years before for Lady Mary Anne Sturt.

For several years after he married, Blandford neither saw nor communicated with Mary Anne, who continued to live in outward amity with her husband Charles Sturt at their beautiful house, Crichel, near Wimborne in Dorset, during which time she bore him a son and two daughters. Blandford, for his part, was occupied with two house removals, with plant-collecting and gardening, and with the raising of numerous progeny. But George and Mary Anne's love for each other had not been extinguished, and in 1796 an event occurred which undermined whatever intentions of virtue and restraint had, until then, governed their thoughts and actions: Mary Anne's brother, the Hon. Cropley Ashley Cooper, who later succeded his brother as the sixth Earl of Shaftesbury, married Lady Anne Spencer, one of Lord Blandford's sisters. Thus was formed a close family tie between the Sturts, the Shaftesburys and the Spencers, within which it was inevitable that the two lovers would meet and indeed could, in circumstances which precluded comment or suspicion. The former friendship between George Blandford and

Charles Sturt was warmly resumed; the Blandfords together visited the Sturts at Crichel, and at another of their properties, Brownsea Castle, a house romantically situated on an island in Poole harbour. The result was not hard to foretell: the smouldering embers of George and Mary Anne's love for each other were rekindled – and this time there was no dousing the flames. The affair reached its culmination in the birth of a daughter to Mary Anne in January 1801, and in May that year Charles Sturt brought a case against Lord Blandford for Criminal Conversation (the contemporary expression for adultery) with his wife.

After the catastrophic case was over, Sturt published a long pamphlet[1] vindicating himself from the charge of complicity in his wife's adultery, which had been one of the leading points in the stout defence mounted on Blandford's behalf by the Attorney General, and one which, evidently, had cut him to the quick. In this pamphlet Sturt recalled ruefully the many visits Blandford (then a bachelor) had made to his house soon after the two had first met at Lord Shaftesbury's home, St Giles, a few miles from Crichel. They had quickly taken a liking to each other and, wrote Sturt: 'I invited him to Critchill; he came with eight or nine horses, servants in proportion, and lived in my house for near nine months.' Somewhat bitterly he commented: 'I received him . . . at a time when Blenheim was not so agreeable to him . . . and he came to me, and was hospitably entertained with an establishment nearly as great as my own, for several months at a time, and at different periods.'

Charles Sturt and Lady Mary Anne had married in 1788; it must therefore have been a bitter discovery when (according to him) he learned some twelve years later, from letters he intercepted between his wife and the Marquess, that his wife 'had been persuaded by the vile and unmanly acts of Lord Blandford to withdraw her affections from me the year after she had married the man of her own choice.' In 1791 Blandford had married, and the close friendship with the Sturts ceased, until Anne Spencer's marriage to Cropley Ashley in 1796 revived it again in the most agreeable way. Nothing could have seemed more open and natural: Blandford visited his friend of many years' standing, now connected by family ties, as a married man and the father of a family. Sturt was to repeat many times over that he at no time nurtured the slightest suspicion of the true state of affairs between Mary Anne and the Marquess, until accidentally at Christmas 1800 he came across a letter from her to Blandford; thereupon he intercepted others which plainly revealed that they were lovers, and that the child Mary Anne was within a few weeks of expecting was Blandford's.

The story of this love affair, which is a tale of both passionate romance and sordid and elaborate deception, is largely unfolded in the series of letters between the main characters in the melodrama, which Charles Sturt was to publish after the court proceedings.

In a letter to Mary Anne in March 1801, George Blandford wrote: 'You know that my love for you is not a sudden thought; you know that it is grounded on near eleven years intimacy; you know that I married to get the better of it, and that that failed; you know that I tried an absence from you for four years, and that that failed also . . .'. They had renewed their love in 1798; from then until discovery intervened, George and Mary Anne corresponded through devious means. Blandford would often write a letter to one or both of the Sturts on perfectly mundane subjects, this 'innocent' letter forming the outer covering, or 'envelope', for another missive which would be surreptitiously extracted by Mary Anne – the enclosure, couched in very different terms, being for her eyes alone. At other times his letters were concealed in gifts of Parmesan cheese, books or gowns. Mary Anne sent hers in her husband's parliamentary bag (Sturt was Member of Parliament for Bridport). If, as Charles Sturt repeatedly and energetically asserted, he at no time suspected any untoward behaviour, his dismay, mortification and sense of betrayal must have been overwhelming when he uncovered the clandestine correspondence.

Although he may not have nurtured any outright suspicions, nevertheless Sturt was not entirely un-critical of their mutual friend, the Marquess: in November 1800 he wrote to Lady Shaftesbury (wife of the fifth Earl, and Mary Anne's sister-in-law) in a distinctly complaining vein:

---

43. Whiteknights in 1776, by R. Godfrey, after Governor Pownall.

44. The Spring, from *A Descriptive Account of the Mansion and Gardens at Whiteknights* by Thomas and Barbara Hofland, 1819.

My dear Lady,

We are not very gay here, but dress very fine: the
Marquis, with his fingers loaded with rings, and my wife
with trinkets, ear-rings, lion-clasps, and handsome gowns,
which the Marquis constantly gives her. Whenever he
comes he makes it up by his profusion of presents, which,
in my opinion, would be more proper for the Marchioness,
though, I believe, she is no great favourite. He is a damned
odd fellow, and I do not know what to make of him. I
forgot to add that my ears are continually assaulted with
his woeful compositions. The death of the wren is his
subject now.

Not surprisingly this letter was seized upon in court by the Defence
as indicating that Sturt must certainly have had doubts about the
propriety of the relationship between the Marquess and his wife.

It was some six weeks after writing to Lady Shaftesbury that
Sturt said he made the discovery of the letters between his wife and
Blandford. Mary Anne was nearing her confinement: shattered and
outraged though he was, her husband decided that he would not
risk a calamity occurring either to her or to the baby which might
result from confronting her with his discovery of her infidelity, but
he resolved that as soon as she was sufficiently recovered from the
birth he would sever all relationship with her. Meanwhile, a painful
and difficult period lay ahead during which he would have to feign
ignorance of the real situation in deference to his wife's condition.

Charles Sturt did, however, unburden himself to the Shaftesburys: living in the country within a few miles of each other, Mary
Anne and her sister-in-law were probably on close terms; at any
rate, Lady Shaftesbury broached the subject of her relationship with
Lord Blandford. We do not know in detail how their conversation
went, except that Lady Shaftesbury did not reveal that Sturt knew
of the affair, but she may have given counsel in a general way as to
the impropriety of Mary Anne's conduct and warned her of the risk

---

45. The Swiss Cottage: note the flower baskets, a Reptonian feature much in
evidence throughout the gardens. From the Hoflands' book.

46. Fountain in the Botanical Gardens, designed by Lady Diana Beauclerk: note
the china barrel seats. Through the trellis archway can be seen the Conservatory.
From the Hoflands' book.

she ran of discovery. Mary Anne thereupon wrote to Blandford, telling him about her sister-in-law's intervention which had obviously gone to the extent of advising her to cease corresponding and to break off the relationship: 'I would love you, but my friends advise me against it, and their advice is my first consideration . . .'. This provoked a series of long and hysterical letters of protest from Blandford, in which he vilified Lady Shaftesbury for interfering between them. At this moment Mary Anne evidently ceased writing to him, although his letters (now monitored and presumably copied) probably continued to reach her. Blandford was plunged into despair by her silence:

> I have no letter from you to-day; none since Thursday: this completes every thing; however, I shall make no further comments upon your inhumanity: I only think it right to tell you, that you have succeeded in making me the veriest example of wretchedness that, I believe, ever drew breath. *Lady B. is quite alarmed about me, for I burst into tears continually and talk so in my sleep, that she is quite frightened.* Things might have been otherwise; you might have made them so; one piece of wisdom you will have been taught by it, namely, how dangerous it is to let a third person in between ourselves and those we love.
>
> Adieu! That you may profit by my misfortune is still the prayer of one who, had you treated him with moderate kindness, would never have ceased being, for a moment,
>
> Most affectionately and
Unalterably yours
B——

One cannot help sparing a thought for 'Lady B', who must have had a trying time of it.

Meanwhile Blandford and Sturt were exchanging letters of open friendship, right up to the brink of the discovery of the correspondence. One letter from Blandford, written just before Christmas, mentions the pleasurable prospect of a visit to Crichel at the end of January; writing from Whiteknights, he says he 'shall probably not take my gun in hand until then, as we have no pheasants at all, you know, here; and I think partridge shooting poor sport in comparison.'

He also remembers (as an afterthought) that the last day of the year is 'Lady Mary Anne's birth-day; and most sincerely do I hope that she may see many more; and I cannot perhaps wish her a greater share of happiness than her own merits entitle her to . . .'. This friendly letter of good wishes would have arrived in time to rub salt into a new wound: Christmas that year, Mary Anne's birthday and the New Year must have been muted feasts at Crichel; Charles Sturt wrote long unhappy letters to Lady Shaftesbury, depicting his anguish at having to carry on his domestic life in a normal way without letting it appear that he knew the appalling truth. Most painful of all was having to endure his wife's 'kind attention' to himself. He wrote on 26 January 1801 :

> The affectionate conduct of Lady Mary hurts and distracts me more than I can express. I am almost at times led to believe it is all a dream – a delirium . . . But, alas! reflection convinces me of her cruel guile and that all this affection is meant to deceive me; for she knows I am in possession of his picture, his hair, his dirty baubles, and more than suspects I have kept all the correspondence . . .

During this time more incriminating letters from the Marquess were intercepted to fan the flames of Sturt's outrage. One letter, however, was openly addressed, and was wide-eyed in its innocent purpose:

> Dear Lady Mary Anne,
>   Did I not rely upon Charles letting me know when you are confined, I should suspect that it was the case by now, from your long silence. I have not heard from Charles neither for some time. I should be sorry you should hurt yourself by writing much: but I own I shall be glad to receive a line from you, to say you are both well . . .

Mary Anne Sturt was delivered of a daughter on 14 January,*

---

* There is some confusion about the precise date: in the Sturt family Bible it is recorded as 7 January; Sturt's letter gives it as 14 January; the *Gentleman's Magazine* as 15 January. The latter states the birth took place at Brownsea Castle, but all the evidence points to Crichel.

and later in the day her husband wrote to Blandford in the following manner :

> I take up my pen to acquaint you of the safe delivery of Mary Anne of a little girl this morning; they are both very well. She had been unwell for some days. She desires me to thank you for your three letters, one containing a key: being so unwell, she begged me to say, she could not write. Indeed, I can answer for the truth of this, for I have been writing for her to her mother and Miss Calcraft. She is uncommonly well; so much so, that I am going to attend Blandford Sessions to hear what can be done for the poor, poor indeed and miserable, indeed many they are. I am quite sick of Critchill, so much misery around me. You have heard of my poor keeper's accident. Believe me,
>
> > Dear Blandford, yours,
> > C. Sturt.
>
> My horses are at the door.
> Jan. 14, 1801.

During the legal proceedings importance was attached to this letter as proof that Sturt had known all along of the situation and had condoned it. Sturt strenuously denied this, stating that the letter had been written in the presence of a witness, and in order to maintain the fiction that he had not discovered the correspondence.

Blandford's speedy reply to his friend opens a new chapter in effrontery :

> Many thanks to you, dear Charles, for your early and very pleasing intelligence. I most sincerely congratulate you on Lady Mary Anne's being so well, and pray that she may continue to. *I hope also that my little god-daughter* will thrive, and shall be very glad to hear from you again soon that they are both going on well. Pray tell Lady Mary Anne, that I hope she will not think of writing a syllable to me till she feels herself strong, and assure her of my kindest regard and congratulations. As I suppose she may read letters though not write them, I shall write to her in a few days. I was very sorry to find, by your last letter but one, that you was still plagued and harassed by

your annuitants; there is no time that one feels the want
of riches so much as when an opportunity offers that one
could oblige a friend in! Pray give me one line soon, and
believe me,

Yours, dear Charles
Blandford

White Knights,
Sunday.

Blandford also wrote to his Mary Anne, in terms which make
one blush for the foolish fellow, and which reveal him as having lost
all contact with the realities of the situation, no doubt under the
influence of frustated emotions:

That Heaven, my more than ever beloved Mary Anne,
who has so indulgently granted my prayers for your safe
deliverance, may still continue to shield you under its
safeguard, is my constant and ardent prayer! However
we may have had hitherto separate concerns, we can have
but one now; but one point to look to, and that one the
dear pledge of our eternal love! Oh, my wife! my dear, my
adored wife! the blessed mother of my child, what a poor
conveyance language is to express the feelings of a heart
really overcome with affection and love. I love you ten
millions of times more than ever I did. My joy at hearing
you was safe, and my ecstasy at knowing that you was
comparatively free from pain, was more than I really can
express. Suffer, my adored Mary Anne, that the dear
babe, who alas! I have not yet seen, may so cement us in
love and affection, that no machinations of others may
ever have a chance of succeeding in causing even a temporary coldness between us! Love the father in the child,
my dear, and never be ashamed of the workings of nature
and sympathy! Love my poor *Georgiana for the sake of your
George*, your Blandford, your husband, your devoted half!
Heaven knows, and Heaven only knows, how I love you,
my dear Mary Anne; and Heaven will reward me yet for
my constancy. Oh! could I now press my child and its
dear mother to my arms; I could do it with the greatest
innocence! It appears more like a romance than a real
narration of facts, that I should be separated from a

mother and child I adore! When you do write, my dear, write as if you acknowledged me as your husband, for so I am by every divine law! I thought a month ago that I had arrived at the utmost pitch of loving, but I find that I was mistaken, and that I now love more than ever, for I love you now as my wife and the mother of my child. Adieu, my love: I must not write too much to agitate you; I will write again soon, but you must expect tautology.

Most religiously and unalterably yours,
Blandford.

No one will be surprised to learn that the baby was not named Georgina or Georgiana; and Lord Blandford was neither present at the christening (as much to Charles Sturt's indignation he proposed to be), nor was he a godfather. The baby was baptized Emilia on 1 February by the Rector of Crichel; Lady Mary Anne, the children's governess and the nurses were present, but Charles Sturt was not. Indeed, he had as planned removed himself from Crichel as soon as his wife was well enough to rise from her bed, leaving a note with one of his servants addressed to the Marquess, in the event of the miscreant appearing at the house in Sturt's absence:

Your cruel, dishonourable, and atrocious conduct, my Lord, compels me to forbid your putting your feet in my house. My servants have received positive orders to refuse you admittance, and to take every step, however disagreeable, to prevent you.

Yours, &c.
C. Sturt.

Thursday,
22d January 1801.

Although Mary Anne may have suspected that her husband knew about her affair with Blandford, it was not until the third week in February that he actually informed his wife that she and her lover had been discovered. It is clear that Sturt had by then taken legal advice, and that he had been advised not to communicate directly with his wife; he therefore wrote to the Rector of Crichel, the Reverend Mr Marsh, the following dignified letter:

My dear Sir,

I discovered, in the end of December, with the greatest horror and astonishment, a criminal correspondence between Lord Blandford and Lady Mary Anne, my wife: and I have most melancholy and decided proof, besides, that the child of which she has been delivered lately was his. I was compelled, at the time, to conceal this shocking discovery, from Lady Mary's advanced state of pregnancy; and have delayed the communication to the present moment, in order to be allowed due time for her recovery, not wishing that even my wrongs and sufferings should supersede the feelings of humanity. But I need hardly add, that I have had no connexion with her since my acquaintance with her misconduct, and that I never can see her again, or suffer her to remain any longer under my roof. I desire, therefore, that you will have the goodness to represent me upon this unhappy occasion, and that you will take every proper means to carry my wishes into effect. It gives me great pain to request this of you; but having no friend in the country now, and advised not to have an interview with Lady Mary, I am, distressing as it is, obliged to solicit your friendship on this melancholy occasion.

I remain, dear Sir,
Your faithful and obliged friend,
C. Sturt.

February 23, 1801.
Dorant's Hotel, Albemarle Street.

One cannot but feel for the unhappy Rector in having this disagreeable task imposed upon him; indeed, according to Charles Sturt, he at first refused to undertake the commission, and needed some persuading.

In the first week of March, Lady Mary Anne left Crichel with baby Emilia and went to London to her mother, the Dowager Countess of Shaftesbury, at 18 Lower Seymour Street, Portman Square. The two elder children, Henry Charles, aged six, and Mary Anna, aged ten, remained behind in Dorset in the care of their uncle and aunt, Lord and Lady Shaftesbury. The consequences of Mary

Anne's actions now began to crowd in upon her : she was distraught at the possibility that she might not be allowed to see her other children; her adultery and duplicity left her without rights in the matter. Her own family must have been aghast, but they stood by her, her mother giving her and her baby shelter, and her uncle, the Hon. Edward Bouverie (the Dowager Lady Shaftesbury's brother) weighing in with support and advice. He had been present at a meeting with Lord Shaftesbury (Mary Anne's brother) and Charles Sturt when the latter had declared his intention of pursuing Lord Blandford in the courts.

Bouverie now (6 March) wrote to Sturt, telling him that he had seen Mary Anne soon after her arrival at her mother's house in London, and that she was in 'a situation of distress beyond my power to describe. She lamented exceedingly not having had an opportunity given to see you; or that you would not acknowledge the receipt of her letters, as she had constantly written to you . . .'. He begged on his niece's behalf that she should be allowed to see her children, reminding Sturt that Mary Anne was a devoted mother : 'let me entreat a compliance as soon as possible to my request, in full; as by it some alleviation may be obtained for a very suffering and an unfortunate mother.'

This *cri de coeur* was answered the very next day by Charles Sturt, who readily agreed that Lady Mary Anne had ever been an exemplary mother, that she could certainly have access to the children, and that they could also see their grandmother (the Dowager Lady Shaftesbury), 'whose attachment and love for them I know to be equal to their mother's'. Sturt continues, however :

> Be assured, my dear Sir, whatever I can do, under the present circumstances, to alleviate the sufferings of Lady Mary Anne, I will; but to be diverted from pursuing the steps I have been advised to against Lord Blandford, is impossible. I am determined to punish him with the utmost rigour. His treachery, his black ingratitude deserves no mercy from me, nor will I show him any.

Charles Sturt was evidently desirous of behaving in a humane fashion towards his wife, and in a postscript to this same letter he told Edward Bouverie that he had not answered Mary Anne's (no doubt distraught) letters to him, being under legal advice not to do so, adding: 'To add to distress, I trust, is not my disposition.'

Blandford went on writing long, passionate and pleading letters to Mary Anne. It seems unlikely that she received them – certainly she did not write to him, as he sadly states in one letter that he had had no word from her since before the birth of their child. But it may well be that Mary Anne, now completely under the tutelage and protection of her own family, acquiesced in the interception of her lover's letters. If they were sent (by Edward Bouverie, perhaps?) to Charles Sturt, it may have been to provide evidence that Blandford was indeed the seducer, and Mary Anne more sinned against than sinning. Although they stood by her, the Shaftesbury family must have been horrified by the scandal, and still more so by the prospect of the whole affair being paraded in public in a court of law.

Blandford refused to believe that the recent train of events had altered anything: on 19 March he wrote Mary Anne a very long letter protesting his unchanging love for her, and recalling the length of their attachment. He, the hopeless romantic, is prepared to find the world well lost for love, and reminds her of a plan they had, it seems, already discussed – namely, to fly away together abroad, Switzerland being the chosen refuge, where Blandford has many friends: 'Let us, my adored Mary Anne, taking with us our beloved —, grasp at the only happiness now within our reach . . .'.

In his letters, Blandford was wont to refer quite often to his lonely, solitary state; in one he describes himself as 'like a single pin in the world; my father and mother rather wish me ill than well'. But he had found a friend and supporter in his first cousin and contemporary, William Spencer, son of Lord Charles Spencer. Through him, George received news of his beloved – that she was well, and suckling her child. 'I see no soul but W.S. I hate the sight of all the world . . .'. And it was through William Spencer that Blandford devised a new and 'safe' method of communication, which he explained to Mary Anne in another lengthy missive on 22 March: he would direct his letters to her via William Spencer at his London address, and the latter would ensure their safe delivery by himself addressing the outer cover; she was to do the same in reverse. Blandford assured Mary Anne of the perfect safety of this plan; he longed now to hear from her: 'Tell me all you wish, but tell me you still love me. You run no risk now, I assure you, my dear; you may safely unbosom yourself to me; this do, my dear, once more sign yourself "Your unalterable Mary".' He yearned to fix a time when she would appear with their child in her arms at a window – he would be in the street to see them. Blandford's house, 21 Portman Square, was, it so happened, just round the corner from the house in Lower Seymour Street where Mary Anne was living. He had already seen her at a window, quite by chance – now he would like to arrange to glimpse her again; his passion for her and his misery are clear on every page. But this new and 'safe' means of communicating with Mary Anne proved no more secure than previous devices – the letters continued to be intercepted, which points to the explanation that Mary Anne herself had renounced all communication with her former love.

As so often in our hero's life, the bizarre and ludicrous are a mere hair's breadth away from romance and drama: at about this time Blandford launched the following invitation to the man he had so greatly injured:

Dear Charles,

If you are disengaged on Monday next, we shall be very happy in your company at dinner, at half past five. I should not have written you this formal note, had I been able to meet with you.

Yours &c.
Blandford

Don't trouble yourself to send an answer; we shall not wait for you after half after five. Fincastle and Thornton dine with me.

✳✧✳✧✳

The Monday in question, by an ironic coincidence, was to be the day Sturt's solicitor served the Marquess with a notice of prosecution. Not surprisingly Charles Sturt was beside himself with indignation and, on meeting one of the gentlemen also included in the invitation, Lord Fincastle, who enquired if they were to meet at Lord Blandford's, declared: 'No, I would see him d—d first. I would never put my foot in his house!'

It is from Blandford's letters to Mary Anne Sturt at this period that we gather some impressions of his thought processes; we also obliquely glean some clues to Susan's character. When the case came to court, Sturt's counsel made much of the purpler passages from the Marquess's letters to his love – and they show him indeed as a foolish and fanciful fellow; but a reading of the correspondence as a whole reveals other aspects of Blandford's attitudes and feelings, which are not wholly discreditable. The underlying characteristic which is revealed throughout, however, is the man's total lack of a sense of reality.

In the letters Blandford wrote to Mary Anne in the spring of 1801 urging her to join her fate to his and to go abroad, he is at pains to describe to her in detail the arrangements he proposed to make for his wife and children: he would share with his wife the income he was receiving from his father (£2000 a year) and the profits of the Whiteknights estate; he has engaged a private tutor for the boys until they go to Eton; he proposes to let his house in London, 'so there will be left for Lady B and the children, at least 1500*l.* per ann. with a comfortable house (Whiteknights) to live in; and when she wishes to come to town, she has many relations who can accommodate her . . .'. Blandford wants neither Mary Anne nor the world to think he had treated his family ill:

> It may be urged against me, that I abandon my wife and children, following the dictates of passion only; but will not this bear an explanation? . . . When a man leaves his wife friendless, and his children without means of subsistence, he may be said to abandon them; but when he leaves his wife surrounded by her relations, and leaves her, knowing that his presence can neither procure her happiness nor comfort; and when he leaves his children amply provided for, and a plan of education laid out for them to follow, he can scarcely be said to abandon them . . .

Thus he reasoned and justified his conduct, and displayed his never-failing fund of good intention. However, knowing as we do the Marquess's state of perpetual indebtedness (he was for instance already raising money on Whiteknights in 1800, a mere two years after its purchase), it is unlikely that his proposed arrangements would have proved practicable.

When Blandford writes about his wife, he obviously harbours no ill-will or even dislike; on the contrary, he seems to have had an esteem for her, and a sympathetic understanding of how unenviable was 'Lady's B's' position in all this. When writing of his plan of elopement to Mary Anne, he says:

> the regrets that I may receive by going, will, I know, be confined to one person; to one who certainly from her merit deserved a better fate, than that of being united with a man who loves, who adores another; but she has friends, and though I am aware she would suffer on the first surprise, yet she is prepared for all that can happen; her reason will soon show her that she could look for no happiness and little comfort in the society of a man so much attached to another, as she knows me to be; and I am sure also, that, when she hears I am happy, she has regard enough for me to be glad that I went . . .

In another letter, he writes confidently that he is sure his wife would, if he asked her, 'take out a bill of divorce against me'. (Divorce at that time was granted only through a Bill in the House of Lords.) Evidently he had discussed his passionate love for Mary Anne with his wife: 'she not only knows that I adore another, but is perfectly convinced that my sentiments will never change, that she would not have hope even to build on. I know she is prepared for whatever can happen.' Time and again in his letters to his love Blandford excuses his conduct towards his wife by advancing the argument that she will be better off without him:

> I must be an everlasting scourge to her, was I to continue with her; I would do anything to serve her at a distance, but to live with her is impossible. I know, I am certain that she would, after the first change of habit, find pleasures and comforts without me, which she could never experience with me . . .

One cannot help wondering whether 'Lady B' would really have gone so quietly, or whether, as always, Blandford saw the whole scenario through his own eyes, a vision rose-tinted by false optimism and wishful thinking.

Once he knew of the discovery of their correspondence, and the impending court case, Blandford took himself off to Switzerland, probably for some months, so that, he told Mary Anne – in yet another letter that would later be read out in court – he 'might indulge his melancholy amidst the horrors of the Alps'; he was carrying with him, to console his solitude, 'a miniature of his Mary Anne, which he had received from her in the days of their love'. He would also enjoy perusing her letters – they would be quite safe with him, and would be seen by no other eyes! He would leave instructions that they were to be burned after his death – except for one, 'particularly kind', which he desired should be placed in his coffin.

Despite suggestions from Blandford's lawyer that the case might be settled out of court, or tried in the Sheriff's Court in Dorset in order to avoid the publicity of a London trial, the case eventually came to court at the end of May 1801 and was heard before Lord Justice Kenyon. The damages asked for by the Plaintiff were £20,000; the Defendant pleaded not guilty.

Mr Erskine represented Sturt, and Blandford was defended by the Attorney General no less, Sir Edward Law. Mr Erskine had a field-day: lamenting to the jury his misfortune in being obliged to assemble them to give satisfaction in damages for what they would consider 'the greatest injury which it was possible for one man to receive of another – the seduction of his wife', he then expatiated on the regrettable number of similar cases which were again and again brought before the courts. Despite efforts to repress the commission of this crime by the greatest possible severity, he was very sorry to have to say there was little improvement to be observed in public morals in that respect, and, further sorrowing that the Defendant, 'a man of very high and illustrious rank', had not 'conducted himself with any degree of discretion either as it regarded his family, or himself, or the unfortunate Gentleman whom he represented', Mr Erskine then proceeded to outline the case which was causing him so much distress, by introducing the *dramatis personae* and generally setting the scene. Witnesses were called who testified that the Sturts 'appeared to live very happy together' until Lord Blandford, under cover of the family relationship existing between the Sturts and the Shaftesburys consequent upon Lady Anne Spencer's marriage with Mr Cropley Ashley, 'availed himself of the opportunities he had to debauch the Plaintiff's Lady, and to destroy all the happiness of his life'. Such had been the secrecy with which the guilty couple had conducted their affair that proof of their adultery rested entirely in the letters written by Lord Blandford to Lady Mary Anne and eventually intercepted by her husband: 'letters which expressed the most enthusiastic affection for her' and, said Mr Erskine, reminded us of those of Abelard and Petrarch. Extracts from many of these letters were duly read in court. The most damning evidence was provided by the letter written by Lord Blandford to Lady Mary Anne immediately after the birth of her child, acknowledging it to be his.

Despite such weighty evidence, however, Mr Erskine was not to have it all his own sad way. The Attorney General with considerable briskness proceeded to outline the case for the defence, basing it upon two main points. The adultery was admitted to be proved, but, claimed Sir Edward, the Plaintiff had known all along about his wife's affair with Lord Blandford; he had virtually encouraged it, and was therefore an accessory. The exchange of amiable letters between the cuckold Sturt and the seducer Blandford, which ranged from invitations to and from Whiteknights and Crichel to the gift of a carpet or a barrel of madeira, were read in proof of Sturt's complaisance – particularly telling was the letter written by Charles Sturt to Blandford the day of the baby's birth, announcing the event in cheerful and normal tones. After the case Sturt was to say in his justification that the Attorney General had transposed the chronological order of several of the letters, thus giving the impression that he had accepted presents and conducted this friendly correspondence while knowing all the time that his wife was committing adultery with his friend. His position remained that those letters written after he had found the guilty correspondence (which, according to Sturt, was not until Christmastime 1800) maintained the usual friendly tone in order that Blandford might not guess he and Mary Anne were discovered, and that Sturt might have further and complete proof of their guilty conduct.

The second point upon which the Attorney General based his defence was produced somewhat after the fashion of a conjuror who, as a *pièce de résistance*, brings forth a rabbit out of a top hat, and must have caused a sensation in court:

I have then to communicate to you, Gentlemen, that Mr
Sturt, who has thought proper to appear in a court of
justice, to demand damages for the seduction of his wife,
whose society, comfort, and assistance, in the terms of his
complaint, he professes to have lost, lived for years in a
state of avowed concubinage with a Madame Krumpholtz, a celebrated player on the harp. By this woman he
had a child, who was named after him Henry Sturt
Krumpholtz. I shall prove to you, that he has been seen
in bed with her; and if this fact is made out, his Lordship
will tell you, it does repel him from coming here with any
claim to damages. How can he complain of the loss of the
society of his wife, and the comforts of marriage, to whom
that society never was a comfort; but from whom he was
living apart with another woman, withholding those
conjugal rites and endearments she alone was entitled to
expect; lavishing his time and affections on a rival, and
setting her an example of infidelity, which it is not to be
wondered she followed?

Members of Madame Krumpholtz's establishment were called, including one, Sarah Carey, who had looked after the little Henry,
and who gave evidence of the frequent presence of Mr Sturt at
Madame Krumpholtz's house; indeed, she had on many occasions
seen them in bed together. The Attorney General extracted the
utmost advantage for his client from these revelations.

When the judge, Lord Kenyon, came to sum up, he did so in a
ponderous and circuitous fashion; wishing, no doubt, not to be
outdone by Mr Erskine, he also lamented the moral turpitude of the
age, as the *Times* reporter recorded: 'by the assistance of Juries he
had done all he could to suppress offences of this kind, but he pro-
tested that it seemed to him they were in the condition of those who
when they cut off the serpent's head, several more grew in the place
of the one that was cut off . . .'. Finally, he delivered himself of the
opinion that 'this action is not supported on the whole of the evidence', His Lordship's somewhat convoluted reasoning resting on
the straightforward principle that the pot may not call the kettle
black. The jury, however, was not impressed and lost no time in
finding for the Plaintiff, but awarding risible damages of £100
instead of the thousands hoped for and sought. Although Blandford

escaped a financial scourging (which in itself must have been a source of great relief), he emerged from this case a patently ludicrous and scandalous figure, exposed to the ridicule and censure of the world at large. Within his own family the whole sorry tale and embarassing publicity can hardly have improved his already fraught relationship with his parents, while long-suffering Susan would have needed all her cheerfulness and generosity of spirit to rise superior to such mortifications as the public recital of her husband's follies and long infidelity must have laid upon her.

But whatever consequences Blandford had to bear in his own personal life, and in the contempt and ridicule of the world, the framework of his existence was unchanged by the scandal, whereas Mary Anne's life and reputation were in ruins as a result of her unbridled love affair: she and Charles Sturt parted for ever, and she could look only to her family for support in her outcast state. We find no evidence that she and Blandford ever had any further contact. Emilia remained with her mother, but Henry Charles and Mary Anna regarded her as their sister, and it would seem that Charles Sturt was fond of the child; he died in 1812, and in his Will she is referred to as 'dear Emily', and received her portion of the trust (Shaftesbury money) set up at the time of his marriage. Mary Anne is not mentioned in the Will; she survived her husband (and her lover) by many years, but did not marry again. When she died aged eighty-six in 1854 she left her whole estate to Emilia, who died, a spinster, aged sixty-nine.

47. Charles Sturt, a miniature by Richard Cosway.
48. Lady Mary Anne Sturt, a miniature by Richard Cosway.
49. Lord Francis Spencer, by William Owen.
50. George and Charles Spencer, sons of George and Susan Blandford, in fancy dress, a miniature after Richard Cosway.

VII

Living in Arcady

BLANDFORD WAS TO CREATE virtually a new landscape at White-knights, but it is much less clear to what extent he altered the exterior of the house he found when he acquired the property. The mansion dated probably from the second half of the eighteenth century, and a watercolour made in 1791 showing the north aspect of the house, and an engraving of the south and east sides dated 1798 (the year Blandford acquired the estate) show it largely unaltered since Governor Pownall's drawing in 1776. Mrs Hofland described the house in 1816 as a 'handsome modern construction'; by this time, pictures show two great bows on the eastern side, rising the full height of the façade, with a Venetian-style window incorporated, and enclosing the first floor between the bows. The hexagonal construction observed in the 1798 engraving had now disappeared; Mrs Hofland makes no mention that the Marquess added the bows or the veranda which she describes, and alterations and additions may well have been made after 1783, when William Byam Martin bought Whiteknights from the Englefield family. It is known that the architect and surveyor Samuel Pepys Cockerell (1754–1827), was working there during Martin's time, and later on did some work for Lord Blandford.

Although there are no illustrations of the interior of the house in the Hoflands' book, the author gives almost as detailed (and every bit as effusive) a description of the principal rooms as she did of the gardens. Entering the house, she describes how 'Along the whole of this [south-east] front runs a beautiful veranda, supported by light

---

51. 'The Adoration of the Magi' by Carlo Dolci, c. 1635–40. It is likely that this was at Whiteknights in Blandford's time.

iron pillars from the ground.'[1] The veranda (a typical and delightful
Regency adjunct which may well have been added by Blandford)
rose to the first floor, and along its whole length were placed the
'most rare and fragrant exotics growing in classical vases of the
finest forms', interspersed with china barrel seats. So from the beginning we find the same style and themes we had enjoyed in the
gardens invading the house in an enchanting way.

Blandford's love of being in the van of fashion was also reflected
in the arrangement and decoration of the rooms, where nearly all
the contemporary trends were reflected with the ebullience and
extravagance to which we are by now quite accustomed: the
Grecian style; the Egyptian style; Indian ('Histoodanée') touches –
all are represented; indeed, the only style omitted would seem to
have been Gothick: in the grounds, however, there was the romantic
ruin of the Gothick chapel, and several of the arbours had Gothick
details incorporated.

Before allowing her readers to embark on their tour of the house,
Mrs Hofland advises them that the rooms they will see 'are perhaps
unrivalled in their character of combining comfort with magnificence.' Warming to her topic, she continues: 'All here is elegant,
appropriate, splendid, and yet useful; the most fastidious admirer of
simplicity could not find one object which he could denominate
gaudy; nor the lover of grandeur, one circumstance which indicated
deficiency: everything is rich, dignified, and graceful, yet chaste
and unobtrusive.' Our minds thus prepared (without our critical
faculties being subdued), we can proceed.

The two most striking rooms on the ground floor were the
Grecian Room and the Drawing Room, both of which filled the
respective bows and looked out over the lawn gently descending to
the water's edge, at that part of the lake which gave the appearance
of a river flowing through the grounds: beyond, the park extended
to the ruined chapel, and to the north-east the Drawing Room
commanded views over the sheep-walk, the lake and the New
Gardens. Both in France and England 'le goût grec' had, following
the excavations from 1730 at Paestum, Pompeii and Herculaneum,
become the rage as a fashion for furniture, decorative motifs and
costume; but the Neo-Classical style often owed little to its classical
Greek origins. The Grecian Room at Whiteknights would appear

to have justified its name: the walls were painted to represent *verd antique* Ionic columns upon a ground of Sienna marble; there was a stove 'of a new and elegant form, in bronze with appropriate Grecian ornaments', and a marble bust of Artemis. Here, and throughout the house, the lamps and pendant lights were in the Greek style. The furniture coverings and the curtains in the Grecian Room were of a gold and silver 'India chintz'. The Grecian theme was not, however, slavishly adhered to, as there were twin cabinets full of fine French china, and disposed around the room gilt Dresden china jars, silver filigree ornaments, and tables with books and drawings.

The Drawing Room – the counterpart of the Grecian Room, but looking out over the east and north – must have been particularly splendid: the walls were hung with pale peach-blossom coloured cloth, the floor being carpeted in the same colour. 'The curtains of this room are of a rich purple silk, intermixed with peach-blossom coloured sarcenet [a very fine, soft silk], and trimmed with the most splendid fringe, lacings, and tassles of gold-colour silk.' The furniture was covered with purple satin, woven to represent embroidery. In this sumptuously decorated room were hung the most important of Lord Blandford's large collection of old masters: we do not know at what period he acquired his pictures – certainly not as the result of a Grand Tour, for, unlike so many of his contemporaries, he had been denied this experience. One gets the impression that the art collection at Whiteknights was a veritable 'fruit salad' of artists and themes – but a gentleman of taste *had* to have a picture collection! There were throughout the house canvases by Carlo Dolci, Ludovico Carracci, Rubens, Titian, Bronzino, Parmigianino, Salvator Rosa, Panini, Guido Reni, Veronese, Correggio, Caravaggio and Tintoretto. The Dutch and Flemish schools were represented by Rembrandt, Teniers, Ruysdael, Cuyp, Paul Potter, Van de Velde, Pieter de Hooch, Ostade, Rubens and Van Dyck. But despite this dazzling galaxy of names, one feels that Blandford's picture collection consisted chiefly of minor works by major artists: it was certainly not for its art collection that Whiteknights was so widely celebrated. When the greater number of the pictures were eventually sold, Mary Russell Mitford attended the auction, and her verdict was that they were 'very good and very bad'. [2]

But Mrs Hofland was, of course, duly impressed: she was particularly struck by the pictures in the Drawing Room, remarking somewhat grandly and patronizingly that they were 'striking and affecting, even to those who are wholly unlearned on the subject of Painting.' She mentions specifically 'The Death of Darius' by Carracci: Darius 'sinks back in his chariot, overwhelmed with despair; his misfortunes have reached their acme, and hard indeed must be the heart that can refuse to sympathise in his distress. The Madona, by Carlo Dolce [sic], is exquisitely beautiful, and the expression of modesty is so fine that it becomes almost divine.' A Guido Reni of the suffering Christ she found 'too affecting for its situation; the eye that has gazed upon it cannot soon return to the objects of delight which surround it.' One appreciates it must have sounded a dissonant note in the peach-coloured Drawing Room with its purple silk curtains.

In the Dining Room, where the curtains were of blue cloth trimmed with velvet, and the mahogany chairs had blue morocco leather seats, there were more old masters and, on a bracket over the sideboard, a bust of Lord Blandford by Christopher Prosperi (fl. 1800–15). In the Billiard Room there was an equestrian portrait of him by the German painter Peter Eduard Ströhling (b. 1768), and another portrait by Richard Cosway (c. 1742–1821). There were some portraits of the children – but none of the Marchioness.

The elegant staircase, which after the first flight branched into two semi-circular ascents, was lighted by a dome. The Duchess's (Lady Blandford's) Dressing Room adjoined the Library, its three windows opening southwards on to the veranda. It must have been a charming room, and here there was an original touch – could it have been Susan's? – the walls were painted with views of Reading, Caversham and the surrounding countryside: Mrs Hofland's account makes no mention of the artist. She tells us that the Dressing Room was furnished with 'Chinese crape of azure blue, enriched with brocaded flowers, and is ornamented with the most judicious taste, in the Histoodanée style.' It is impossible not to remark upon the absence of any other distinguishing sign of Susan Blandford's presence or influence in the house and gardens: Mrs Hofland makes no reference to her, other than to point out 'her' Garden and 'her' Dressing Room. We can only hope Susan derived some enjoyment from it all, and was allowed some say in the creation of this acre of Arcady.

The most important and interesting room (or rather, sequence of three rooms) on this floor was the Library. In the First Room was Lord Blandford's collection of ancient missals, and displayed on the library-table in a glass case were the two most famous books in this considerable collection: the Bedford Missal and a rare edition of *The Decameron*.

We have already told how in 1786 Blandford had acquired the Bedford Missal for the sum of £698 5s. Now in the British Library – a most exquisite and romantic object – it was executed as a book of devotion for the Duke of Bedford in 1422, when he was Regent of France; it contains the only portraits in existence of John, Duke of Bedford and his wife, Anne of Burgundy.

As for the rare Valdarfer edition of Boccaccio of 1471 – it was the only copy known to have escaped the Florentine bonfires lit by the eloquence of Savonarola towards the end of the fifteenth century. Blandford had purchased this *Decameron* at the Duke of Roxburghe's sale on 17 June 1812 for £2260, in sharp competition with his cousin, the second Earl Spencer – and Napoleon Bonaparte. This, incidentally, was the largest sum yet given for a single volume, and was not to be eclipsed until 1884. The sale was the occasion of the founding of the Roxburghe Club by the bibliographer Thomas Frognall Dibdin (1776–1847), whose patron was Lord Spencer. The members of the Club were bibliophiles, many of whom, like Lord Blandford and Lord Spencer (the President), had taken part in the auction; they dined annually on the anniversary of the sale, and must have made a most congenial company.

There were many other treasures and rarities in Blandford's Library, including a copy of the second edition, on vellum, of Luther's Bible. The Marquess had collected not only Bibles and missals, but also many fine modern books, and, not surprisingly, a considerable number of botanical books, both ancient and modern. Whereas the description of his array of prestigious pictures leaves one cold, here in the Library, as in the Gardens, Blandford seems to come into his own: the image (largely self-made, one must confess) of the spendthrift, licentious fool fades, and one is charmed by the enthusiasm and the knowledge of the collector, eagerly following his own tastes and bent.

In the Second Library Room was housed still more of Blandford's book collection, and also divers specimens of china, sculpted ivory and wood, and numerous objects in bronze, silver filigree, crystal and amber – he must have been a veritable magpie! And, in this room a 'most magnificent grand piano-forte', as well as a small moveable organ 'of pure gold'. This room affords us another example of contemporary taste and fashion: the decorations are in the Egyptian manner. Sirius and Isis replace Artemis as the presiding deities; one wall is painted to represent an Egyptian landscape, and the suspended lamps are Egyptian in style. The taste for Egyptian motifs had been fired by Napoleon's Egyptian campaign in 1798. Accompanying Bonaparte on his campaign and heading an archae-ological expedition to Egypt had been the archaeologist and engraver Denon: his *Voyage dans la Basse- et Haute-Egypte*, copiously illustrated, was published simultaneously in both London and Paris in 1802. Directoire and early Empire French styles reflect the Egyptian influence very strongly, and the fashion soon caught on in London and lasted for a number of years. Despite the long years of inter-mittent war with France throughout the eighteenth and early nine-teenth centuries, English society never wavered in its predilection for all things French. As early as 1750, when the beautiful Gunning sisters had arrived in London, taking society by storm, the only art in which they felt themselves to be deficient was that of understand-ing and speaking French, and their father complained that it cost him 'a guinea a month to teach 'em!' [3]

The Third Room of the Library was called the Boudoir: here it was evidently intended that inmates or visitors of a studious mind might retire and read or write in peace and seclusion. It had a large plain bookcase against the principal wall, and various valuable pictures and interesting curiosities were displayed around.

A general description of the bedrooms by Mrs Hofland states that their character 'is that of simple elegance and solid comfort . . .'. They sound rather charming and uncontrived: it appears they were decorated in similar fashion – 'with fine coloured cottons lined with green', china ornaments, and pictures principally by 'modern' artists such as Romney and Nasmyth.

As to the diversity of styles and the brilliance and variety of materials and colours which were to be found in the principal rooms on the two main floors of the house, it is possible that Lord Blandford may have drawn some of his inspiration for the décor of Whiteknights from an unusual man, the author and virtuoso Thomas Hope (1770?–1831). Hope was a student of architecture, and had visited architectural remains in Egypt, Greece, Sicily, Turkey and other places; he was very rich, and himself had a large collection of vases and marbles. He had purchased in 1799 a London house in Duchess Street, near Cavendish Square, which he proceeded to arrange and decorate in a manner to illustrate his tastes and theories, encompassing both classical and oriental styles; much of his art collection was displayed here, and in 1804 he opened his house to visitors. Three years later he published a book, *Household Furniture and Interior Decoration*, which contained full descriptions of the rooms there, as well as many illustrations. The house and the book had a marked influence on contemporary taste in interior decoration, and John Cornforth writes: 'The dramatic-sounding colouring [in the Duchess Street house] seems to anticipate Beckford's schemes at Fonthill and the Duke of Marlborough's at White Knights as described by Hofland in 1820.'[4] As well as a London residence, Thomas Hope had a country property, at Deepdene, near Dorking, where part of his collection still remains.

One is further tempted to see a connection between Hope and Whiteknights in the fact that at the beginning of the Hoflands' book there is inserted an essay, 'On Modern Gardening', by Thomas Hope, Esq. It was included as part of the Introduction to the main work, because, in Mrs Hofland's words, the theory expressed therein 'appears to the author in perfect unison with the taste displayed by the noble possessor of White-Knights'. And indeed the long and eloquent dissertation is an enthusiastic proclamation of the virtues of the Picturesque style which was so much in evidence there. Mrs Hofland affords us no enlightenment as to the author of this essay other than his name – somewhat primly remarking that she 'is induced to transcribe it entirely, under the full persuasion that the judicious reasoning and profound knowledge of the subject evinced by that gentleman, will not fail to give pleasure to the enlightened, and carry conviction to the uninformed, but candid enquirer.' Quite so.

When Lord Blandford returned to England after the ignominious
and painful episode of the Sturt case, he seems to have addressed
himself, at least temporarily, to the realities of life, inasmuch as he
now sought once more to enter Parliament. For six years from 1790
he had been Member of Parliament for the county seat of Oxfordshire, succeeding his uncle Lord Charles Spencer (of Wheatfield),
but in 1796 his uncle, a popular local figure, had taken on the seat
once more. When he finally relinquished it in 1801, the representation of the county remained in the family, but once more by-passed
Blandford (perhaps not surprisingly in view of the wide publicity
given to the Sturt affair); whether it was a direct result of this scandal
one cannot say, but Blandford never again represented the family
interest either for the county or for Woodstock. The succession in
the county seat was now taken up by his younger brother, Lord
Francis, aged twenty-one, upon whom the Marlboroughs were
more and more to fix their hopes: in 1800 he had married Lady
Frances Fitzroy, daughter of the Duke of Grafton, and over the
coming years Lord Francis would increasingly assume the role and
take on the functions that should rightly have been the province of
his elder brother, such as commanding the Oxfordshire Cavalry
volunteers and the Oxfordshire Militia and Yeomanry. All this must
have been humiliating for Blandford, marking both his parents'
disapprobation and his own poor standing in local opinion and
esteem. However – perhaps as part of an attempted rehabilitation
after recent scandals – a new parliamentary seat was contrived for
him in 1802: it was not a local seat, but Tregony, in Cornwall.

Blandford was never to make a mark in politics, however. One
receives the impression that he went through the motions of being a
Member of Parliament as being the 'done thing' for one of his rank,
and possibly in an attempt to show a scornful world that he was not
the ludicrous lightweight he seemed to be. He started politically as a
Whig, following his forebears, but the resumption of war with France
in 1803 found him a Pittite Tory, and when William Pitt the Younger
formed his third coalition government in 1804, Blandford was included in the administration (somewhat ironically, one may be
forgiven for thinking) as a Commissioner of the Treasury. There
were at this period several members of the family active in politics:
the Duke's brother, Lord Charles, sometime Postmaster General,

who adopted the 'trimming' tradition of his family; Lord Francis, a 'trimmer' too, made a showing, moving the address congratulating the Government on the victory at Trafalgar. Commenting on their different political stances at this time, Dr Rowse observes that between the extremes represented by Lord Blandford, a Pittite Tory, and his uncle, Lord Robert Spencer, a Foxite Whig, were 'the Duke, whose main idea was not to upset George III, and Lord Francis, whose leading idea was not to upset his father.'[5]

In the autumn of 1805, Nelson's victory at Trafalgar delivered England from the threat of invasion, and gave her the command of the sea; but six weeks later, at the battle of Austerlitz, Napoleon's crushing defeat of the forces of Tsar Alexander of Russia and the Emperor Francis II of Austria made him master of Italy and southern Germany, and encompassed the overthrow of Austria. These heavy tidings hastened the death of William Pitt towards the end of January 1806; he was succeeded as Prime Minister by Lord Grenville (1759–1834), a Whig, allied to Fox, and a supporter of Catholic Emancipation; he headed the 'Ministry of All Talents', which lasted until March 1807.

Blandford was on friendly terms with the new Prime Minister, and he lost no time in lobbying him with a view to remaining in office in the new administration: on 7 February 1806 Lord Grenville wrote regretfully that owing to various difficulties he had had 'to relinquish the hope I had entertained that I might be enabled to propose to Your Lordship, that you should retain your seat at the Treasury Board . . .'.[6] Nothing abashed, Blandford cheerily assured Lord Grenville that his Lordship's 'inability . . . to meet my wishes in the New Administration will not at all slacken my Zeal to support Your Lordship's Government, & to pursue that line of Conduct towards which I am impelled by a sense of Duty to my King & Country, & of personal regard and consideration for Your Lordship.'[7] Finding that fine words were buttering no political parsnips, Blandford tried another tack: he applied to be called up by writ to the House of Lords; his request to the King was passed through Lord Grenville and, the King acceding, Blandford hoped to take the title of Churchill. The Duke, however, was not favourable to the proposition that his less-than-worthy son should adopt this proud name, though acquiescing to his use of one of his other subsidiary titles. Accordingly, Blandford was called up by a writ in his father's Barony as Baron Spencer of Wormleighton. He was introduced into the House of Lords on 17 March 1806 by Lord Grenville and by his father-in-law, the Earl of Galloway (who appeared under his English title of Lord Stewart of Garlies).

Now a member of the House of Lords, Blandford still yearned for office, and although Lord Grenville ceased to be Prime Minister in March 1807, he continued to receive requests from his importunate friend. On 10 August that year, Blandford wrote: 'As sudden Changes *have* happened, *are* happening, and *may* happen again', he cannot help troubling Lord Grenville with a private inclination of his wish for a situation in the Government.[8] There is no direct reply to this broad hint, and later in the month Blandford writes again, this time seeking the command of a militia regiment: two days later, on 28 August, Grenville replies that such appointments are made by the Lords Lieutenants of the Counties, and that it is not within the power of the Government to put his name forward.[9] Three months later, on 13 November, the Earl of Galloway died aged seventy; he had held the post of one of the King's Lords of the Bedchamber: before the month was out Blandford was appealing to the long-suffering Grenville that he might be considered to fill the vacancy which now occurred.[10] There is no record of any reply to this request, but we know that Lord Blandford was not appointed to this post. Truly his motto should have been '*Nil desperandum*'.

❖❖*

Meanwhile Lord Blandford's plant collecting and gardening activities continued, and his appetite for new and rare plants was voracious. At Whiteknights he was forever bursting the boundaries he himself had made, and 'colonising' other areas of his estate. To the Botanic Gardens were soon added the New Gardens and the Woods (through which we have been guided by Mrs Hofland); and throughout the parkland he planted many choice and beautiful trees. We have already been the amused witnesses of a mild horticultural skirmish between the Marquess, Sir Joseph Banks and William Townsend Aiton. In 1805 we once more find the irrepressible Blandford importuning Sir Joseph for plants from Kew Gardens.

From Sir Joseph Banks to W. T. Aiton:

May 21st 1805

The following List of Plants was given to me two Days ago by Lord Blandford who has demanded them in rather a peremptory manner, some of them I see can't with propriety be parted with, possibly none of them ought to be sent away. Of that you are the best Judge, be so good as to favor me with your opinion upon it as soon as possible.

It is unfortunate that my Lord Blandford shou'd so continually require from you & from me Plants that ought not to be spar'd from the Gardens, & so seldom those that can with propriety be parted with, but you & I must do our Duty to the King without partiality to my Lord, by always letting him have those that can be spar'd & as constantly refusing to part with those that ought not.[11]

Although it was nearly two months before Aiton replied to Sir Joseph, he was evidently in an amenable frame of mind and prepared to oblige the persistent nobleman. Aiton to Sir Joseph Banks, 16 July 1805:

. . . I am flatterd you will approve that the Plants inserted in the enclosed List may be offerd from His Majestys Collection at Kew to the acceptance of the Marquis of Blandford, I have thought so more particularly on this Acc. They have been exhibited in Blossom before the Royal Family & have been much admired by their Majesties, they are rare Plants being to my knowledge in no other Garden than the Kings from which Collection they can be spared with propriety, the Garden already possessing duplicate Plants of the several kinds mentioned in the List.

I shall wait with great pleasure to obey your Commands, in order to forward the Plants for the Marquis of Blandford in the Way His Lordship may choose to direct.[12]

From Sir Joseph's letter (written on the same day), it would seem that he did feel his Superintendent had been somewhat dilatory, for his letter to Blandford runs:

My Lord,

I have at last received from Mr. Aiton a List of Plants which can with propriety be spared from the Royal Gardens at Kew . . .[13]

Banks goes on to say that, on hearing from the Marquess that they are acceptable to him, he will give instructions for them to be prepared for collection. Blandford must have been regarded as a serious collector for both the distinguished Director and the highly possessive Superintendent at Kew to have been prepared to oblige him – albeit not without heaving a sigh or two!

Part of creating the picturesque effect at Whiteknights involved architectural schemes: Lord Blandford employed one Francis Bernasconi to give the chapel its *à la mode* Gothick façade in 1810 (his account for this work amounted to £42 6s); he also did stucco work on the bridge. Bernasconi's account is countersigned by Samuel Pepys Cockerell, the surveyor and architect; he was a descendant of the famous diarist, and brother of the East India Company nabob, Sir Charles Cockerell, for whom in 1805 he had designed and was building Sezincote, a fantastic and unique house in the Indian style: Humphry Repton made the gardens there following the same theme. Another illustrious patron of the 'Mughal' Indian style was the Prince Regent; he had been introduced to this style by William Porden (1755–1822) – a student of S. P. Cockerell – who built the stables at the Royal Pavilion, Brighton. Later, after a visit to Sezincote, the Prince commissioned Repton to make plans in the Indianesque manner for the Pavilion and its gardens, which were published in 1808.

Samuel Pepys Cockerell had in fact worked at Whiteknights before, during the tenure of William Byam Martin, for whom he designed entrance gates and a bridge; the sketches for these were exhibited at the Royal Academy in 1785. Some twenty-five years later, he was back adorning the chapel and titivating his own bridge at the behest of the subsequent owner. There is no record of any other work Cockerell may have done for Lord Blandford, but it is easy to see that as a patron of the fantastic and exotic, the Marquess would have delighted to call in the architect so recently made famous in those styles, and it may have been Cockerell's influence which produced the 'three Oriental arches surmounted by crescents' that we observed inside the entrance to the Botanic Gardens.

A few years later, Blandford was to employ another purveyor of the fanciful – a well-known architect, garden designer and inventor of garden ornaments and buildings who rejoiced in the name of John Buonarroti Papworth (1775–1847). Although, according to Mrs Hofland, Blandford himself designed some of the ornamental constructions at Whiteknights, Papworth was working there in 1815, designing fountains and long arcades; he also created many of the elaborate and unusual covered seats and arbours which were to be found at every turn throughout the garden walks.[14]

The works of all kinds which were carried out at Whiteknights were much discussed, and aroused keen curiosity – both among those who were genuinely interested in plants and gardening, and also among the many people who were eager to visit the property of a nobleman whose other activities had rendered him an object of scandalized interest. In the summer of 1807, Mary Russell Mitford (whom we have already met as a friend of the Hoflands) visited Whiteknights, writing afterwards to her father:

> I am very happy I have seen Lord Blandford's, my darling, as I should, if I had not, always have fancied it something superior. In good truth, I was greatly disappointed. The park, as they call it (if about eighty acres, without deer, can be called a park), is level, flat, and uninteresting; the trees are ill clumped; the walk round it is entirely *unvaried*, and the piece of water looks like a large duck pond, from the termination not being concealed. If the hothouses were placed together instead of being dispersed, they might make a respectable appearance; but as it is, they bear evident marks of being built at different times (whenever, I suppose, he could borrow money for the purpose) and without any regular plan. Their contents might be interesting to a botanist, but gave me no great pleasure. The thing I best liked was the garden in which the conservatory is situated; the shrubs there are really very fine, particularly the azaleas, and the American honeysuckles both pink and yellow; the rhododendrons are superb . . .[15]

Some ten years later, in October 1817, Miss Mitford was once

again at Whiteknights, this time in the company of Thomas and
Barbara Hofland, who were busily working on their book; she
wrote all about it to Sir William Elford on 11 October:

> It was that notable fool, His Grace of Marlborough, who
> imported these delightful people into our Boeotian town.
> He – the possessor of Blenheim – is employing Mr. Hofland
> to take views at Whiteknights – where there are no views;
> and Mrs. Hofland to write a description of Whiteknights
> – where there is nothing to describe . . . There is a certain
> wood at Whiteknights, shut in with great boarded gates,
> which nobody is allowed to enter. It is a perfect Blue-
> beard's chamber: and of course all our pretty Fatimas
> would give their heads to get in. Well, thither have I been,
> and it is the very palace of False Taste – a bad French
> garden, with staring gravel walks, make-believe bridges,
> stunted vineyards, and vistas through which you see
> nothing. Thither did I go with Mrs. Hofland – 'the two
> first modest ladies', as the housekeeper said, that she
> remembered to have been admitted there. *Nota bene*, the
> Queen and Princesses had walked over it the week before.*
> But the master was absent, and we had the comfort of
> laughing at it as much as we chose . . .[16]

These somewhat scathing accounts are in marked contrast to the
eulogistic descriptions of the Hoflands. It seems only fair to remark
that at the time Miss Mitford paid her first visit to Whiteknights,
none of Blandford's plantings could have been more than seven or
eight years old, and that the Hoflands had the advantage of finding
a more matured garden to describe with pen and brush. However,
Miss Mitford is a good splash of cold, clear water in the face; no
doubt the Hoflands, having been commissioned by Lord Blandford,
were bound to play 'the customer's game', and describe in uncritical
enthusiastic terms the effects their patron had called into being.
Indeed, perhaps Lord Blandford had inspired (or instructed) them
to describe and paint the garden and woodland scenes as he himself
saw them, through the long-distance, rosy time-lens of his own imagination – such an imagination as all true landscape gardeners

---

* She must have been referring to the visit of the Queen and Princesses in August
1817, which is described in due course.

must possess. Certainly the pleasant oil paintings of Thomas Hofland show ripened landscapes where Lombardy poplars, for instance, have soared beyond the possibility of their actual height at the time he painted them; and the groves and glades so felicitously described by his wife assume a rate of plant growth which would delight and excite the most hopeful of gardeners.

Miss Mitford must have had a happy and hilarious time with her friends, wandering about the grounds at Whiteknights and poking endless fun at the absent Marquess. Indeed, so enthused by the whole project did she become that she contributed a sonnet to the Hoflands' *magnum opus*, inspired by the Fishing Seat. It in every way matches the hyperbolic flights indulged in by her friends.

The Fishing Seat: Whiteknights

There is a sweet accordant harmony
  In this fair scene – this quaintly fluted bower:
  These sloping banks, with tree and shrub and flower
Bedecked; and these pure waters, where the sky
In its deep blueness shines so peacefully:
  Shines all unbroken; save with sudden shade
  When some proud swan, majestically bright,
Flashes her snowy beauty on the eye:
  Shines all unbroken; save, with sudden start,
When from the delicate birch a dewy tear
  The west wind brushes. E'en the bee's blithe trade,
Or the lark's carol, sound too loudly here:
  A spot it is for far-off music made,
Stillness and rest – a smaller Windermere!

M.R.M.[17]

Miss Mitford was the first to admit her prejudice, writing in the same letter to Sir William Elford:

> I have been a great deal with them [the Hoflands], and have helped Mrs Hofland to one page of her imperial quarto volume . . . and to make myself amends for flattering the scenery in verse, I comfort myself by abusing it in prose to whoever will listen . . . .

Somewhere between the Hoflands' euphoric flights and Miss Mitford's more astringent judgements must surely lie the truth; and as with the human countenance, so also with works of art (in which I include gardens and man-made landscapes), beauty to a large extent ever lies in the eye of the beholder.

To the contemporary gardening *cognoscenti*, however, and at a time when many amateurs such as himself were keen gardeners and plant collectors, Lord Blandford was judged to be among the foremost.[18] John Claudius Loudon (1783–1843), the eminent landscape gardener and horticultural writer, had first visited Whiteknights in 1804, and for many years following he was to revisit the woods and gardens, writing commentaries of how, despite changing fortunes, they were progressing or surviving, of such great importance did he rate the collection there. And apart from the interest and great variety of plant life at Whiteknights, the Marquess's sheer profligacy as a collector was the subject of amazement and comment. Even the erudite Loudon (who, incidentally, had bankrupted himself on his ambitious horticultural publications) was moved to report on Blandford's wild extravagances: 'The greater number of these costly plants were furnished from the Hammersmith nursery; and, in 1804, the late Mr Lee informed us, that the Marquess of Blandford's bill with him exceeded 15,000*l*!'[19] The nursery he refers to here was the famous Vineyard Nursery, founded by James Lee and James Lewis Kennedy about 1745 on the site of a former vineyard, at the place where Olympia now stands.

In the gardens and arboretum the Marquess had planted many newly introduced American trees and shrubs (Loudon remarked particularly on the extensive collection of *Crataegus*, or thorns), and he was never content with only one plant of a rare species if more were to be had; Mr Lee had further vouchsafed that he had sold 'several plants of the same species to the marquess when they were at twenty guineas, and even thirty guineas each'.[20] No wonder Blandford's account with the Vineyard Nursery grew to such mammoth proportions.

---

52. 'A Modern Living Room' from Repton's *Fragments on the Theory of Landscape Gardening*, 1816.
53. The Pantheon after the fire of 1792, by J. M. W. Turner.

Rich.ᵈ Cosway, R.A Delᵗ.   I.S Agar Sculpᵗ.

J.D.F.

There is an amusing story concerning the extent to which what one can only describe as 'collector's mania' had seized Lord Blandford; it appears in the biography of Edward Budd, a famed sportsman and florist. Budd had told the author

> that sixty years back (*c.* 1807) there were no more than three varieties of geranium known in Great Britain. They were, he thought, the oak-leaf, the Bath scarlet, and the variegated. 'At about that period,' said Mr Budd, 'the Duke of Marlborough* had a famed floral collection at White Knights. His Grace was one day inspecting the choice collection of a celebrated Chelsea florist, when seeing some marvellously-beautiful flower, he inquired the price, and was informed seven guineas. Finding the dealer had but two more, he purchased the three for twenty-one guineas, destroyed two of the flowers and said, "Now the Duke of Marlborough has the only one in England".'[21]

It seems clear that Blandford was more successful as a collector than as a creator of garden landscape, and that in his unbounded enthusiasm he crammed into the 280 acres of the Whiteknights estate more than they could with convenience or harmony contain. It was too small a canvas for his enthusiastic brush: he would not forego a single novelty, neither treillage tunnels, nor gardens modelled on those at the Château de Chantilly, nor would he deprive himself of a greenhouse or a grotto, a fountain or an arbour or two. Having imbibed the Hoflands' descriptions, then to walk the length and breadth of the Whiteknights terrain certainly confirms one in this opinion. And while I will not join Miss Mitford in decrying the lake as a 'large duck pond', I am bound to admit that that agreeable stretch of water in no way calls to mind Lake Windermere. Nevertheless, the Whiteknights gardens, whatever Miss Mitford thought of them, were renowned: the King had paid a visit around

---

* The author, writing retrospectively, has made a mistake: Lord Blandford did not become Duke of Marlborough until 1817.

---

54. George, Marquess of Blandford, by I. S. Agar after Cosway. This portrait probably dates from the time of his succession: note the ducal stance and the Column of Victory at Blenheim in the background.

1810, just before his grave illness, and Miss Mitford herself tells how she visited the gardens hot in the footsteps of the Queen and a posse of Princesses.

During June 1814, the whole country was agog with excitement at the visit of the Tsar Alexander I of Russia and King Frederick III of Prussia, accompanied by a galaxy of princelings and nobles and attended by a glittering entourage. This visitation of England's allies was to celebrate the overwhelming of the Corsican tyrant, and took place during that euphoric period which elapsed between Napoleon's first abdication in early April 1814 and that fateful day, 1 March 1815, when, escaped from his incarceration on the island of Elba, Bonaparte landed near Cannes, setting all Europe a-quaking, and began those hectic Hundred Days which had their climax at Waterloo.

On 7 June 1814, the Tsar and King Frederick arrived in London, and throughout their three-week visit much public interest was displayed in every detail of the royal programme. It would seem that a visit to Whiteknights by the royal guests was mooted and, needless to say, Miss Mitford, who lived in the neighbourhood of Reading, got wind of this rumour and saw in it an irresistible opportunity to sharpen her pen (her wit needed no honing) on our Marquess. Writing on 11 June 1814 to her father, she reported that a regiment of Light Dragoons was said to be in Reading to be in attendance on the monarchs when they made their proposed descent on Whiteknights: 'It is almost impossible to believe that this report can be true; not so much on account of Lord —'s character, as his notorious poverty. He could scarcely find credit for a collation to stay the royal stomachs . . .'[22]

Inspired to verse by the prospect of this visit, she took up her pen and dashed off a verse, which she avowed to her father was 'the first libel I ever had the honour to compose':

> *Epigram on the intended visit of the Emperor (of Russia)*
> *and King (of Prussia) to the Marquis of Blandford*
> *at Whiteknights near Reading*

> To gaze, with eager, yet discerning, eyes
> On all our Island boasts of good and wise;

To greet in England men to England dear,
The Hero-Monarchs come. What calls them here?
Here, where preside, mixed up by courtly rule,
Th'Adulterer, Spendthrift, Fiddler, Knave and Fool;
Well for our Prince, well for our Country done,
To show of this rare species more than one.[23]

Miss Mitford had observed what a later generation can also perceive: that 'Prinny' and our Marquess were cast in the same mould. She toyed with the idea of publishing this witty epigram which so delighted her (and, no doubt, her friends) and her publisher too considered doing so, but prudently drew back when the verse was declared libellous by a lawyer. In the event, the visit to Whiteknights never took place – perhaps none was planned. Their Imperial and Royal Majesties *et al*, however, did visit Blenheim on Wednesday, 15 June, the day after they had been received in Oxford.

Some seven years on, we have an account of Whiteknights from another visitor, Mrs Arbuthnot, the great friend of the Duke of Wellington. In January 1821 she was staying at Stratfield Saye, the home of the Duke, where a large and fashionable house party was assembled, including the Russian and Austrian Ambassadors and their wives, and Lord and Lady Castlereagh. On 14 January Mrs Arbuthnot wrote in her journal:

> . . . we rode a large party from Stratfield Saye to see White Knights, a place belonging to the Duke of Marlboro, where there is the finest garden in England, quite beautiful. It consists of 36 acres, laid out with the greatest taste. From the profusion of evergreens the place looked quite like summer, & it is impossible to express the beauty of the American plants. We could only take a very hurried view of it, for it is eight miles from Stratfield Saye, and we did the whole in three hours . . .[24]

No doubt they had to curtail their visit through lack of time, otherwise Mrs Arbuthnot would have realized that the pleasure grounds extended to much more than thirty-six acres. But the impression she received demonstrates how well furnished were the gardens, that even in deepest winter they gave such a beautiful effect.

VIII

Kith and Kin

URING ALL THIS TIME we have few insights into the relationship of George and Susan, but we do find one or two 'signposts' in the letters Blandford wrote to Mary Anne Sturt. In one (written before the birth of their child, probably late December 1800–early January 1801), no address, but clearly written from 'home', Blandford writes: 'You [Mary Anne] ask me about my reception here; it was as usual; but we disagreed in less than an hour after I arrived, and scarcely spoke till next day.' In other letters Blandford made it plain that he had discussed his love for Mary Anne with his wife; perhaps Susan had known even before the fatal disclosures that there was 'another', but the blazoning abroad of the affair must have added to her pain and mortification.

Other aspects of their life together may have been easier: their new house, with its so fashionable décor, and the elegant Library and its remarkable collection of books; musical interests; their growing family, and the veritable maelstrom of activity and planning in the grounds – all these could have afforded opportunities for mutual interest and enjoyment. And we may be sure our Marquess was a liberal and congenial host: there is a vastly entertaining account of a visit to Whiteknights, around 1814–15, by Captain Gronow. This dashing figure and indefatigable writer of reminiscences had recently returned from the Peninsular campaign in Spain; he was about twenty at the time, and an exact contemporary of George Sunderland, with whom he had been at Eton. Gronow describes how 'at this charming house' which was 'kept up with a splendour worthy of a royal residence'[1] he found a large house party among whom were Lord Grenville, the former Prime Minister (who had evidently not been deterred from staying by Blandford's badgerings for office) and his wife, Lady Grenville, who was herself a noted gardener at their home, Dropmore, near Beaconsfield in Buckinghamshire. Among the other guests were Lord and Lady Macclesfield, neighbours in Oxfordshire; Mr Matthias, an author; Lord William Fitzroy, etc. A tremendous fluster was caused by Captain Gronow's Sicilian soldier servant, who attempted to kiss Lady Macclesfield's maid, whom he met on the staircase; the maid took refuge in her mistress's bedroom, whither the lusty Sicilian pursued her; Lady Macclesfield's screams brought help, and the Sicilian took refuge under the bed, whence he was subsequently expelled with the aid of the fire irons!

Whatever may have been the true nature of their relationship over these years, it seems that a cross-roads was reached in the Blandfords' marriage around 1812; in that year's edition of *Boyle's Court Guide*, different addresses in London are given for the Marquess and Marchioness: 37 St James's Street for him, 10 Cadogan Place for her, while their country address is given (as it was to remain in succeeding years) as Whiteknights. Ever since the early years of their marriage the Blandfords had rented a town house, and for some time prior to this change, their joint London address had been listed as 44 Grosvenor Square. The entry for 1812 in *Boyle* must be significant, marking the stage at which the couple no longer sought to conceal the state of their marriage from the outside world. It also helps us to place an undated document[2] which seems to be an attempt to regulate George and Susan's separate arrangements in London.

This interesting document is written in what appears to be Blandford's hand; it is extremely difficult to decipher, but I judge it to be the rough draft of a memorandum seeking to create a *modus vivendi* for the now 'semi-detached' couple. It is impossible to put a precise date to the paper, but various clues, such as the watermark of the paper (1808) and the mention of 'Holydays with the Boys', lead me to place it somewhere between 1808 and 1812 – probably 1811.

There is no indication as to whether this memorandum was ever put into more formal shape, nor whether it ever formed the basis of mutual discussion or correspondence between George and Susan Blandford. It is a guide as to how he, at any rate, envisaged the practical organization of their life: it makes it clear that while each partner was to have a separate and independent house or apartment in London, both parties would undertake certain joint obligations as to the conduct of their social and family life, some of which was to continue to be in common.

Lord Blandford was 'To have a Cover at Lady B^d's table whenever I choose to dine there', – unless, Lord B considerately mentions, 'L^{dy} B may wish to dine from Home'. He is to have a 'good Best Bedroom' furnished to his liking whenever he wishes to sleep in her house; conversely, 'L^{dy} B to have the same apartments in my House in Town as she would have were she solely resident there . . .'. They would continue on certain occasions to entertain together: 'L^{dy} B to preside at any dinners I may give when there are Ladies or when I wish her to dine occasionally with me alone . . .'. One cannot resist the impression that Lord B was quite eager to have his cake as well as eating it.

As to their country life: Whiteknights was to continue to be their family base, but one can just detect a faint note of conciliatory pleading – is it possible that the agreeable and seemingly compliant Susan had at last shown some fight? The italics are mine: 'L^{dy} B to consider W.K. as the joint country house of Lord B^d and herself & *not to object to going there occasionally with Lord B & [with] Lady Caroline, or to pass the Holydays with the Boys.*' In 1811, two (and possibly three) of the boys would still have been at Eton; Caroline was thirteen that year, and it is clear from other references that she lived with her mother until she married some ten years later.

The finale of this significant memorandum runs:

> Lord B considers it impossible that L^{dy} B can be otherwise than satisfied with all this, as the plan of having her living entirely by herself is completely provided for; L^d B Reasserts having nothing to do with her House, nor himself with her Housekeeping –
> L^d B only binds himself to this plan for one year or should his Father die before that time to that period.

By modern standards this document would seem to form a basis for a reasonable and civilized (albeit a somewhat male-oriented)

arrangement, by which the façade of their marriage was to be preserved, and their family life continued in the country, while each
partner could have a wide measure of personal liberty in London;
and it appears that the Marchioness was quite as eager to have some
measure of private life as her Lord. In the event, we have no details
of how the Blandfords organized their domestic life beyond knowing
that from 1812 they lived separately when in London. Until 1817
when Lord Blandford succeeded his father and Blenheim became
the main focus of his life, there are several references to Lady
Blandford being at Whiteknights with her husband and children.

As to Blandford's relationship with his family, it had for years
been fraught with misunderstanding. Immediately following his
marriage in 1791 a semblance of goodwill had been achieved, largely
through the gentle offices of his aunt, Lady Pembroke, but the truce
was shortlived. In 1798 the Duke had bought Whiteknights and
leased it to Blandford – the very least he could do for his son and
heir – but there is no evidence that things between father and son
were improved. It was a sad business, although certainly not unique
in the annals of family relationships.

We glean a good deal about family affairs at this time from the
correspondence between Dr James Blackstone, the family lawyer
and one of the fourth Duke's trustees, who lived in Woodstock, and
Lord Auckland; the latter was not only a family friend, but also a
close counsellor to whom Blackstone reported regularly. Although
Blandford was so ill-regarded by his parents, Dr Blackstone seems
ever to have been scrupulously fair to him, and by his advice (whether
to the Duke and Duchess, or to Lord Blandford) never sought to
trouble further the muddied waters.

As for Lord Francis Spencer, thirteen years Blandford's junior,
ever since Lord Henry's death in 1795 he had increasingly become
the favourite son. We have no evidence that he tried to 'edge his
brother out' – rather he appears as a go-between, but Blandford
must have resented his parents' obvious favouring of the younger
brother, and have felt keenly the weakness of his own position,
seeing with dismay that Francis was usurping his patrimony. The
dukedom and Blenheim were, of course, inalienable, but large tracts
of property such as the Cornbury estate were settled by the Duke on
his younger son, and in 1815, after years of lobbying, the Duke

procured a peerage for Lord Francis, who became the first Baron
Churchill of Wychwood, and founded a cadet line of the family.

Earlier on, Blandford had been anxious to make some conciliatory gesture towards his parents – more especially towards his
mother; it was, of course, in his own self-interest to do so, but cold-
heartedness was never a fault of his, and he may genuinely have
wished to break the deadlock in their relationship. Evidently he
consulted both Dr Blackstone and his brother Francis: they had
been as one, at the time, in advising Blandford to wait for a propi-
tious moment to proffer his olive branch. Such a moment presented
itself towards the end of October 1811, when the Duchess (then aged
sixty-eight) was taken very ill, and her life was thought to be in
danger. Dr Blackstone gave a detailed account of the whole episode
to Lord Auckland: on the morning of 24 October, the Duchess had
fainting fits, and seemed *in extremis* – she rallied, however, and the
chaplain administered the Sacrament to her; afterwards (according
to a pre-arranged plan) the chaplain urged her to have her son the
Marquess sent for; to this suggestion the Duchess agreed

> on Condition of his not seeing the Duke, & of not staying
> longer than necessary for the interview – A despatch was
> sent to White Knights, for Lord B who Arrived about 6 &
> has just ($\frac{1}{2}$ past 7) left me after calling upon me to relate
> all circumstances. On his Arrival L^d F [Francis] brought
> a Message to him from the Duke saying he was too nervous
> to see him but considered this as the beginning of a recon-
> ciliation. He was then conducted to his Mother who
> shook hands with him, & told him he must ask his Father's
> forgiveness not hers. She wished him only to acknowledge
> that she had ever stood his friend, which he s^d he instantly
> Acknowledged – she then talked Calmly about his
> Children, hoping he w^d breed them up Well; that she
> would like to live a little longer, but the Medical Gent^n
> knew best – On the Whole L^d B was affected with the
> interview. On his retirement, a Cold Collation was given
> him; and he received a Message from his Father that he
> wished to see him: he described this interview as One
> Scene of Sobbing by the Duke whilst he was on his knees
> before him. And After^{ds} he rec^d a Message by L^d F that
> when things were a little quieter he would be received . . .[3]

Blackstone seemed hopeful that a reconciliation had been achieved, and the Doctor gave his opinion that the Duchess might survive a day or two; she struggled on however, and, indeed, a month later was declared to be out of danger, although still very ill. 'The poor Duke upon being told of her Amendment, went into her, and feeling her hand, burst into Tears.'[4] The 'Amendment' in the poor Duchess's condition was fleeting, for she died two days later, on 24 November.

It would seem that some better relationship was achieved after the affecting interviews Blandford had with his parents as his mother lay near to death. It would also appear that now, left by himself, and bereft of his close companion of nearly half a century, the Duke, while becoming even more of a recluse, at the same time softened towards other members of his family, and one cannot resist the impression (borne out by other testimony) that Duchess Caroline had been the sterner and more unrelenting parent.

After the tragic death of Lady Charlotte in 1802, her daughter, Elizabeth Martha Nares, had visited her grandparents at Blenheim, but her widowed father had not been invited; within a year or two of the Duchess's demise Professor Nares (he was to become Regius Professor of Modern History at Oxford in 1813) was asked to accompany his daughter, now in her teens, and was most kindly received by the Duke.

The youngest of the daughters, Lady Amelia, also fell in love beneath her station, with a Captain Henry Pytches Boyce; her father at first persuaded her to give him up, but during the last days of her mother's long illness, Lady Amelia was observed conducting clandestine interviews with her lover in the park. Lord Francis intervened, and Amelia told him that she intended to wait until some time after her mother's death, when she would ask her father for his consent to her marriage. We hear no more details – but Lady Amelia Spencer was married to Captain Boyce in September 1812. And it was well indeed that the ageing and now lonely Duke did not alienate another daughter, for in this same year death swept away 47-year-old Elizabeth (married to her cousin John Spencer); and a year later Caroline (wife of Viscount Clifden) would die, aged forty-four – so only two of the five lively daughters, Anne, Countess of Shaftesbury,* and Amelia Boyce, would remain to lighten his darkling years.

At this point in our story, another witness appears to furnish us with details about the Spencer family: George James Welbore Agar-Ellis (1797–1833) was the eldest son of the second Viscount Clifden and his wife Lady Caroline Spencer, and was therefore the Duke's grandson and Lord Blandford's nephew. Some thirty years younger than his uncle and aunt, he was the close contemporary of their children. He was educated at Westminster, and in 1814 went to Christ Church, Oxford; he later became a Member of Parliament and a Privy Councillor, and was created Baron Dover in 1831. Now, in 1814, when he was about seventeen, he started to keep a diary from which we glean illuminating glimpses of his kinsfolk in several generations.

Around Christmas 1814 a large family party was gathered at Blenheim, among whom were Lord Blandford, his wife, and three of their children – Charles (now aged twenty), Henry (eighteen), and sixteen-year-old Caroline. George Agar-Ellis and his (now widowed) father Lord Clifden, were also there. The days were passed in the traditional country way, with riding and wild duck shooting, and a good deal of eating and drinking. On 18 December, Agar-Ellis was out riding with his father and Dr Blackstone: 'We talked of Lord Blandford's folly – He is more in debt than ever, & it is hardly possible for him to avoid an execution at Whiteknights.'[5] It must have been rivetting for the young man to hear this talk about his elder (if not better) kinsman. A few days later (23 December) we read young George's views on his Blandford relations: 'The Marquess seems rather *Penseroso* (well he may be) – Charles is dull – & has got his father's bad manner – Takes snuff, & wears rings. Such Bete!!! – Henry is to be pitied† – Lady Caroline will some day shew sport, or I am very much mistaken – '.[6]

Long-drawn-out Christmas and New Year gatherings are often occasions for tension and disagreements: from Agar-Ellis we learn that Christmas-time at Blenheim in the early nineteenth century was no exception to this rule. One night at dinner Dr Blackstone got

---

* The Hon. Cropley Ashley, her husband, succeeded his brother as sixth Earl of Shaftesbury in 1811.

† This may be a reference to his fragile health.

drunk and quarrelled with Lord Blandford; Agar-Ellis deemed the latter 'insufferable'. His uncle was clearly in a contentious mood, and endeavoured to entrap Lord Shaftesbury (his brother-in-law) into political arguments, '& so quarrel with him. He has not yet exactly succeeded, but they have both shown sport – '.[7] Sport or no, Agar-Ellis hoped his uncle would leave Blenheim soon: spacious though the Palace is, it apparently was not large enough to contain Blandford comfortably as a member of the family party. On 29 December our diarist recorded: 'The Marquess is grievously offended because the Duke has sent to him to say that he hopes he & his family will not stay longer than Monday next – He [presumably Blandford] lays it all upon Francis & wants to pick a quarrel with him about it – Francis has behaved very sensibly – '.[8]

It is clear that the Duke preserved his privacy and solitude even at this familial season, choosing to communicate his wishes through a third party: Blandford was (not surprisingly) greatly upset and, reported Agar-Ellis on 30 December, 'He says it is turning the Eldest Son out of the House – & the like nonsense – He intends now to stay till Thursday. This is a dreadful thing for the rest of the company, for he is altogether grandissima bestia . . .'.[9] Although too young to have been on the Grand Tour as yet, George Agar-Ellis seems nevertheless to have acquired some showy French and Italian expressions.

If her husband was determined to outstay his welcome, Susan Blandford was not – moreover, she had a refuge hard-by at Kirtlington, with her uncle, Sir Henry Dashwood; she left Blenheim on 2 January. In Agar-Ellis's entry in his diary for that day we get confirmation that Susan was well liked in the family: 'L^y Blandford went away to the great sorrow of the House. Lord Blandford made his son Charles go with her because he is jealous of him here.'[10]

In February 1815, Agar-Ellis was again at Blenheim to celebrate his grandfather's birthday; he does not mention the Blandfords as having been there – perhaps it was too near the *froideur* caused by the Duke's request for his son to shorten his previous visit. But the following year George and Susan were once more at Blenheim with their children for Christmas and the New Year, and Blandford was there in early February 1816, when Agar-Ellis described an 'immense party' given to mark the Duke's seventy-seventh (and, it was to prove, his last) birthday. George Blandford's visits to the family seat seem to have been confined to festive occasions, while Susan was a more frequent guest, quite often staying there with Caroline and one or more of the boys.

George Agar-Ellis quite clearly disliked and despised his uncle, and had no great opinion of Charles or of his other cousin, John (his exact contemporary), whom he described on one occasion as 'her [Lady Blandford's] Tarpaulin sailor Son . . . Dull Boy & in the way'.[11] While enjoying Agar-Ellis's pungent comments on his relations, we have to recall that he himself was barely eighteen, and his vivid, descriptive phrases resound with youthful intolerance. The Blandfords' eldest son, George Sunderland, was some four years older than his cousin, and although there are plenty of criticisms in Agar-Ellis's diaries of Sunderland's drinking and indebtedness, nevertheless he obviously enjoyed the company of this wild young man; a year or two later, when the two cousins met in Paris, they spent (or mis-spent) a good deal of time together.

Although the male members of the Blandford family did not, on the whole, find favour with Agar-Ellis, the young man quickly formed a warm and confidential relationship with his Aunt Susan. As we know, Lady Blandford had a separate establishment in London from her husband, and Agar-Ellis records many calls upon her – sometimes to breakfast with her and Caroline, or to escort her to the theatre; Lady Blandford also visited the Clifdens at Roehampton from time to time. One rather unusual expedition upon which he accompanied his aunt is described by the young man in his diary entry for 18 September 1816: after driving Lady Blandford in her phaeton to see the Philanthropic Society, they then went on to see 'the Female part of Bethlem, at which she was a good deal frightened . . .'. In the eighteenth century Bedlam, as the Hospital of St Mary of Bethlehem in the City was known, was quite one of the sights of London and frequently visited by foreign and provincial sightseers. In 1815 the Hospital moved to a new site in St George's Fields, Lambeth (now the Imperial War Museum), where conditions and treatment of the lunatics were considerably improved (although still horrific by modern standards).[12] Around this time the mad mercifully ceased to be a public spectacle; and it is likely therefore that Susan Blandford's interest would have been inspired by genuine concern for the wretched inmates, probably aroused by her contact with the Philanthropic Society.

Susan Blandford was now in her late forties; it is frustrating that we have no likeness of her at this time, but we get the impression that she was a thoroughly likeable, warm-hearted woman. She no doubt found it a comfort to have within the family circle a sympathetic listener, and one to whom she could confide without indiscretion or disloyalty her anxieties about her difficult and dissolute sons. As their contemporary and frequent companion, her nephew made the ideal confidant; he also understood without being told the unhappy state of her marriage, and the lack of sympathy or support she found in her husband.

Caroline Spencer, now in her late teens, was beginning to go about in society with her mother, and it was of course both convenient and delightful for them both to have in London a young and lively escort. The relationship between the two young cousins, George Agar-Ellis and Caroline, was somewhat arch. At Christmas 1814, he had commented that Caroline would, in his view, one day 'shew sport'; nearly two years later, after dancing one evening with her at Blenheim, he noted (not, one senses, without a certain satisfaction), 'she makes visible advances to me, & squeezes my hand on all occasions';[13] and a couple of weeks later, '. . . Lady B's daughter Caroline makes large eyes at me, & squeezes my hand. She would not dislike to be Lady Clifden – but I should.'[14]

Although Caroline was obviously making the running, George was increasingly aware of his cousin's burgeoning charms: in September 1816 we find him noting, 'Caroline very delightful – She is very pretty; with an exceedingly alluring figure.' And the following spring, after Caroline and her mother had spent an evening at Roehampton with the Clifden family: 'Passed a very pleasant evening – Caroline Spencer sang beautifully.'[15] Evidently the larky schoolgirl had blossomed into a beautiful and talented young woman. The two cousins were to continue to meet quite often, but their relationship never developed beyond the flirtatious calf-love stage. Both of them married in the same year, 1822, George Agar-Ellis espousing Lady Georgiana Howard, daughter of the sixth Earl of Carlisle, and Caroline, a few months afterwards, marrying Mr David Pennant.

We get further glimpses of Blandford family life from George

Agar-Ellis's pen during the summer and autumn of 1815, when he became closely involved with his cousin Sunderland's candidacy in the county Parliamentary election which took place as a result of Lord Francis Spencer's elevation to the peerage in August. On 27 July Agar-Ellis saw Lady Blandford at an entertainment; also there was Lord Blandford, who, according to his nephew, 'is very sulky because Francis has got a Peerage, & his son is brought forward, & come in for the County.'[16] The next day Agar-Ellis went to Blenheim where he found his cousin who, with only two days to go to nomination day, had found no one to propose him; a letter had already been written opposing his nomination by one Coker, and generally much opposition was expected.

However, by 31 July family and friends had rallied round, and at the nomination meeting, which was held in Oxford, Sunderland was proposed by his great-uncle, Lord Charles Spencer (who had himself represented the county for many years in the past, and was locally very popular); his seconder was Dr Cook, President of Corpus Christi College. Agar-Ellis, who attended the meeting, recounted that on Sunderland's name being proposed there was 'much hissing through the hall, & very little applause'.[17] The opposition candidate was a seemingly inoffensive gentleman, Mr William Henry Ashhurst, who throughout the ensuing campaign was to prove much less combative than his promoters and supporters, one of whom declared at the nomination meeting that 'He loved the County of Oxford, and wished to see it throw aside the slavery of its attachment to the House of Blenheim.'[18]

At the Palace there was a good deal of pessimism as a result of the meeting: Dr Blackstone was very despondent, and felt that the contest would not be worth its cost (a prudent professional view); he told Agar-Ellis that 'the county are to a man against the Blenheim Family . . .'[19] and that he would advise the Duke that the contest should be abandoned for the present time. However, by early August things began to look up, and Agar-Ellis reported: 'Sunderland improved in canvassing – Much liked by the farmers – He is what they call, a personable man . . .'.[20]

The battle now joined was waged with eloquence and acrimony in succeeding issues of *Jackson's Oxford Journal*: long (often vituperative) letters were published, frequently over *noms-de-plume* such as 'Vindex', 'A Freeholder', 'Scrutator', 'Independence' and 'Verax'. George Sunderland was well supported by his family: Agar-Ellis was energetic in helping his cousin with his campaign; from the middle of August, Lady Blandford was at Blenheim for weeks on end, assisting her son in his contest; and John Spencer, his sailor brother, also came to join the fray. Lord Blandford – piqued though he may have been at the outset by Sunderland's candidature – now busied himself by writing to influential persons, drumming up support for his son.

The campaign was a long-drawn-out one, lasting over two months, and by the middle of September the candidate for the Blenheim interest would seem to have deteriorated in his conduct. On 17 September, Agar-Ellis wrote in his diary: 'Sunderland has made a pretty mess of this Election business . . . Besides this, he has completely lost himself in this house [Blenheim, presumably] – by his drunkenness – obstinacy – indolence – shocking temper – duplicity – & bad manners . . .'.[21] By the third week in September, the family gathered at Blenheim was angry and mortified: 'They have at length come to a final resolution here, to give up the election on account of Sunderland's bad conduct',[22] reported Agar-Ellis. Certainly it would seem to have been deplorable, even by the robust standards of the eighteenth century: George Sunderland and his brother John were constantly getting drunk, and his adversaries were not slow to take advantage of their disreputable conduct. Agar-Ellis exploded in his diary: 'What a beast & fool Sunderland is . . .'.[23] The next day he reported: 'Lady Blandford very unhappy – Sunderland is not to be allowed to darken the doors of this house with his presence. Tant mieux . . .'.[24]

By 8 October, the family's decision was confirmed: the election was to be given up – presumably the family did not wish to court the humiliation of a crushing public defeat. Sunderland was much angered, but a few days later he wrote a graceful letter to the Freeholders of the County of Oxford, announcing his retirement from the contest, largely on the grounds that the opposition had gained a strong advantage against him by starting their campaign much earlier; he thanked his own supporters, and promised that he would present himself to the electors on a future occasion.[25] On 12 October the election was held, and Mr Ashhurst duly became the new Member of Parliament for the County of Oxford.

The twilight of the fourth Duke's long life was drawing on: although leading the life of a recluse, and deeply absorbed in his preferred occupation of astronomy, he was still the patriarchal head of the family, and Blenheim continued to be the gathering point for all the branches of the family, whether at peace or at war with one another. The Duke depended more and more on Lord Francis (at last Lord Churchill, to his father's satisfaction), but he remained to the end very much 'his own man', and an amusing sidelight is cast upon his habits at this time by Dr Blackstone, who, in a letter to Lord Auckland dated 23 March 1814, wrote:

> The Duke has taken to riding, & will I hope Continue it. It is Amazing how Sly he is grown. I have discovered it in a good many instances in which it used to be otherwise. I do not know whether to attribute this to increasing Age or from the Necessity he feels of being so, from the Servants & others who surround him & have Compleat influence over him, but he is grown quite Cunning!!![26]

Undoubtedly His Grace was a great eccentric, and we cull one last example of this characteristic from Captain Gronow: no doubt the episode lost nothing in the telling, but we know the Duke was most unwilling to receive unexpected guests from the account of his reception of the great Lord Nelson and his companions many years before. Captain Gronow wrote:

> The Duke had been for some time a confirmed hypochondriac, and dreaded anything that could in any way ruffle the tranquil monotony of his existence. It is said that he remained for three years without pronouncing a single word, and was entering the fourth year of his silence,

---

55. Mary Russell Mitford, by A. Burt, 1836.
56. Barbara Hofland, 1823 (artist unknown).
57. Captain Rees Howell Gronow, by J. C. Armytage.
58. The Reverend Edward Nares; a miniature by Anna Dovetin, 1827.

when he was told one morning that Madame la Baronne de Staël, the authoress of *Corinne*, was on the point of arriving to pay him a visit. The Duke immediately recovered his speech, and roared out, 'Take me away – take me away!' to the utter astonishment of the circle around him, who all declared that nothing but the terror of this literary visitation could have put an end to this long and obstinate monomania.[27]

When the Duke was found dead in bed on 30 January 1817, it marked the end of a reign that had lasted more than half a century. We have perhaps been more concerned with the unusual, not to say quirky, side of his character, but in his care Blenheim waxed in beauty, fame and prestige. The fourth Duke of Marlborough's true memorial, which has endured already nigh on two hundred years, is the splendid parkland scene created under his aegis by Capability Brown. It is likely that the visionary concept of these two men – the ducal patron and the great 'Improver' – may last yet, despite economic and social changes, for the 'Great Spencer's' descendants, now seven generations on, cherish and strive to perpetuate the noble picture conceived by their forebear and wrought by Lancelot Brown.

59. A gaming table at Devonshire House, by Rowlandson.
60. 'The Inexpressible Air of Dignity', by Gillray, 1803.

IX

Paradise Lost

The shadow of the dome of pleasure
Floated midway on the waves;
Where was heard the mingled measure
From the fountain and the caves.
(*Samuel Taylor Coleridge, 'Kubla Khan'*)

WHEN THE FOURTH DUKE OF MARLBOROUGH had acquired the Whiteknights estate for his son and heir, it was no doubt the fervent hope of both his family and their advisors that a new and more hopeful chapter had begun in Blandford's life – a period which would see a stability in his affairs which hitherto had been conspicuously lacking. But Blandford had almost certainly not sloughed off all the burden of indebtedness which he had incurred from his earliest days of adult independence; as we have seen, as early as 1800 he was endeavouring to raise money on the Whiteknights estate.

Meanwhile, nothing daunted, he was launching out on his fantastic plans for the gardens. One feature alone, much to be remarked upon in future years – the wall of *Magnolia grandiflora* – was planted in 1800, using twenty-two plants at the current price of five guineas each – somewhere in the region of £60,000 today! We are not surprised to know that Lord Blandford's account with the nurserymen Lee and Kennedy soon reached astronomical proportions, attracting comment from several sharply pointed pens.

Nor were gardening and plant-collecting the only outlets for Blandford's propensity for over-spending: the bookshelves in the splendid new Library rooms had to be filled, and we have seen how the house was 'done over' in the latest and most fashionable styles of decoration. New and handsome pieces of furniture were commissioned for the rooms; the walls were hung with valuable masterpieces, and the display cabinets filled with a great variety of precious, curious or beautiful objects. Even the Marquess's love of music and music-making must have been costly, entailing as it did the hiring of musicians and bandsmen for the concerts and entertainments he loved to give. On our tour through the gardens, we were shown several places especially arranged for outdoor musical parties, and very delightful they must have been.

One would have thought that gardening, plant-collecting, bibliomania, painting and music would have amply fulfilled even Blandford's breadth of creative interest, and given his enthusiasm and energy full rein: not so. No doubt fancying himself as a patron of music and the theatre, he had become involved in a totally unnecessary and, as it was to prove, unsuccessful and financially damaging venture – the reconstruction and revival of the Pantheon.

The original Pantheon,[1] constructed on a site at the conjunction of Oxford Street and Poland Street, had been opened in 1772, and was one of the most remarkable places of entertainment in London. Designed by the architect James Wyatt (1746–1813), with a vast cupola, large central hall and gallery, and a subterranean tea room, its interior decorations and furnishings recalled the Pantheon in Rome, and it accommodated up to two thousand people. Hailed by Horace Walpole as 'a winter Ranelagh'[2] and immensely popular when it first opened, the novelty of its theatrical performances, masquerades, exhibitions, balls and concerts declined over the ensuing decade. After the King's Theatre, Haymarket, was destroyed by fire in 1789, the Italian opera and ballet were transferred from there to the Pantheon, but a fire on 14 January 1792 gutted this building also – the scene was so spectacular that it was sketched by J. M. W. Turner (1775–1851). Rebuilt after a fashion, the Pantheon (and its unfortunate shareholders) passed through divers vicissitudes until 1811, when it was leased by a Colonel Greville (the proprietor of the Argyll Rooms, which were popular for music, dancing and various theatrical entertainments), who formed a committee of noblemen and gentlemen in the hope of adapting the building once more for theatrical use; among his backers, who laid out about £50,000 for the project, was the Marquess of Blandford.

Although the new Pantheon opened for 'burlettas'* in February 1812, the building was subsequently found to be unsafe and was closed a month later by order of the Lord Chamberlain. The architect John Nash was at once employed to oversee the necessary repairs, and Blandford seems to have been the chief spokesman for his fellow promoters, writing a series of urgent letters to the Lord Chamberlain on the subject. But a team of surveyors headed by Wyatt and including John Soane and S. P. Cockerell reported that the building was still unsafe, and it remained closed for a full year. There was another fire during the winter of 1812, and the following spring Blandford again solicited the Lord Chamberlain for a licence, which was refused. Nevertheless, the Pantheon reopened, without licence, as an 'English opera house' in July 1813 – the proprietors were summonsed and fined; the season was doomed; and in December it was closed for good. In October 1814 all the fittings were sold at auction against arrears of rent. Colonel Greville and his aristocratic supporters, including our luckless Blandford, faded from the scene, certainly the poorer – some, perhaps, the wiser.

And so the sorry tale of Blandford's debts continued. In 1812, the Duke took a major step towards relieving his son's indebtedness: the whole estate of Whiteknights was mortgaged (via the trustees) to Archibald Traill, Sir Charles Cockerell (of Sezincote fame) and Henry Traill, for £45,000 plus interest. That the purpose of this transaction was to pay off Blandford's debts is made abundantly clear in the deed: reciting that 'the said Duke was desirous of relieving the said Marquess and of wholly exonerating him from the payment thereof . . .'.[3] But even this major settlement proved only to be a palliative: by December 1814 the young Agar-Ellis had overheard the Duke's lawyer, Dr Blackstone, talking to his father, Lord Clifden, while out riding about the alarming state of his uncle's finances. Ten months later, in October 1815, when Agar-Ellis paid a visit to his uncle and aunt at Whiteknights, he found that a crisis was impending, for a bailiff was actually present in the house. He noted in his diary for 29 October: '. . . unless Lord B can raise several thousands immediately, there will shortly be a great crash.'[4] His nephew was obviously of a resourceful turn of mind, for he tells us that he 'Recommended Lady Blandford to remove all her valuables

* Comic operas or musical farces in one act with a limit of four performers.

from Whiteknights, as whenever an execution comes (& come it must *"aut serius aut citius"*) they will be liable to be seized with the furniture &c.'[5] No doubt his Aunt Susan was grateful for such practical advice.

There is no evidence that, faced with imminent financial collapse, Blandford resorted to any form of tardy economy: on the contrary, in this same year John Buonarroti Papworth was busily designing and erecting arbours and seats at Whiteknights. In early December, Agar-Ellis recorded that he had received a letter from his aunt: 'She says Lord Blandford can get no money' – and added, somewhat spitefully, 'tant mieux'[6] But at this dark and seemingly desperate hour in the Blandford fortunes, 'something turned up' to rescue our lordly Micawber – to the surprise of all and, one senses, the irritation of some. On 1 March 1816, Agar-Ellis wrote in his diary: 'Lord Blandford has borrowed fifty thousand pounds on Post Obits from Crasus Farquhar (a rich West Indian) – He is consequently much up in the world.'[7]

We have another, most illuminating, account of Lord Blandford at this time from Captain Gronow, one of whose earlier visits to Whiteknights we have already mentioned. Gronow always had agreeable memories of the Marquess: 'He was always very kind to me,' he wrote, 'and I lived a good deal with him and his sons when I was a young man.'[8] In 1816, he had driven down to Whiteknights with him:

> During our journey, Lord Blandford opened a sort of cupboard, which was fixed on one side of the coach in which we travelled, and which contained a capital luncheon, with different kinds of wine and liqueurs. Another part of this roomy vehicle, on a spring being touched, displayed a sort of *secrétaire*, with writing materials, and a large pocket-book; the latter he opened, and showed me fifty Bank of England notes for £1000 each, which he told me he had borrowed the day before from a well-known money-lender in the city, named Levy. He stated that he had given in return a post-obit on his father's death for £150,000 . . .*

* Gronow states that Blandford had the money through this man Levy; but the author thinks Agar-Ellis's account may be more accurate in detail. Gronow was writing after 1857, whereas Agar-Ellis was not only a close relation, but also writing at the time of the event. Levy may have been an agent in the transaction.

This episode illustrated Blandford's frenetic lifestyle and mood; and a subsequent quotation from the Captain shows him also to have had a sadly prophetic sense, for after telling his friend how he had borrowed this vast sum of money, he had added:

> You see, Gronow, how the immense fortune of my family will be frittered away: but I can't help it; I must live. My father inherited £500,000 in ready money, and £70,000 a year in land; and, in all probability, when it comes to my turn to live at Blenheim, I shall have nothing left but the annuity of £5000 a year on the Post Office.* [9]

Despite these momentary flashes of foresight, Blandford continued on his helter-skelter course towards bankruptcy. But, for a moment, in this spring of 1816, with his feckless and optimistic nature, he must have felt quite flush, with his fifty £1000 notes. It was around now that he laid down the book about Whiteknights from Mr and Mrs Hofland, who, obviously delighted with this prestigious commission, abandoned all other work to concentrate on it.

The large loan negotiated by Blandford at the eleventh hour was to put off the direst consequences of his indebtedness for nearly three years, and during this period of relative respite, the most important change was to take place in his life and situation: on the morning of 29 January 1817, his father was found dead in his bed at Blenheim, and George, Marquess of Blandford entered into his noble inheritance of titles and domains, as fifth Duke of Marlborough and Prince of the Holy Roman Empire.

✳︎❖✳︎❖✳︎

When his father succeeded to the dukedom, George Sunderland moved up in the hierarchy, taking his father's erstwhile title of Marquess of Blandford; he was, at the time of his grandfather's death, twenty-three years old and, as we have already seen, a fairly wild young man and often the cause of great concern to his relations. He was also, like his father, frequently short of money – although

---

* Lord Blandford was referring to the Post Office Pension granted in perpetuity by Queen Anne to the first Duke of Marlborough and his heirs. It was commuted for a capital sum in 1884.

(again like his father) he does not seem to have allowed this inconvenience to have markedly affected his lifestyle. He must have been very good-looking – one of his contemporaries at Eton, Lord Monson, had described him as 'one of the handsomest lads I ever saw'.[10] Nor can he have lacked fire and courage, for he was among the leaders of the famous 'rebellion' of the boys against their headmaster, the redoubtable Dr Keate, the brutality and frequency of whose beatings is part of Eton's folk history. On his appointment to the headmastership in 1809, Keate had found that discipline in the school was poor, and the new headmaster had set about his task with reforming zeal: presently, in June 1810, a great row – boys versus headmaster – flared up. George Sunderland was in his last year at the school, and was among the 'ninety grown-up boys'[11] who were flogged for their insubordination. Despite his severity, Dr Keate was generally liked by the boys, who, certainly in the light of the ensuing episode, bore him no malice.

In 1815, Sunderland and some cronies including Captain Gronow (with whom he had been at Eton) were in Paris, in those glorious summer weeks following the Battle of Waterloo, when (as in the previous year after Napoleon's first abdication) a large part of London society invaded the French capital. These young gentlemen were astonished to see the ferocious Dr Keate, the terror of their schooldays, partaking of an ice cream 'at Tortoni's on the Boulevards'. His former pupils at once invited him to join them at the best dining place in Paris – Beauvilliers, where, according to Captain Gronow, the Doctor 'ate as if he had never eaten before, and paid his addresses, in large bumpers, to every description of wine; and towards the end of dinner, expressed his delight at finding that his old friends and pupils had not forgotten him; concluding "a neat and appropriate speech" with "Floreat Etona".'[12]

On his return to England, Sunderland soon found himself involved with the County Parliamentary election, where we know he conducted himself atrociously, and finally withdrew from the contest; and because of his behaviour he had been ejected from the patriarchal home by his disgusted relations.

Lord Sunderland (or Lord Blandford, as he was soon to become) was of course among the most eligible of London's bachelors, despite his financially encumbered estate, because he was the heir to a duke-

dom. An even more glittering catch was the sixth Duke of Devonshire, described by Gronow as 'young, graceful, and distinguished',
and who, the Captain also tells us, 'was hunted down by mothers
and daughters with an activity, zeal, and perseverance – and, I am
sorry to add, a vulgarity – which only those can conceive who have
seen the British huntress in full cry after a duke.'[13] Among the most
beautiful of the girls in society at this time was Lady Elizabeth
Conyngham, daughter of the Lady Conyngham who was for so long
the close friend and companion of the Prince Regent. Lady Elizabeth had many admirers, but her mother had high ambitions for her
daughter, and discouraged those young men who were not in line for
a ducal coronet, or in possession of one: the Conynghams had fixed
their eyes upon the Duke of Devonshire, but while they were pursuing this fine quarry, George Sunderland fell desperately in love
with Lady Elizabeth, and asked her to marry him. Throughout the
later months of 1816 and the first part of the following year, there are
mentions in Agar-Ellis's diary of this affair. It is quite clear that the
'crafty Conynghams', as he terms them, were hoping that their
daughter would become Duchess of Devonshire, but that while
pursuing one duke these prudent parents were careful not to lose
the other; throughout the autumn therefore they blew hot and cold.
Interestingly enough, Lady Blandford (who was Agar-Ellis's source
of information) seems to have been unenthusiastic about the match:
on 8 September 1816, Agar-Ellis wrote: 'Had a long conversation
with L[y] Blandford about Sunderland & L[y] E. Conyngham – those
wretched Conynghams will get him at last.' A week later, on 13
September, he called on Lady Blandford, who 'had had a long visit
from those crafty Conynghams, who are now beginning to be
devilishly afraid of losing Sunderland . . .'. In mid-January 1817,
Sunderland and Agar-Ellis found themselves in Paris together,
where they amused themselves, among other things, in going to
some little theatre where they were diverted by semi-naked girls.
But on 16 January, Agar-Ellis noted that 'Sunderland is in a melancholy way about Lady Conyngham's rejection of him for her
daughter . . .'. The Conynghams were also in Paris at that time, and
George Agar-Ellis endeavoured to intercede for his friend with Lord
Conyngham, who, however, only held out faint hopes for the melancholy Sunderland. But although the Conynghams had evidently

decided to pin all their hopes on the Devonshire match, in Gronow's words, 'the favourite bolted'; and indeed, it was not only the Conynghams who were destined for disappointment – the young Duke escaped all his pursuers, and lived and died a bachelor. Presently, the lovely Lady Elizabeth married Lord Strathaven, later to become the Marquess of Huntly.

Possibly on the rebound from his disappointment over Lady Elizabeth, Lord Blandford, as he now was, proceeded to become entangled in a most discreditable way with a girl not yet seventeen, Susannah Adelaide Law. She was the daughter of respectable bourgeois parents, her father being a provision merchant in Dublin, at this time living in Seymour Place, Bayswater Square, London. Susannah Law and the Marquess met in the early months of 1817,[14] whereafter he proceeded to call upon her frequently. Professing an ardent affection for her, Blandford persuaded her to marry him, in-sisting however that the marriage be performed in the strictest privacy, for family reasons. On 16 March 1817, Susannah Law and Lord Blandford went through a marriage ceremony at her parents' house, in the presence of her mother and her sister Gertrude. The marriage was solemnized according to the rite of the Church of England, by a brother of the Marquess, who was (so he said) a clergyman: Mrs Law entered the marriage on the fly-leaf of a Prayer Book. The young couple went to live in Lord Blandford's house in Manchester Street, calling themselves Captain and Mrs Lawson: Lord Blandford settled £400 a year on Susannah, which she was to say she always regarded as a 'marriage settlement'.

At this juncture, Agar-Ellis once more sheds some light on a family scenario: on 30 March 1817 he met Blandford, who was 'in raptures about a mistress he has got, & to whom he has given a settlement. If the Woman behaves well, I think, from what I know of Sunderland's* character, he is settled for life with her . . .'.[15] Nearly a month later he found that his cousin 'seems rather out of spirits – but talks in raptures of his mistress, whose name I find is Lawson – He has settled three hundred† a year on her for life; in

---

* Agar-Ellis has made a slip of the pen. Sunderland had of course just become Blandford.

† A mistake: the settlement was £400.

case he leaves her – *Quel Sot, mais c'est son affaire*.'[16] One cannot help pondering the muddled chivalry which on the one hand provides against desertion, yet on the other does not hesitate to bamboozle a young girl into a fake marriage.

Presently, Susannah discovered that Blandford's 'clergyman' brother was not a clergyman at all, but an army officer: it was naughty Lord Charles, who had connived with his brother in this cruel deception. Mrs Law, predictably much upset, confronted Lord Blandford with his shameful conduct: probably the girl, swept off her feet by this young and handsome nobleman, had genuinely been taken in by his explanations and assurances, but it is hard to believe that Susannah's parents could possibly have thought the secret marriage to have been *bona fide*: an entry in a Prayer Book could never have been regarded as a legal certificate of marriage. As a result of parental protestations, Blandford (who had to admit the invalidity of the marriage) promised to take Susannah to Scotland, where, according to Scottish law, a marriage could be regarded as legal by being publicly recognized.

In March 1818, Susannah Lawson gave birth to a child – a girl, who was named Susanna; and in August 'Captain and Mrs Lawson' with their five-month-old baby went to Scotland, accompanied by some of his jolly friends (among them Colonel James Stewart, an uncle on his mother's side, and his cousin Lord Garlies), with whom he was to shoot grouse. 'Mrs Lawson', baby Susanna and a maid travelled north by mail coach, and were lodged in small hotels or lodging houses throughout the time of Blandford's various sporting visits. Blandford later insisted that they never went about in society together while in Scotland, and that at no time was Susannah regarded as his wife; his testimony was supported by two of his companions at the time.

The idyll was fast fading: on her return to London (apparently unaccompanied by 'Captain Lawson'), Susannah and her child went to live with her parents. In the autumn of 1818, a friend of Blandford's came to inform her that the arrangements between her and Blandford were at an end, as he was shortly to marry the Marquess of Breadalbane's daughter: Susannah, upon hearing this news, suffered a complete collapse, and was ill for several weeks. The anticipated Breadalbane marriage never took place, but it was not long before the man Susannah had genuinely loved was placed irredeemably beyond her reach – for in January 1819, Lord Blandford married his first cousin, Lady Jane Stewart.

Susannah Law saw Lord Blandford on one future occasion, in 1823, when he had already been married for four years. According to her, Blandford visited her at her home, and 'on his knees implored her to forgive his past conduct and admitted his baseness'; he also recognized the validity of their marriage, and begged her to return to him. Later Blandford reneged on this ill-considered outburst in a carefully constructed note – but he made a rendezvous with her at Lord Charles's house, whither he bid her bring their child to see him. After Susannah Law's association with Blandford had ceased, his mother, the Duchess, was to continue the payment to her of £400 a year for nine years; later the original sum was reduced to £200 per annum, and Susannah had to give up many letters from Blandford which were in her possession, some of them signed 'Your affectionate husband, Blandford'. It does not appear that she ever married again, but the little Susanna grew up to marry 'a man of fortune' and, we hope, to live more happily than her naïve and sorely used mother.

At the time of these events, only very few people can have known of the secret 'marriage', although a considerable number must have been aware that Blandford had a mistress who was called 'Mrs Lawson' – and indeed this seems to be all that such a close friend and relation as George Agar-Ellis knew of the affair (although he knew of the settlement being made on her by his cousin). Probably Blandford's mother knew more of the facts of the case and, feeling family honour at stake, decided herself to continue the allowance to Susannah. The whole story was not revealed until twenty years later, in 1838, when the weekly *Satirist, or the Censor of the Times* (an eighteenth-century prototype of *Private Eye*) made it public. *The Satirist* held that the marriage had been publicly recognized in Scotland, and was therefore valid: if that was the case, Blandford had committed bigamy; his marriage to Lady Jane Stewart was invalid, and their children bastards. Upon this, the family had to take action, for an even more serious implication lay at the heart of these libellous attacks: by an Act of Queen Anne, the dukedom of Marlborough can pass through the female line if male issue fails. If the arguments advanced in *The Satirist* prevailed, the lawful heir to the dukedom was Susanna, the child of Blandford and Susannah Law, and her issue. In the libel action brought by the family* the details, which were perforce paraded as to the indubitably dishonourable behaviour of the Marquess of Blandford, his brother and some of his friends, must have been humiliating to those concerned, but *The Satirist* lost the case and the whole question of the legality of the marriage with Susannah Law (whether in England or Scotland), with its troubling implications for the succession to the dukedom, was settled once and for all.

Despite the shaky state of Marlborough's financial affairs, the beauty and fame of the Whiteknights gardens waxed yearly, and in the late summer of 1817, the new Duke and Duchess were honoured by a royal visitation. About noon on Monday, 18 August, a positive bevy of royalty and, as the *Reading Mercury* put it, 'several Noble Personages' arrived at Whiteknights.[17] Queen Charlotte, now over seventy and in the last year of her life, was accompanied by two of her fifteen children, the Princesses Augusta and Elizabeth, both – although in their late forties – still unwed, and harnessed to family and court life as if they were *jeunes filles*. Several other members of the Royal Family also arrived in their carriages to join the Queen and the Princesses on this pleasurable occasion.

Before proceeding on their tour of the grounds, the company partook of 'an excellent *déjeuné*'. Afterwards, the Queen, with the Duchess of Marlborough, drove in an open garden chaise, but most of the other grandees preferred to walk. The day was a little clouded, and it started to rain before the tour was completed. There were many other guests invited for this occasion, and the Duke's band added an agreeable touch. Driven in eventually by the rain, the 'Royal Visitants' were treated to a 'splendid collation'. The report in the *Mercury* noted that 'nothing was omitted by the Duke and Duchess of Marlborough, for the amusement and gratification of their Royal and Noble guests, and their entertainment was evidently

---

* The case was known as Regina *v.* Gregory (the publisher of *The Satirist*) and was brought in the name of the Earl of Sunderland.

productive of the highest pleasure.' Despite the rain, the greater number of guests stayed to witness the departure of the royal party and their 'Noble Entertainers', as the *Mercury* described the Duke and Duchess – ending their euphoric account of the day on an optimistic note: 'whom we hope, notwithstanding their magnificent acquisition of Blenheim, will frequently honour and enliven this neighbourhood by a residence at White Knights.'[18] Little did the reporter know how near this lovely 'pleasure dome' was to being dismantled.

Earlier that same year, Agar-Ellis had again discussed his uncle's situation with Lord Shaftesbury (also his uncle, who, more-over, does not seem to have been very discreet as a trustee), according to whom the Duke's financial affairs were 'in a bad way, as he owes considerably more than 600,000£ – He, Shaftesbury, seems thoroughly tired of being his trustee, as well he may be – but to use the late D^{ss} of M's phrase, "he has made his bed, & must lie upon it".'[19] One cannot resist a twinge of irritation at the priggish pleasure this twenty-year-old seemed to take in discussing his older relation's discomfiture.

One who was disposed to take a more sympathetic view of the Duke's difficulties was his brother-in-law, Professor Nares, who had already visited Whiteknights in April 1817, when he had written of the delights of the gardens and the precious books in the Library; now he made another visit, in mid-March 1818, when among his fellow guests were Dr Lee, Vice-Chancellor of Oxford University, and his wife. Although by this time the Duke was on the verge of bankruptcy, life at Whiteknights was still conducted in fine style: the mornings were passed in the park and gardens, or the Library, where the Duke's own knowledge of plants and books added greatly to the pleasure of his guests; in the evening, while the assembled company was at dinner, a military band of seventeen musicians played, and afterwards in the Drawing Room, there were concerts 'with many eminent performers from Oxford and elsewhere. The Duke himself was so proficient as to be able to play on almost any instrument, and many of the prettiest pieces were of his Grace's own composition.'[20]

Many years after the fifth Duke's death, copies of sheet music from his personal collection were sold at auction, giving us a clear

indication of his musical tastes, and of the works which would probably have formed part of the concert programmes at both Whiteknights and later at Blenheim. Among his preferred composers were
Beethoven, Mozart and Donizetti; Czerny, Haydn and Crotch;
Moore ('Irish Melodies'); Purcell, Croft and Handel[21] – what a
galaxy of delight!

Edward Nares must have been a loyal and understanding man,
for he ends the description of his visit to Whiteknights with this
sympathetic and illuminating comment on his brother-in-law:

> I write these things for the sake of bearing my testimony
> to the extraordinary attainments of the Duke, whose
> pecuniary embarrassments have since expos'd him to
> much obloquy. I have been acquainted with him from
> very early days, and know the many disadvantages under
> which he labour'd, and though I cannot pretend to vindi-
> cate every detail of his life, I shall always consider him an
> injur'd man.[22]

Nares had known George Blandford (as he then was) since those
now faraway days at Blenheim when, as a young don and the friend
of Lord Henry Spencer, he had taken part in the theatricals there,
and had so met and fallen in love with Lady Charlotte – and we
know the ensuing sad story. During these years when Nares had
been so much at Blenheim and welcomed equally by all generations,
Blandford had been in his early twenties; the young don would have
had every chance to observe the relationship between the Duke and
Duchess and their children, and would possibly have borne out the
statement that the Duchess had an antipathy towards her eldest
son:[23] Edward Nares himself had bitterly sad and personal reasons
for knowing how hard Duchess Caroline could be, and what influence she wielded with her husband. Now, nearly thirty years older
and a most distinguished man in his own right, Professor Nares saw
with sadness the disgraceful and pathetic condition to which his
talented, debonair friend of such long standing had descended: the
ridicule and obloquy to which George Spencer was exposed grieved
him and, without disturbing the sleeping dead, he made a plea for
the better understanding of his friend and kinsman.

Meanwhile, Thomas and Barbara Hofland were hard at work

on the book commissioned by the Duke in 1816; they often stayed
in the neighbourhood of Whiteknights, and their friendship with
Mary Russell Mitford waxed in intimacy. In early October 1817,
Miss Mitford wrote to a friend, Mary Webb: 'we had Mrs Hofland
the authoress with us and you would so have enjoyed the conversa-
tion.She is the wife of the celebrated landscape painter and we have
been together backward and forwards the whole week. Mr Hofland
(who is even more delightful than his wife) being taking views at
Whiteknights . . .'.[24] We know already what a pleasant and hilarious
time this trio had together, wandering through the groves and
gardens. It took the Hoflands between two and three years to complete their superbly illustrated, comprehensive account of the
gardens and house at Whiteknights, and, by the time the work was
nearing completion, the bubble of the Duke's finances had burst.

When he inherited the title and Blenheim, the Duke's personal
vast indebtedness had not been to any effective degree alleviated:
very fortunately for generations still unborn, the essential wealth of
the inheritance, whether in treasures, lands or money, was safely
entailed. In 1819, the Duke's creditors closed in upon him, and only
by despoiling Whiteknights could he conceivably hope to meet their
now insistent demands.

In early 1819, the Duke of Marlborough must have told the
Hoflands that, owing to his dire financial straits, he would be unable
to honour his commitments to them. We learn this indirectly in a
letter from Mary Russell Mitford to Mrs Hofland of 3 February
1819; evidently it was necessary for the Hoflands to go to Whiteknights, and Miss Mitford writes: 'I only wish your business was of
a pleasanter nature. I am afraid the Duke of Marlborough speaks
truth with regard to his concerns, poor man!'[25] ('Poor man' indeed –
but poorer Hoflands!) Miss Mitford later refers to 'these miserable
fifty copies' of the book, which (luckily perhaps) were all that had
been printed, the costs for the production of which had been borne
entirely by the Hoflands; now it was only from the sale of these that
they were likely to see any reimbursement, she wrote to Sir William
Elford, 'for the paintings – drawings – journeys – his wife's writing –
and, which is worst of all, the whole of the engraving. Not an engraver
in London would strike a single stroke on the Duke of Marlborough's
credit: and the Duke of Marlborough had not (to use his own

elegant phrase) "a brass farthing" to repay Mr Hofland.'[26]

It must have been a disastrous situation for Thomas and Barbara Hofland: she had put aside her highly profitable writing activities; he had foregone other commissions for pictures, in order to concentrate on the creation of their joint masterpiece for their lordly patron. Their friends proceeded to do everything in their power to promote the book, and it is evident from the following that Hofland had tried (unsuccessfully) to take some legal action to secure some payment from the Duke:

> I don't think they will ever get anything but the sale of these 50 copies – for the Chancellor* has no respect for the Arts – and the Duke's vanity will now be as much mortified by this catalogue and description of pictures and books which are there no longer, as it would once have been gratified. Nothing can be more pitiable than this loss to Mr Hofland. They are excellent people.[27]

Barbara Hofland must indeed have been a delightful person, for, even in her state of anxiety and righteous indignation at the turn of events, her sense of humour did not desert her. Sir William Elford had the benefit of hearing from Miss Mitford an account of a ludicrous incident witnessed by Mrs Hofland when she had been at Whiteknights – no doubt to discuss the sorry state of their business affairs. The Duke had left the house at the same time as Mrs Hofland,

> taking away with him the contents of the larder, half a cold turkey, and three-quarters of a ham. After he had driven off, he remembered that he had left behind some scraps of a loin of mutton, and actually went back to fetch them. The servants are not on board wages, observe; and the housekeeper, knowing they could not get even a twopenny loaf without twopence, and naturally alarmed at this clearance of eatables, ventured to ask His Grace for

* Presumably the Court of Chancery.

---

61. Rustic Orchestra Seat in the Woods at Whiteknights, which could accommodate the Marquess's whole band. From the Hoflands' book.

62. Sketch for a covered seat at Blenheim: note the Palace in the background, and the similarity of this seat to those at Whiteknights (artist unknown).

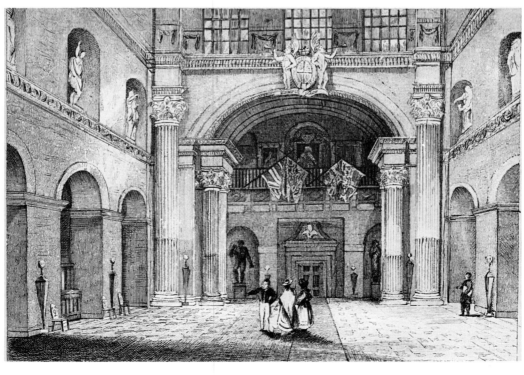

money. After much stuttering, he gave her ten pounds.
All this time, for him and his son there were waiting three
carriages with four post-horses each – one of them empty.
Is not this stopping one hole in a cullender? Mrs Hofland
saw the whole transaction. You should hear her tell the
story, with the Duke's stuttering, Lord Charles's dandy-
ism, and the poor housekeeper's dismal whine. She cannot
help laughing in the midst of her troubles. [28]

During that spring rumours were rife as to what was going on at
Whiteknights, and of course Mary Russell Mitford fed Barbara
Hofland's curiosity with all the tit-bits of news she could gather:
Lord Rivers had looked at the place with a view, it was thought, to
renting – but had veered off, considering 'the house damp, and dis-
liking the trouble and expense of the gardens'. [29] Miss Mitford had
also heard that books and pictures had been seized in payment for
debt. On 12 September 1819, she announced with a tone of great
relief to Sir William:

> The Hoflands' splendid publication (that can't be called
> a book, for the engravings are the soul of that great work)
> is out at last – and they are in great luck not to have got
> many subscribers for the booksellers agreed to take them at
> 7 guineas a copy and the Duke is to have none but for
> ready money – so that they will not lose above 2 or 3
> hundred pounds by this undertaking which considering
> the person they have to do with is a prodigious piece of
> good fortune . . . [30]

The book which Mr and Mrs Hofland struggled against such
odds to produce is a beautiful artefact, and remains today a rare,
vivid and valuable testimony to the fleeting wonder-of-its-day which
was Whiteknights. Despite the way they had been treated by their
patron, the work bears a full-page dedication:

---

63. A design for an 'Egyptian Room' from Thomas Hope's *Household Furniture and
Interior Decoration*, 1807. Similar motifs and features may well have been used in
the Second Library Room at Whiteknights.
64. The Great Hall at Blenheim, in Mavor's *Description of Blenheim*, 1835.

TO

HIS GRACE

GEORGE SPENCER-CHURCHILL

DUKE OF MARLBOROUGH,

PRINCE OF
THE HOLY ROMAN EMPIRE,
MARQUESS OF BLANDFORD,
EARL OF SUNDERLAND,
BARON SPENCER OF WORM-LEIGHTON,

AND

BARON CHURCHILL OF SANDRIDGE,

THIS

DESCRIPTION OF WHITE-KNIGHTS

IS MOST HUMBLY DEDICATED,
BY HIS GRACE'S OBLIGED AND OBEDIENT HUMBLE SERVANTS,

T. C. AND B. HOFLAND

Whether Thomas and Barbara Hofland really felt themselves to be 'His Grace's obliged and obedient humble servants' we may beg to doubt. But this was the nineteenth century and – especially eager as the authors of the work were to attract buyers for their book – they were not going to forego the prestige such a dedication could bring.

The Hoflands now recede from our view. In 1841 they removed to Richmond, which was to be their last home: Thomas died of cancer in January 1843, in the arms of his faithful and devoted Barbara; she died just under two years later, in November 1844.

✳◇✳◇✳

There was nothing for it: the Duke was in effect now bankrupt;* everything at Whiteknights had to go – from the farms, from the gardens, and from the house – to even begin to satisfy his ravening creditors. The first articles to be sold (as distinct from seized) were his precious books: from 7 June 1819, and for eleven succeeding days, the contents of the Library, which the Duke had shown with so much pleasure and pride to his visitors, were auctioned by Mr

* Before 1849 a person had to be a 'trader' in order to 'go bankrupt', so neither as Marquess nor Duke could he have been a *declared* bankrupt.

Evans at 26 Pall Mall, London. Along with the rare items also went
thirty lots of music – compositions, or arrangements by the 'Marquess of Blandford'. Some of the songs had romantic titles: 'Say
Myra why is gentle love?' and 'If then to love thee be offence' (could
that have been composed for lovely, forbidden Mary Anne?). None
of these fetched high prices. Two lots were marked in the catalogue
as 'passed' (that is, withdrawn): Lot 4664, 'The Life, Death, and
Burial of Cock Robin, set to Music by the Marquess of Blandford,
red morocco'; and Lot 3592, 'A Volume containing EIGHTY-NINE
Drawings of Plants, by the Duchess of Marlborough, painted in a
most beautiful and delicate manner'. We have to be glad that, for
whatever reason, these last were not sold; and if we, like the Duke
himself, are sentimentalists, we may like to cherish the thought that
these paintings were at the last minute withdrawn by him because
they represented happier days and shared interests with a woman
he had never loved, but had liked, and perhaps esteemed.

The financial result of the sale of the books was a considerable
disappointment: the book-buying market was, at that time, de-
pressed; moreover, the value owners themselves tend to put upon
their possessions is often highly exaggerated. When George Agar-
Ellis had stayed at Whiteknights in 1815, he wrote that his uncle's
library was valued at £36,000: when the day of reckoning came,
'The produce of the sale was scarcely fifteen thousand pounds. The
collection had probably cost twenty-five thousand.'[31] Even the
wondrous and much celebrated *Decameron* by Boccaccio, bought by
Blandford in 1812 for £2260, was sold to Longman (bidding for
Earl Spencer) for only 876 guineas. It will be remembered that when
Blandford had acquired the book at the Roxburghe sale, his cousin
was then the under-bidder (along with Napoleon): Lord Spencer
must have felt recompensed for his earlier disappointment.* Apart
from the unsatisfactory state of the market at the time, one can only
conclude that Marlborough had ever been a rash, impatient pur-
chaser, and in his enthusiasm to acquire either plants or books he
frequently paid fancy prices.

As usual, we can rely on Miss Mitford to supply us with piquant
details of these events, including an account of an amazing feat of

---

* It is now in the John Rylands University Library of Manchester.

duplicity practised by the sly Duke upon his despoilers. Writing to Sir William Elford on 9 November 1819, she told him:

> Our great Berkshire Bibliomaniac (he of the Boccaccio and the Bedford missal – in other words, the Duke of Marlborough) has had all the contents of Whiteknights sold a fortnight ago, very much against his will, poor man! The *rariss*: books were all gone before – all sold at Evans's, with the sole exception of the aforesaid missal, which the Duke, by an admirable trick of legerdemain, contrived to extract from the locked case that contained it, leaving the said case for the solace of the sheriff's officers. Nothing in sleight of hand has been heard of to equal this abstraction – or rather this abduction – since the escape of the man from the quart bottle. Except the Bedford missal, the poor Duke saved nothing. Everything was sold – plants, pictures, bridges, garden seats, novels and all.[32]

Between the end of September and the end of October 1819, sale days were held at Whiteknights itself or on the farms, when farming stock and equipment, ricks of hay, 'feed of Park', etc., were disposed of; there was also a long list of 'Rare and Excellent Wines' to be sold. During October the pictures went – Italian and Flemish schools and 'most celebrated Modern Masters'; 'Modern furniture & Superb Effects' were up, too, and in the last lap, the remaining pictures, and garden items. Particularly specified were the Chinese Pavilion (or 'Temple'), which we saw on our tour of the Botanic Gardens, with its canopied roof painted in two greens; and an iron bridge, most probably the one 'of elegant and beautiful construction' which bridged the lake at that part of it which seemed like a river, and over which we approached the New Gardens from the direction of the house. Having visited this lovely domain in company with Mrs Hofland, it gives us a pang to learn of its despoilation, and we are consoled to learn that not all the garden seats and summer houses were sold, although the shelves and moveable fittings were torn out and auctioned.[33]

Mary Russell Mitford attended one or more of the sale days: she commented on the 'capricious manner in which things go at an auction where there is no reserve – no power of buying in'.[34] Blue cloth curtains worth fifty guineas as new, fetched a hundred and thirty guineas; 'A table of the most beautiful pollard oak, inlaid with brass and exquisite woods, which cost two hundred and fifty guineas, fetched twenty-three! . . . A sideboard of equal splendour went equally cheap, and some trumpery chandeliers equally dear.'[35] Evidently the hazardous nature of auction sales has not changed in the intervening years.

At the picture sale the prices fetched seem to have been just as erratic: in Miss Mitford's opinion the pictures were 'very good and very bad', and as some had already been taken in discounting bills along with Lots of 'one hundred pairs of shoes, two hundred [yes, *two hundred*!] pair of leather breeches, and some other articles . . .',[36] a suspicion was thrown over the really original paintings,

> which (added to their being wretchedly hung amongst all manner of cross-lights, the highly-finished small pictures high up, and the large ones close to the eye – together with the auctioneer coming from Reading who was as ignorant as all people are who live in, or within five miles of, that town) reduced the value from the 10,000*l*. that was expected to under 2000*l*. You may imagine what wood the man of the hammer is made of when I tell you that, in selling a very fine head of Christ, by Guido – an undoubted and ascertained original, – he never said one word of the picture or the master, but talked grandly and eloquently of the frame. I am very glad of this incredible ignorance, since it let poor Edmund Havill (a Reading artist) into an excellent bargain, and Mr Hofland, I hope, into something still better. He has bought several pictures, particularly an exceedingly beautiful L. Caracci.[37]

One is indeed glad to know that Mr Hofland, whose eye had no doubt spotted choice pictures during his many visits to Whiteknights, was lucky in the sale.

Contrary to Miss Mitford's predictions, the Duke neither sold nor let Whiteknights at this time; indeed he continued to visit the house, although it must have been a bleak place with its empty walls, curtainless windows, and rooms depleted of all the best furniture. But two years after the contents of the house and estate had been sacrificed to appease the Duke's creditors, the final execution took place. Readers will recall that in 1812 the estate had been

mortgaged to, among others, Sir Charles Cockerell, for £45,000:
now, in late 1820 or early 1821, Sir Charles seized the whole property
against the un-repaid debt. When Mrs Arbuthnot made her visit to
Whiteknights on 14 January 1821 she knew that the place had been
taken over by Sir Charles Cockerell: '& it is said', she had noted in
her journal, 'it will be sold in the Spring . . .'. Again rumour had it
wrong: Sir Charles and Lady Cockerell were to inhabit the house
for a number of years.

As far as the creator of the Whiteknights dream was concerned,
however, it was a closed chapter. We have no means of knowing the
Duke's feelings, we can only guess at his despondency at the turn of
events; but, fortunately for him, he was nothing if not buoyant.
There is a saying that if in life one door closes, another opens: now
for George Spencer the great double doors of Blenheim Palace were
open wide to their lawful lord. Bankrupted and discredited he may
have been, but he was the Duke of Marlborough still, and the
successor and caretaker of the splendours of Blenheim and its
domains.

X

Elysium

WHEN THE FOURTH DUKE OF MARLBOROUGH had succeeded to his titles and inheritance in 1758 – nineteen, unmarried, handsome, virtuous, and the friend of the young King – he had been the cynosure of all eyes. A few years later, his marriage to the beautiful Lady Caroline Russell made the young Marlboroughs a grand and glittering couple. But chiefly preoccupied with their growing family, and content with life within the walls of their own large domains, this Duke and Duchess became known as an aloof couple; Blenheim was throughout the near half-century of the fourth Duke's reign the hub of their immediate family's life, and the centre to which the extended kin of nephews, nieces, grandchildren and cousins ever gravitated.

By contrast, when George Spencer, Marquess of Blandford, entered Blenheim Palace as fifth Duke early in 1817, he and his wife Susan were semi-estranged and middle-aged, and their five surviving children ranged from twenty-four to nineteen years old. Although they were all familiar with the house and estate through years of visiting their grandparents, Blenheim would never be for this younger generation the hearth and home it had been for their immediate predecessors.

As for the Duke himself, his closest relations and trustees, who knew him and the state of his affairs best, must have entertained dismal forebodings for the future. To the world at large, George, fifth Duke of Marlborough, was that discredited ass Blandford, whose scandalous, foolish exploits and debts were common gossip. A few people, however, may have seen interesting possibilities for a man they recognized as a botanist and plant collector, or knew to be a gifted musician; while bibliophiles may have looked forward with satisfaction to the augmentation of the Sunderland Library at Blenheim by the celebrated collection of books presently at White-knights.

As for the new Duchess, people probably liked her, as her family circle certainly did; but although well-born, hers was not the brilliant politico-social background of her Russell mother-in-law; and one feels instinctively that Duchess Susan lacked the style and prestige of Duchess Caroline – attracting glances of pity for the public infidelities and follies of her scapegrace husband, rather than the awed respect a snobbish world had accorded her proud and frigid predecessor.

Comparisons, however, are indeed odious, and not many in 1817 can have remembered the earlier, more dazzling succession to the dukedom. In the last years, life at Blenheim must have been dull to distraction, and a new beginning always begets new hopes – if only, in this case, among creditors who now earnestly hoped their bills might be paid.

Perhaps even between the Duke and Duchess there was a spirit of new endeavour: their nephew once more sheds light for us on their troubled and now stalemated relationship. Agar-Ellis had been in Paris when he received the news early in February of his grand-father's death; some weeks later his newly 'duchessed' Aunt Susan wrote him a long letter, giving him 'a good account of the state of the Family, & says that the Duke has not yet quarrelled with his brother [Francis, Lord Churchill] – she also tells me, what I am very glad of, that she is to live at Blenheim . . .'.[1]

From this it is clear that relations between George and Susan had reached their nadir: evidently, even the independent existence they had for some time led in London had not afforded a sufficient easement, and a further, more complete separation had been a possi-bility. So far as the Blandford marriage was concerned, the death of the old Duke may have been providentially timed, and the new Duchess, at any rate, was going to give their altered state of life the benefit of a 'try'.

It is at this point that we get our only direct description of Susan;

it comes from the vivid pen of Miss Mitford, in a letter to Barbara
Hofland: 'The Duchess is an excellent little person, and looks about
her new demesne, with a waiting woman, in a style of old simplicity
and kindheartedness that really does one good . . .'.[2] It is only a
brief, swiftly drawn sketch; but identikits are built up from such
clues. Susan now, in our mind's eye, is short of stature – an active,
bustling person, full of fresh optimism as she inspects the great house
in her new role as chatelaine.

In this same letter, Miss Mitford informs her friend that 'the
mansion [Blenheim] is worse even than the common run of bad
great houses – they kill two oxen and twenty sheep a week, and the
waste, riot, and drunkenness that go forward from morning to night
are sufficient to demoralize any neighbourhood in the world . . .'.
No doubt Duchess Susan's observant eye had already seen much
that was awry in the conduct of the place when she had been her
father-in-law's guest. At any rate, quite soon a new set of rules for
the servants at Blenheim was drawn up – a copy in her hand is in
the Blenheim Papers:[3]

1817

RULES TO BE STRICTLY OBSERVED

The Servants are all to dine at one o'clock, before the
Parlour dinner, both Upper & Under Servants, & to
breakfast & sup at nine – & no *hot* Suppers.

The Butler, or Groom of the Chambers, to see that the
Servants Hall & *Powder Rooms*, are cleaned & locked up
every night *before 11* o'clock.

All the Servants to sleep in the House when the Family is
at Blenheim; unless with special leave for any particular
cause.

The Under Butler to be assisted by all the Footmen in
turns, as there will be no Plate Maid.

The plate to be washed by the 2 Stillroom Maid, & in the
Stillroom; from whence the Under Butler must fetch it.

The plate to be kept & *cleaned in the Pantry*, & the present
dark plate Room to be shut up.

All the Glass etc. to be kept in the waiting room & closets adjoining; & to be cleared out of the dining room every day after dinner.

The Butler to keep the key & take charge of the Ale Cellars; also to superintend *all* the Under menservants, & to keep the Accounts, passing them all with Mr Fellows.

No meals to be allowed anywhere, excepting the Servants Hall & Stewards room. Breakfast excepted.

No Garden Men, or Milkmen to have their meals here.

No Posthorses or *hacks* to be taken into the Stables; being so near Woodstock.

Over the years abuses had no doubt grown up in the great household; but now there was to be a stiff new broom at work. The list ends on a firm note: 'Should any objections be made to these reforms, *those* persons may retire.'

Within a year or two of the fourth Duke's death, his trustees sold off two properties – Syon Hill House at Brentford, and Parkbury Lodge in St Alban's. Marlborough House too now ceased to be a family residence: it was Crown property, and subject to a bewildering number of complicated leases, terminating at different dates. In 1817 part of the lease expired and this magnificent London mansion reverted to the Crown, and was thereupon designated for use by Princess Charlotte (the Regent's only child, and heir to the throne) on her marriage to Prince Leopold of Saxe-Coburg-Gotha in 1816; the following year the Princess, aged twenty-three, died giving birth to a stillborn son; Marlborough House, however, continued to be the London home of Prince Leopold until 1831, when he became King of the Belgians.

It is from this time that we have two of the very few letters from Susan which (to our knowledge) survive: addressed to her husband, and written at the end of July 1817, they give nothing away about their mutual relationship. Businesslike, and agreeable in tone, they deal almost entirely with domestic affairs and social arrangements. Beginning 'My dear Lord', the Duchess enquires of the Duke as to whether she had not 'better send the White Knights plate that I have here,* down when I leave town, & so have the Syon plate when I return for my town use . . .'.⁴ The old Duke's executors had evidently proposed that the plate, linen and china from Syon House should be made available to her: politely, but quite firmly, Susan enquires of her husband if this arrangement is to be carried out. The Syon House linen is reported by the housekeeper there to be 'very little & it is old', but Susan adds, with just a touch of asperity: 'I daresay it is equal to what I get from W. Knights now . . .'. Marlborough House is being run down, and she makes proposals for reducing the staff to a sensible 'caretaking' level. Another mutual domestic preoccupation, mentioned in both letters, was the state of readiness at Blenheim; Susan expresses relief that of the guests she has invited to stay for the forthcoming Races only two look like coming, for which she is not sorry owing to the works in hand, which she fears may well not be finished. All this rings a familiar note across the centuries.

Amid these housekeeping topics a family theme is inserted: Henry, now very nearly twenty years old, had evidently vexed his mother, for she writes: 'I have had a letter from Henry but I do not consider it quite a proper apology perhaps it is from ignorance, as he ends by being sorry – he is very anxious for an answer about a Horse . . .'. Henry, it would seem, was on the scrounge. Her letter ends pleasantly – 'Good Night it is late, Ever your affectn: S.M.'

Two days later, the Duchess is writing again to her 'dear Lord': they have been invited to a ball being given for Princess Elizabeth at Clay Farm† on the following Tuesday: she, Susan, is thinking of going to it, and spending a night *en route* to Oxford. Attending the ball will mean missing the first day of the local race meeting, but she has ascertained that 'none hardly of the Oxford neighbours intend attending these Races – the Abingdons, Dawkins, Dashwoods, Macclesfields, Churchills . . . are all to be absent and as we shall have no sons there nor have anything to do with them,‡ I think attending

---

* She must have been writing from her own London residence, which was at that time 16 Grosvenor Place.

† Probably Clay Hall Farm at Windsor.

‡ Meaning 'officially', i.e. the Duke was not acting as steward.

the second day will be sufficient, especially when they hear Royal Commands prevent us.'[5] The new Duchess is conscientious – wanting to do the right thing, wanting to please people – and the letter ends on a slightly flustered note:

> I cannot leave Town till Monday next at all events and then shall be sadly hurried. All my things are so dispersed but I will do my best to be ready. My coach is not yet ready . . . I shall lose the post if I add more so adieu in haste – I fear we shall not find all ready when we do go to B[n] [Blenheim] – Yrs ever affectnly S.M.

The Duke started his era with verve and style, petitioning the Prince Regent for his authority to reassume the name of Churchill: this request was graciously granted, and the *London Gazette* of 26 May 1817 published the royal decision:

> that in order to perpetuate in his Grace's family a surname to which his illustrious ancestor John the First Duke of Marlborough, etc., by a long series of transcendent and heroic achievements, added such imperishable lustre, he and his issue may henceforth take and use the surname of Churchill, in addition to and after that of Spencer . . .

In addition Marlborough and his issue might bear 'the arms of Churchill quarterly' with the arms of Spencer, and they might in future use 'the supporters borne and used by his said illustrious ancestor'. Thus the family name of the Dukes of Marlborough became Spencer-Churchill. Various reasons may be attributed to this sudden action by the new Duke: a glow of patriotic euphoria remaining from the Waterloo years; a wish to remind people of another 'great duke's' services and victories; and, least worthy – but it springs to mind – perhaps the desire to thumb his ducal and fraternal nose at his annoying brother Francis, who had 'poached' the glorious Churchill name on his creation as a peer in 1815, an event which had been deeply galling to his elder brother.

The doors of Blenheim were soon open to family and friends. Towards the middle of the month, George Agar-Ellis paid his first visit since his grandfather's death: there was quite a gathering of the family – his own father, Lord Clifden, was present, and Lord Charles (Marlborough's uncle) with his three granddaughters.

Agar-Ellis received a warm welcome from his Aunt Susan and from his cousin Caroline, but the Duke himself 'did not seem above half glad to see me', [6] the young man confided to his diary: perhaps uncle and nephew shared mutual opinions of each other, and the Duke may have resented his nephew's confidential relationship with his wife.

A mark of local esteem and approbation must have pleased the newly fledged Duke: on 6 August 1817 he was admitted to the Honorary Freedom of the Corporation of Oxford, and later that month, to celebrate the beginning of their reign, the Duke and Duchess gave a party at Blenheim. There were over seventy guests who included a goodly representation from the City and University of Oxford, and the county. Among the close family attending were Lord John and Lady Caroline; Lord Charles came over from Wheatfield with a bevy of his grandchildren; and from Kirtlington came a collection of Dashwoods, including the Duchess's mother, the Dowager Countess of Galloway. Among the Woodstock representatives were the Mavors and the Blackstones.

Details of the organization for the party survive in the Blenheim Papers: [7] the lamps round the Court, steps and Portico were to be lighted by nine; on the steps were to be stationed the stable people, as the guests arrived, and the other servants ranged in the Hall to announce the company and to conduct them through the Bow Window Room to the Grand Cabinet, from whence all the double doors were to be opened as far as the Dining Room, creating a splendid vista. Dinner was to be served precisely at half past five, and directly afterwards the rooms were to be lighted; two servants were designated to attend to the lamps and candles throughout the evening.

There was music, of course – and, from their instructions, the band would seem to have had a busy and peripatetic time of it. While the company was arriving, they were to play in the Hall, 'then in the Dining Room as they pass to the Saloon. They will afterwards return to the Hall and play during the Dessert at the Door leading to the Saloon. When the Ladies retire they will cease and be ready to re-commence in the Library when the Gentlemen go to the Drawing Room.' [8] The Duke was not unmindful of his music-makers' creature comforts: refreshments would be served to them in the Colonnade. One stringent note, however, was sounded: 'on no account whatever must anything be taken into the Library . . .'.

But behind the jaunty façade of this new beginning, much was amiss in the life of George and Susan Marlborough – both between themselves, and with regard to family and financial matters. Susan had resolved to go and live at Blenheim, despite any intentions she may have previously had to the contrary; but when Agar-Ellis returned to England from France towards the end of March and called on his aunt, he recorded that he had seen 'the Duchess of Marlborough, who with her title has gained nothing but misery – as her Sons & Husband combine to plague her. Her hopeful Son, the young Marquis, has been making disgraceful riots at Hells* in London – taking up money from the Jews etc. etc.' [9]

On 27 March, Agar-Ellis again visited the Duchess, who 'opened to me the whole account of her son's and Husband's proceedings, which are as bad as anything can well be.' [10] It is tantalizing that we are not vouchsafed any details of these 'proceedings'. Blandford had just taken up with the unfortunate Susannah Law, indeed their illegal marriage ceremony (in which his brother Charles had played such a shameful role) had taken place only ten days or so before, but it seems unlikely that his mother would have known about the liaison so soon – and even more unlikely that she would have learned about the 'marriage' at this stage. But her eldest son's current debts and riotous behaviour would have been quite enough to cause her acute anxiety, combined as they were with her husband's perennial and increasingly grave financial entanglements.

Fathers and elder sons are proverbially at odds with each other, and more especially so where a great inheritance is involved. In 1818 the Duke of Marlborough clashed with his heir, the Marquess of Blandford, who with his trustees had resort to law against his father. Blandford had become alarmed (and, no doubt, angered) when he realized that his father had 'been cutting and intends to continue cutting Ornamental Timber on the Demesne Lands of Blenheim . . .'. [11] Counsel's opinion was sought at the end of January 1818. The wrangle continued throughout the year; in September,

---

* Hells, also known as Subscription-Houses or Slaughter-Houses, were gaming houses of which there were a number in London at this period.

George Agar-Ellis rode over to Blenheim; his uncle was not at home, but he walked 'through the rooms, which made me melancholy – & then about the gardens, & took a farewell of the trees, which will probably all be cut down very soon.'[12]

Blandford persisted in his objections to his father's tree felling, and took him to court: when the case was heard on 19 December 1818, the Vice-Chancellor was 'clearly of opinion, that this Court had no jurisdiction to interfere with the legal ownership of the Duke of Marlborough . . .'.[13] It had been said, he continued, that 'the Duke of Marlborough might tomorrow lay the whole of this estate to waste, and reduce this noble mansion and spacious domains to a barren heath . . .', but 'it could not be supposed that the Duke of Marlborough would so far forget what was due to his honour as to deal improperly with this property.' Judgement was given for the Defendant. Blandford, who must have felt fairly certain of his case to have pressed it against his father, would have been chagrined by this turn of events which, for a while at any rate, may have created a chill between father and son.

This year saw another interesting development: by a Decree of Chancery of 1 May 1818,[14] it was ordered that the Will and Codicils of the fourth Duke were to be executed. From the mass of papers concerning this transaction, which involved both trustees and beneficiaries, one provision of particular interest emerges, namely, a clause which directed that a yearly sum not exceeding £30,000 should be paid (at the discretion of the trustees) to the fifth Duchess for her separate use, and for the maintenance and use of all or any of her children and grandchildren. It seems a clear indication that the old Duke was determined to make proper (and separate) provision for his daughter-in-law and her family by his now-despaired-of son; and it was perhaps a mark of his esteem for Susan, and the recognition of her sterling and stable qualities, as well as of the fact that she and her children could hardly hope now or in the future to be decently maintained by her spendthrift husband. It was no doubt by grace of this provision in the old Duke's Will that the Duchess was able in some measure to mitigate her eldest son's dishonour by paying an allowance to Miss Susannah Law for so many years.

On 13 January 1819, the Marquess of Blandford was married at St George's, Hanover Square, London, to his first cousin, Lady

Jane Stewart,* the 21-year-old daughter of the eighth Earl of Gallo-way (Susan, Duchess of Marlborough's brother). It is remarkable how often first cousins married each other in those days: keeping the families and fortunes together would often have been a factor in planning such matches, while for the persons themselves, con-sanguinity and propinquity often went hand in hand. Society was less open, and certainly less mobile; families paid long visits to their relations, and, in the case of the Spencers and the Stewarts, the two families were neighbours in Oxfordshire, through the Dashwoods at Kirtlington. History now repeated itself: as we know, it had been through his friendship with Sir Henry Dashwood that George Spencer, then Marquess of Blandford, had met Sir Henry's niece, Lady Susan Stewart, at Kirtlington; when they married in Septem-ber 1791, it was in the wake of the ludicrous 'Gunninghiad', and was accompanied by much public comment, more especially as the bridegroom's parents were known to disapprove of the match and, indeed, had not attended the marriage ceremony. By contrast, there is no suggestion that George Spencer-Churchill and Jane Stewart were wed other than with the consent and approval of their families; and Blandford must have counted himself lucky indeed that no whisper of his scandalous conduct disturbed the harmony and happiness of the marriage celebrations.

George Blandford was in his twenty-sixth year and had, as we know, in the previous twelve months or so contrived to fall into both debt and disgrace: like father, like son, indeed. But to the chilling account of this young man's affair and mock marriage with Susannah Law must be added another tale of equal shame.[15]

Among Blandford's numerous cousins was Harriet Spencer:

---

* Jane Blandford, later Marlborough, bore her husband four children; she died in 1844. The sixth Duke married twice again; his second wife was Charlotte Flower, daughter of Lord Ashbrook whom he wed in 1846, and with whom he had two children; she died in 1850. In 1851 Marlborough married another cousin, Jane Stewart, daughter of the Hon. Edward Richard Stewart (Susan, Duchess of Marlborough's brother); she bore him one son, and survived her husband by forty years, dying in 1897.

---

65. George, fifth Duke of Marlborough, a miniature (artist unknown).
66. Matilda Glover, a miniature (artist unknown).

some five years younger than him, she was the younger daughter of William Robert Spencer (the second son of Lord Charles Spencer of Wheatfield) and his wife Susan. William was almost the exact contemporary of his first cousin, the fifth Duke, of whom he was the sometime friend and confidant, acting as a 'post office' for his letters to Lady Mary Anne Sturt in the final stages of their love affair.

William possessed a diversity of gifts: a not inconsiderable poet, he also wrote operas; he spoke fluent German and French, and enlivened any company he inhabited with his mimicry and wit. By his talents and temperament, as well as through kinship, William Spencer was drawn into the brilliant, louche Whig world of the Devonshire House set, where his other cousins, Georgiana, Duchess of Devonshire and her sister, Henrietta, Countess of Bessborough (daughters of John, first Earl Spencer* and his wife, Georgiana Poyntz), with Lady Melbourne (mother of William Lamb), were the reigning deities.

In 1791, when he was in his early twenties, William Spencer had married Susan Spreti, the widow of Count Spreti: she had been born Susan Jenison-Walworth (a German family of English origin), and a link already existed between William and herself in that her brother Francis had married a daughter of his fascinating and talented aunt, Lady Diana Beauclerk. From the earliest days of their marriage, William and Susan Spencer moved in a brilliant and varied circle, and in their own drawing room entertained a diverse company of the literary, political and artistic worlds.

Very soon William fell victim to that endemic disease which was the bane of the Devonshire House world – gambling: and he had few resources to squander or possessions to pawn. Nor were William and Susan a happy couple: although outwardly united, for the most part they led their own lives. Susan Spencer was not only unfaithful

---

* John Spencer of Althorp (1734–83), created first Earl Spencer in 1765, was the grandson of the third Earl of Sunderland and Lady Anne Churchill, younger daughter of John, first Duke of Marlborough, and his wife Sarah.

---

67. The miniature of George Spencer-Churchill by George Sanders, 1818, left as an heirloom to Blenheim in Susan's will.

68. Lady Jane Stewart, Marchioness of Blandford, later sixth Duchess of Marlborough; a miniature by Sanders, 1818.

to her husband, but promiscuous, and worse – she transgressed one of the few 'house rules' of their world – she was indiscreet. Of the two, she was by far the less liked, and as the net of debt increasingly entangled them both, Susan was criticized as avaricious, and despised for her shabby, begging ways; while debt, drink and laudanum did their destructive work, and took their toll of William's brilliance and good looks.

The children of this raffish couple, three boys and two girls, must have suffered to some degree from their parents' rackety and debt-laden lives; but they always found a warm welcome from their Cavendish and Ponsonby relations,* joining the veritable tribe of children – both legitimate and illegitimate – which romped through the gilded salons, without invidious distinctions being made. But if the moral code of the Devonshire House set was shallow and amoral, it was neither cold nor dismissive: Georgiana Devonshire and Henrietta Bessborough were essentially warmhearted, and had a true sense of the responsibility owed to the offspring of the liaisons of their golden circle.

Perhaps as a reaction to the circumstances of their childhood and youth, two of the Spencer sons went into Holy Orders – Aubrey George Spencer eventually becoming Bishop of Jamaica, and George Trevor Spencer, Bishop of Madras; while the elder girl, Louisa (later Mrs Edward Canning), became a devout Roman Catholic. But Harriet, the younger daughter, born in 1798, was destined to come to grief: perhaps she, more than her siblings, had been affected by the worsening relationship between her parents, and was subject to even less supervision or guidance from her mother. By the time she was eighteen or nineteen, Harriet was consorting with a group of wild and profligate young men, several of whom were the contemporaries and friends of Lord Sunderland. To their loose and immoral ways must be added lack of chivalry, for Harriet's conduct (or rather, want of it) became widely known, and her reputation tarnished – a most serious consequence for an unmarried girl in those days.

Until then, Harriet's name had not been linked with that of her

* Cavendish and Ponsonby: the family names of the Dukes of Devonshire and Earls of Bessborough.

cousin, George Sunderland (now Blandford). But in 1817 – the year of his illegal marriage to Susannah Law – he seduced his foolish, ill-behaved cousin, and got her with child: he was twenty-four, and Harriet nineteen years old. The consternation within the family circle can be imagined: there was no legal or social impediment to prevent George and Harriet marrying, but there can be little doubt that the idea of the Marlborough heir contracting a marriage with a penniless cousin of ill repute was not one that either Blandford or his family were ever likely to have entertained.

Although the facts were hushed up, rumours were rife – and among these ran the scandalous whisper that Harriet's child was not Sunderland's, but his father's, the Duke's. It shows the nadir to which Marlborough's reputation had descended, that such a charge could have currency. However, a consideration of the carefully re-searched arguments advanced by Dorothy Howell-Thomas in her book, *Lord Melbourne's Susan*, leads me to accept her opinion that Harriet Spencer's daughter was the child of George, Marquess of Blandford and not of his father, the fifth Duke of Marlborough. And to her cogent reasoning, I would add one additional fact: at the time when this child would have been conceived, the middle-aged Duke was in the first flush of a new love for a young girl, and at the beginning of an association which was to be both profound and durable, the account of which belongs to the next chapter.

All those who knew about this squalid and distressing affair between Blandford and Harriet Spencer censured the girl's parents for their lack of care for their daughter. Righteous indignation may relieve strong emotions, but luckily for poor Harriet in her downfall, practical and kindly help was also at hand: Lady Bessborough had always been very fond of her much younger cousin, and as soon as she knew of Harriet's condition she consulted with other members of the family, and she and her husband undertook to assume all responsi-bility for the child. It is likely that within hours of her birth in the spring of 1818, the baby was spirited away to the Bessboroughs' house at Roehampton in Surrey. No record has been found of her baptism; she would probably have been privately baptized without an entry being made in the relevant parish register; named Susan Harriet Elizabeth, she bore the surname Churchill, not Spencer.

Little Susan remained in the care of the Bessboroughs for the first three years of her life, but when in 1821 Lady Bessborough died, her daughter, Lady Caroline, and son-in-law William Lamb took on the care of the child, and Susan Churchill was for the next eight or nine years brought up at Brocket Hall, the Hertfordshire home of the Melbourne family. With Lady Caroline's death in 1828, the happiest years of Susan's childhood were over; but Lord Melbourne (as he became in that same year) never abandoned responsibility for her education and welfare. After some years at an English boarding school, she was sent to a school and family in Switzerland. In 1837, she married Aimé Timothé Cuénod, the son of the minister of a parish near Lausanne. Lord Melbourne (by then Prime Minister) gave his consent, and attended to all the necessary legal formalities for his ward's marriage, appointing trustees to manage her not inconsiderable dowry, which was probably provided by the Bessborough family and himself. This story has a good ending: Susan Churchill's marriage was long, fruitful and happy; throughout her life she kept in touch with her English friends, and she died in about 1882.

So much for the child – what of the mother, the unfortunate Harriet? She took refuge with her mother's relations in Bavaria, and about a year after the birth of her child she became betrothed to her cousin, Count Charles von Westerholt; they were married in Ratisbon in October 1819. The Westerholt family were told that Harriet had borne a child, though they may not have known the extent of her public disgrace. But her father-in-law's approval seems to have been conditional upon Harriet's being received once more into English society. At this point, the fidelity and generosity of William Spencer's kin were once again to be proven: the young Duke of Devonshire (Georgiana's son) espoused his unfortunate cousin Harriet's cause, and gave a great ball at Chiswick House the following April in honour of the young von Westerholts, at which Count Charles's parents were present to witness the rehabilitation of their daughter-in-law. We have a somewhat middling account of the occasion from Mrs Arbuthnot, however, who recorded: 'It was very fine but not very gay & the occasion of its being given kept many persons away . . .'.[16] And she rather bleakly summed up the effectiveness of the Duke's warmhearted gesture: '. . . as no one spoke to her [Harriet], I do not see that it will assist much in patching up her

broken reputation.' Society's rejection of Harriet makes chill reading; but fortunately she was not to make her home in England, but
in Ratisbon, Germany, where her husband's family made her welcome. And joy may have entered her life once more when, in the
autumn of 1820, she gave birth to a son. But hers was not to be a long
life: Harriet von Westerholt died in 1834, aged thirty-six, pre-
deceasing both her parents.

It seems extraordinary that neither the Susannah Law affair nor
this last sad and unsavoury saga were winded by the scandal-mongers
of the press. A number of people must have known about Susannah
Law and her child (even if not about the fake marriage): one can
only conclude that Blandford's companions who accompanied him
to Scotland in that summer of 1818 must have been truly discreet;
and Susannah's own family, who may, rightly, have felt some complicity in the fradulent marriage ceremony, would probably have
judged it in the girl's interest to remain silent – indeed, the settlement
upon her, continued by the Duchess, may well have depended on
their discretion. It was of course quite a commonplace event for
gentlemen to take mistresses among the bourgeoisie, with the then
almost inevitable consequences; at any rate, it was not for twenty
years that the whole disgraceful story became public knowledge. As
for Harriet Spencer and her child: we have seen how her tribe closed
in and around this scandal, forming a wall of silence, and it was over
a century before that tale would be told.

These scandalous family secrets must have weighed heavily on
Susan Marlborough; and quite apart from her fear of exposure, her
kind and generous spirit would surely have revolted against the
dissolute and unfeeling conduct of her son towards two young and
innocent girls. This was the time, too, of the Duke's financial crash,
resulting in the dismemberment of Whiteknights – a humilating and
depressing consequence, which cannot have failed to affect her, for
perhaps she too had loved the place. Finally, events in Marlborough's
personal life may have changed his attitude towards her to the point
where a combination of all these factors made her life at Blenheim
unendurable. Around now – probably in 1819 – Duchess Susan
packed her bags, and left Blenheim and her exasperating, faithless
husband.

Silence surrounds this dramatic event. Even George Agar-Ellis has nothing to say about his aunt's departure from Blenheim, although he was often to be in her company in the succeeding years; and in her son's generation there is a yawning gap in the Spencer-Churchill archives:* the sixth Duke ordered that all his personal papers should be destroyed on his death – which, in view of his conduct as a young man, was understandable.

When her husband had succeeded as Duke, Susan, although nearing the end of her tether, had 'shown willing', and with a ready spirit had tried to make a fresh start with this new chapter of their life. Within two years or so, this woman, whom we have come to feel was so likeable and so full of good will and intent, had had enough. Susan Marlborough must indeed have been outraged beyond all endurance to have taken this drastic step. She had already borne so much, could she not have doggedly 'soldiered on'? She was, after all, at an age when she might have found refuge in the prestige of her position. and the opportunities it offered her; her children, relations and friends would have rallied round her; Blenheim Palace is vast enough, one would have thought, to accommodate two separate modes of life. But no such considerations can have weighed enough with her, and presently we will explore the reason why, in this author's view, Susan, Duchess of Marlborough departed those marble halls. There is evidence that she may have made occasional visits, but from this time on she was never to resume her role as chatelaine of Blenheim or reigning Duchess.

✳❖✳❖✳

However sharply the winds of misfortune blew, George Spencer-Churchill was a man of many parts, and several consolations: to gardening, music, painting and book collecting must be added romance. It might be supposed that these employments could have ensured a happy existence – and indeed, combined with his inborn, unquenchable optimism and natural resilience, these ploys may have lightened the disastrous consequences of his follies. Certainly, despite his financial *débâcle* at Whiteknights, the new Duke lost no time in getting to grips with the gardens of his splendid new domain.

Marlborough did not tamper to any significant extent with the

* Blenheim Papers, now in the British Library.

grand plan created by his father and Capability Brown – although, as we have seen, he was soon to be busily cutting down trees in the grounds, thereby causing alarm to his family and trustees. The fifth Duke's gardening and landscaping activities were to be geographically confined in the main to the area round and above the Grand Cascade, and to the wide expanses of garden to the east, south and west of the Palace, contained within the boundary created by the great lake – and they would be considerably limited in their extent by sheer lack of money.

Apart from the grand 'improvements' and plantings of Capability Brown, the fourth Duke had also created his New Gardens round about, and below, Brown's Grand Cascade, where he caused the whole area to be cleared and replanted. About 1774–5, the long-neglected Bernini fountain had been placed in position near the foot of the Cascade; and the Duke also removed statues from the top of the North Court of the Palace, and had them placed among the plantations in his New Gardens. Forty years on, 'Great Spencer's' son started to make his own mark: we shall see that, like so many of the achievements of this gifted but unstable (and perhaps unlucky) man, his works at Blenheim were to be largely ephemeral.

In 1817, the 'Tenth Edition, Improved' of Dr Mavor's guide was published; from the text it is clear that additions and alterations were already under way at Blenheim. A Flower Garden was being made below the East Front of the Palace, beneath the windows of the Bow Window Room and the private apartments. The former Duchess's Flower Garden was already being planted with choice American hardy species which, as we know from our tour of Whiteknights' gardens, were among the Duke's favourite plants; and over the next few years, he was to remove an enormous number of American trees and shrubs from Whiteknights to Blenheim. Also in the Flower Garden he had recently installed an aviary: constructed in wood and wire-work, it was from a design of Henry Hakewill (1771–1830), who had worked at Blenheim in the time of the fourth Duke. Dr Mavor tells us that it was a construction of 'considerable elegance and expense' (of course!): crescent-shaped, it formed two wings tacked on to each side of a 'small neat Temple'; each wing had six compartments 'stocked with gold and silver pheasants, some curious doves, and a pair of Curassoa birds . . .'.[17] The Duke's fantastical taste is again in evidence.

These additions, of course, were just the beginning: during the succeeding years the Duke was to develop some eighty acres of garden, beginning with the Arcade Garden laid out on the western side of the house (where now lie the water terraces constructed by the ninth Duke in the 1920s), and moving on to the broad stretch which leads towards the Grand Cascade, with the hillside falling down to the lake. Here the fifth Duke created a series of gardens displaying different species and varieties of plants, and repeating in a very different context the theme he had developed at Whiteknights.

This newly developed area was not at that time accessible to the public, and over the years local curiosity was much exercised as to what was the character of the Duke's private gardens; we ourselves have to wait until the publication in 1835 of the twelfth edition of *A Description of Blenheim* before we learn the details; even then, we do not learn them from the good Dr Mavor. The learned Doctor had been on cordial, not to say friendly, terms with the fourth Duke, but this pleasing intimacy had not been handed on to the succeeding generation. Although the Doctor was only some eight years older than the new Duke, the latter probably thought him a prosing old bore, and suspected that this former boyhood tutor and friend of his father most likely disapproved of him, and deplored his 'improvements'. At any rate, while Marlborough obviously could not bar Dr Mavor from those parts of the Palace and grounds which were open to the public, the new private gardens remained tantalizingly shut to him. Bravely glossing over his natural disappointment, however, Dr Mavor resorts to somewhat fulsome blandishments: 'The Duke, who is known to possess more botanical taste and skill than any other nobleman in the kingdom, is now laying out a very large piece of ground which, when finished, will be the finest botanical and flower garden in England . . .', and while he regrets the exclusion of strangers from these gardens, he expresses the earnest conviction that 'when finished, they will doubtless be opened for the admission of occasional visitors'.[18]

Meanwhile, a neighbouring botanist, Dr Joseph Bowles of Faringdon Hall, Berkshire, a Fellow of the Linnaean Society and of the Royal Horticultural Society, had been admitted to the holy ground, and had written a description of the Duke's private gardens

which equals Mavor's for length and flowery terminology. Poor Dr
Mavor could hardly let his comprehensive and renowned guide to
Blenheim go to press without a description of this major development in the gardens, which was of great interest to so many. One
can hardly bear to think of his mortification as, emerging from the
Palace on the west side after a conducted tour of the house, he has to
hand his readers over to a new guide!

> These apartments open immediately to the Gardens, and
> *we copy from the pen of Dr Bowles*, of Faringdon Hall, the
> following description of this charming, picturesque spot,
> the whole embellishments of which are executed not only
> under the inspection of his Grace, but by his constant
> direction and co-operation [author's italics].

And so it is from Dr Bowles that we learn of how, from the
Arcade Garden (just by the house) one passed to the New Holland or
Botany Bay Garden, with its beautiful plants from New Holland and
Norfolk Island, and then to the adjoining Chinese Garden, planted
with camellias and other shrubs of Chinese origin:

> From this Garden, which is about eight acres, we proceed
> to the Terrace Garden, where the character of the scene
> changes, and becomes one of grandeur united with beauty.
> Clumps of the choicest American and other hardy and
> exotic plants ornament and appear to hang on the slopes,
> which descend with bold, yet easy swells, to the lake . . .

Here Doctor Bowles was not to be outdone by the other Doctor in
his praise and appreciation of His Grace's talents and skill:

> The present Duke, the Claude of Landscape Gardening,
> has arranged the points of view with such consummate
> skill, that every view is a complete picture, in a style of
> beauty consistent with itself, and with the characteristics
> it requires.[19]

One next came to the Dahlia Garden – half an acre filled with some
two hundred varieties; from there a walk leads into the Rose Garden,
planted with a thousand sorts of roses, standard and dwarf. We
might have been back at Whiteknights!

Now the ground began to fall away as one approached the

Grand Cascade, where, further developing his father's New Gardens, with their Italian fountain and classical statues set among the trees, the fifth Duke had created a Rock Garden on a large scale, on the slopes above and near the Cascade. Before gaining entrance to this Rock Garden, or *Flora Petraea* (as it is somewhat pretentiously called in the guide), the visitor found himself confronted by a seemingly insurmountable barrier of rock, which consorted well with the crashing waterfall and romantic 'Salvator Rosa' effect of the man-manipulated scenery. Visitors might sustain a few moments of dismay at being thus barred from the pleasures and mysteries beyond, when – wonderment! – at the touch of a hidden spring the mass of rock revolved, as if by magic, on its axis, admitting them to 'a spot in the highest style of picturesque beauty'.

In this area of about an acre, the Duke had, using local limestone, contrived rocky scars on the face of the steep bank, with stairs which passed obliquely from one level to another. The rocks formed emplacements for a large assemblage of rock plants collected from far and wide, which Dr Bowles described in detail.

Near the Rock Garden was to be found a Druids' Temple, 'formed by an immense tablet of rock, supported by huge pillars of unhewn stone, overgrown with moss'. This curious feature further contributed to the romantic atmosphere, and 'the imagination, already excited by the wondrous beauties of the place, carries us back to the far olden time . . .'.[20]

A year or two before these two learned local Doctors were compiling their glowing descriptions of the Blenheim gardens, another visitor had also gained access to the sanctum: J. C. Loudon, that great horticultural pundit and now the eminent 'Conductor' of the *Gardener's Magazine*, in which he published a long critique of all he had observed during a tour of the Palace and the grounds. Reading the two accounts one is reminded of the sharp contrast between Mrs Hofland's flowery descriptions of Whiteknights, and Miss Mitford's cool, critical account of the place, although Loudon's article is both more balanced and more knowledgeable than Miss Mitford's witty, sarcastic letter which so entertained us some chapters back.

Loudon was no stranger to the Duke of Marlborough's gardening proclivities for he had often visited Whiteknights, continuing to do so long after the Duke's connection with the place had ceased. Now, in August 1833,* sixteen years after the fifth Duke had succeeded, Mr Loudon descended on Blenheim to see and record what was afoot there; it was not his first visit, but the last one had been in 1810.

His interest was chiefly directed at the gardens and grounds, and he passed somewhat rapidly through the Palace and its apartments. No sooner was he in the gardens than he at once perceived a feature which displeased him: he strongly criticized the manner in which the private gardens had been divided off from the parts which were open to public access, finding the high dividing fence 'stuck full of furze bushes, so as to render it [the private garden] impervious to the sight: a very great deformity.' It certainly does sound ugly.

In the first part of the gardens which he traversed, Loudon noticed large plantings of azaleas, rhododendrons and other flowering shrubs, all intermingled with flowers; and a feature which pleased his knowledgeable and appreciative eye was the manner in which many of the beds of shrubs and flowers were 'bordered by young oaks, twisted so as to form a wreath, care being taken, in pruning them, never to cut the leaves. In some cases, the common oak is used for this purpose, and in others, the Turkey: both form very beautiful edgings.'[21] A feature which struck him as harsh and ugly, however, was the way the earth in the beds had, in many cases, sunk anything from seven to eighteen inches below the level of the surrounding lawn, due to the removal of the subsoil at the time of planting. At this juncture in his tour, Mr Loudon was in conversation with the Duke's head gardener, Mr Jones, who had been in His Grace's service at Whiteknights and Blenheim since 1802. Mr Jones, no doubt abashed by the critical questionings of the eminent gentleman, declared he was 'as well aware of these faults as ourselves, but has not had hands enough to remedy either them, or several other glaring defects.' One cannot help wondering how pleased the Duke may have been at this interrogation of one of his employees by a visitor to whom he had given particular permission to view his private gardens.

However, Mr Loudon was greatly impressed by the species and

* The entry in the *Gardener's Magazine*, under 'Notes on Gardens and Country Seats', is entitled merely 'Blenheim. August 11.' Since it appeared in volume X, published in April 1834, I have presumed the account was written the previous August.

varieties of plants and shrubs, commenting:

> No expense, or, perhaps, we should rather say, no effort,
> has been spared to obtain not only fine plants, but also
> large specimens of them. There are quantities of large
> Magnolia conspicua, tree paeonies, purple magnolias,
> Pavia carnea and rubra, choice azaleas, kalmias, hybrid
> rhododendrons, wistarias, and, in short, of all the more
> rare and beautiful trees and shrubs procurable at the
> nurseries . . .

He also remarked upon the varieties and size of the heaths, which
seemed to be thriving, some of them attaining three to five feet in
height. Among the trees which were doing well were tulip trees,
Judas trees, *Virgilis* (*Cladrastris lutea*, or yellow-woods), *Ailanthus*
(trees of Heaven), *Nyssa aquatica*, liquidambar, sassafras, and
Balearic box. 'Anyone with the love and practice of gardening,'
wrote Loudon, 'cannot but be bewitched by this catalogue of
"sweets".'

He was, however, critical of the manner in which the trees and
shrubs had been scattered around the area, giving a 'spotty frittered
appearance'. Loudon also had some stringent comments to make
with regard to the covered seats, of which there were a number
(echoes of Whiteknights), which, in his view, struck a dissonant
note – one in particular: 'a circular piece of green trelliswork, with
gilt balls, which we consider the *ne plus ultra* of bad taste and absurd-
ity. It would disgrace a cockney tea-garden . . .'.

By the time Mr Loudon arrived at the Rock Garden, he had very
little time left to do justice to it, but nevertheless appreciated that
here the Duke had created something unusual and remarkable. He
formed the 'decided opinion' that this Rock Garden could be ranked
with other celebrated gardens of similar genre; and although he had
some technical criticisms to make, his assessment was that: 'On the
whole, this rock garden, defective as it is, appeared to us the only
redeeming point in the duke's gardening operations at Blenheim . . .'.
Loudon's appraisal of the Duke as a gardener is indeed severe; yet,
even with our limited opportunities to judge, one feels the justice of
this measured criticism: 'We have seen no evidence, either at White
Knights or Blenheim, of taste or skill in gardening as an art of design:

we have seen a great love of rare plants, without well knowing what
to do with them . . .'.

In all, Mr Loudon found that he was in agreement with another
critical visitor, who had preceded him some years before, in 1828:
signing himself 'An Amateur', he too had published his considered
opinion on the Blenheim gardens in the *Gardener's Magazine* – and
he (for one supposes it was a 'he') had been even harder on the unfortunate ducal gardener than Loudon. Evidently our unidentified
'Amateur' was familiar with Blenheim in both the fourth and fifth
Dukes' time, as well as with Whiteknights. He singled out some
English gardens where the 'superior taste of the proprietors' had
created original scenes such as 'Nature's self might envy' – and
listed Blenheim (as it had been) with Dropmore and Red Leaf.*
Then, in a massive footnote, 'An Amateur' proceeded to deliver a
swingeing judgement on the fifth Duke as a gardener:

> The taste of the noble proprietor of this princely place,
> however well it may have been exerted at White Knights,
> seems either to have fallen rapidly into decline, or never to
> have been sufficiently elevated to bear application to a
> garden on an extensive scale . . . Where the gardens were
> formerly laid out to accord with the adjoining pile, where
> once long and broad gravel walks, lined by lofty and regu-
> larly planted exotic shrubs and trees, led the eye to the
> longer and loftier avenues of the park, are now little
> meandering paths, little arbours or berceaux, little
> clumps of all shapes, little shrubs, the greater part of the
> old, large, and handsome evergreens being cut down; and
> this littleness attached to the finest private residence in the
> world; and 'the Despoiler' cited as one of the most scient-
> ific and accomplished of our landscape-gardeners![22]

'Amateur' is merciless – and unlike Mr Loudon he did not mention
any redeeming features in the Blenheim gardens: perhaps the
footnote was already too long.

Many are the articles written in our contemporary horticultural
journals describing present-day gardens, great and small – but I,
for one, cannot call to mind any such critical assaults upon their

* Dropmore, near Beaconsfield, Buckinghamshire, was the home of Lord Grenville;
Red Leaf, near Penshurst, Kent, was the home of William Wells, Esq.

creators or owners as were heaped upon the fifth Duke of Marlborough's head by these pundits. (Indeed, one may feel that there
is today a dearth of objective appraisal in this field: sufficient that
the owners struggle to maintain them, with or without assistance;
sufficient that the lawns are mown, and the weeds pulled.) One
cannot but feel a twinge of sympathy for our poor Duke for the
lambasting he received at the hands of two such critics, in his
favourite (and most innocent) occupation, coupled as some of the
technical appraisals were with snide allusions to His Grace's personal
morals. One wonders if he wilted beneath their censure. Some years
later, however, he received from J. C. Loudon a remarkable accolade,
which in justice should stand beside the criticisms; in his major work,
Arboretum et Fruticetum Britannicum, published in 1838, Loudon was
to write: 'Among the planters of arboretums in Great Britain during
the nineteenth century, the first place belongs to George, [fifth]
Duke of Marlborough.'[23]

XI

Dearest Girl

WE DO NOT HAVE to search far afield to find the reason why, sometime around 1819, the Duchess of Marlborough left Blenheim Palace: her husband had acquired a mistress – a local girl, young enough to be his daughter – called Matilda Glover.

Mystery surrounds the circumstances of this girl's birth and life up to the time she met the Duke, probably in 1817. Exhaustive searches have failed to reveal any record of her birth, but from her death certificate she would appear to have been born in 1802. An interesting entry appears in the diary of Joseph Farington, RA (1747–1821) for 5 June 1821: 'Mr Charles Bowles of North Aston, Oxfordshire called . . . He spoke of his neighbour, the Duke of Marlborough who, he said, resides at Blenheim, but his affairs are in a very bad state and his conduct very improper. The Duchess has not lived with him for two years or more. He has taken a girl born in low life at Woodstock, and she is now in his keeping . . .'.[1]

One curious coincidence was that the fourth Duke had a friend of long standing – Richard Glover, who died, aged about eighty, in 1822; he was the son of the poet Richard Glover (1712–85), who had been left a legacy by Sarah, Duchess of Marlborough in 1744 to write (with Mallet) the Great Duke's life. Richard Glover the younger was on terms of close friendship with the Marlborough family, and was frequently at Blenheim and Marlborough House. He would appear to have been a man of property, probably unmarried, and with many friends among the aristocracy. When he died he left bequests to both the Duke and Duchess of Marlborough,

and to other members of the family. But although it is most tempting
to seek a clue here to Matilda Glover's antecedents (Glover could
have been her grandfather or great-uncle), no evidence has been
found of any connection between them.

In contemporary context, the label 'low life' might suggest
that Matilda came from a lower-middle-class family, rather than
from working-class stock – merchants perhaps, or small professional
people; and we know that her mother at any rate was alive. There
had been Glovers in the district of Woodstock in the early seven-
teenth and eighteenth centuries (two were Mayors of the town).
Since Woodstock was at one time the centre of the glove-making
trade (gloves are indeed still made there), there may have been a
connection between that occupation and the surname: there was a
'Matilda le Gloveres', but at a very much earlier period than the
one with which we are concerned. [2]

Apart from the mystery surrounding our Matilda's birth, we
know that she had some measure of education because she wrote to
the Duke (although he often complained that her letters were very
short). From her portrait, she looks pretty enough, with dark
ringlets; we are told she had an attractive singing voice, and that
she had a pony (perhaps given her by the Duke), and could ride.
Matilda Glover was barely sixteen when George Spencer-Churchill,
then in his early fifties, fell in love with her. The course of their love
affair, which was to be (for him certainly) deep and abiding, is
traced for us in the large number of letters written by the Duke to
Matilda over a period of twenty years, and preserved in the family
of one of their descendants.* [3]

It is probable that Matilda Glover's home was in Bladon, as
several of the letters are directed 'Miss Glover. Bladon'; the village

* The greater number of the letters are undated. I have therefore had to group
them in periods of time according to any clues afforded by the text, the date of the
watermark on the writing paper, the address from where the letter was written or
to where sent, postmarks, etc.: I have given dates wherever possible.

69. Lady Caroline Spencer-Churchill; a miniature by Sanders.

70. David Pennant, Caroline Spencer-Churchill's husband; a miniature by
Sanders.

71. Their daughter, Caroline Pennant; a miniature by Mrs Robertson.

lies a mere quarter of an hour's walk south-west of the Palace, just outside the park walls. We get glimpses of the first days of their friendship in letters from the Duke, making woodland trysts in or around the park: 'This is a beautifull day, if it lasts, my dearest Girl, I am going to Bladon Hill to shoot. If you come any time, you must come on your Pony, as it will be wet and too long a Walk – a great Trail for you. Let me know by Long [a servant] what you mean to do. Most aff. yours, My dearest Girl. M.M.*

Another day: 'My dearest Poppet, Will you meet me at Burleigh Wood at one if you are pretty of will; don't come if you don't find yourself quite equal to it, then I will come to you at the new Pond at 2 . . .'. This letter cannot be before 1818 (watermarked), so it is possible Matilda was in the early stages of pregnancy. In this same letter, a domestic rather than a romantic note is struck: 'I send you £12, I must owe you £3, for I have no change – I would rather have the Pig for dinner on Monday, I prefer Roast Beef on Sunday . . .'. Evidently the Duke was to dine with her two days running – whether in her own home or in the lodge where she would soon be ensconced is not clear.

Many of his letters to Matilda were written from Whiteknights, right up to the time he had to abandon it forever, sometime in 1821. When he was parted from her, he seems to have written every day; Matilda was not such a good correspondent. From Whiteknights he wrote: 'My dearest Girl, I wrote you a long letter yesterday, but my dear Girls is very short – I hope you will write me a longer one tomorrow . . .'. Soon Matilda would see Whiteknights for herself; in a letter from there marked 'Tuesday, 11 o'clock', the Duke writes: 'Tomorrow I shall get a Letter from my dearest Matilda & you know how happy it will make me; I hope in my Letter tomorrow or Thursday to tell you if I can confirm about your coming here – This place looks beautifull & I long for you to see it . . .'. His attachment for Whiteknights is very evident in his letters, and it was also clearly the place where their love affair first blossomed. Many years later,

---

* MM stands for Marlborough Marlborough, a manner in which he frequently signed himself.

---

72. George, fifth Duke of Marlborough as an old man, a miniature (artist unknown).

George was to write: 'My dear, You really should recollect that White Knights was the first Place you and I were ever comfortable together, that on *that account alone I have reason to regret the loss of it . . .*' (his emphasis).

Although we now know that Marlborough was in the thrall of a real and lasting love, his letters to Matilda seem to lack the headlong passionate unreasoning transports of those he had written to Mary Anne Sturt some twenty years before. He was deeply in love with this girl, but it was an autumn love – and perhaps the more stable and profound for that reason. There were no more wild plans to flee to foreign lands (Blenheim was a sheet anchor, and probably he was too broke), and no more suggestions of divorce. When the lovers had a tiff, the Duke's tone was one of amused indulgence: 'My dear little cross Patch, I will send the little chaise for you at 12 if it is not too soon for you, & I will meet you at the forward gate at ½ past 12.'

Soon, Matilda was with child: perhaps it was at this point that the Duke installed her in a home of her own, where they could be 'comfortable together'; it was almost certainly the Home Lodge,* situated within the park a few hundred yards from the Triumphal Arch, the gateway from Woodstock to Blenheim. This may have been a cosy and convenient arrangement for the Duke and Matilda, but (in this author's opinion) it constituted, with the advent of their first child, the final breaking point with the Duchess. With this 'love nest' established not a mile away, the situation must have seemed to her intolerable. We know that, once made up, hers was a resolute mind, and so Susan packed up and quit the great unfriendly Palace, and her unfaithful, uncaring husband.

She was in a better position than many wronged wives at that time, for she had some independent means, thanks to the provision made by her father-in-law in his will; and for the last ten years or so, she had had her own separate London establishment. She could depend on the loyalty and affection of her own numerous family, and her husband's relations seem to have afforded her their understanding and moral support.

With the advantage of hindsight, moreover, we know that the Duke's new infatuation was no passing affair; and perhaps the

* Now the agent's house and known as China Corner, owing to its proximity to the China Gallery built by the fourth Duke, which was demolished in the 1840s.

Duchess sensed this. With Matilda Glover he tasted not only physical passion, but also companionship and domestic joys which he may never have known either with the woman he had married for convenience, or with his previous paramours. It would seem his restless heart had come home to rest at last with this simple, lowly born girl less than half his own age.

But touching and enduring although Marlborough's devotion to Matilda Glover was to prove, it made him unseeing and unfeeling towards those who had claims on his consideration and loyalty. Though his wife was inevitably the chief sufferer, the affair must have caused divisions and mortifications within his family circle. Caroline, now twenty-one, continued to live with her mother; of the sons, Blandford scarcely appears in the Duke's letters, save when these two were tussling over the cutting down of the trees at Blenheim; we know that Blandford saw a lot of his mother, and it may well be that he took her part – although he himself was hardly in a position to be censorious. As to the attitude of Lord Charles and Lord John, it may have been somewhat ambivalent: they could scarcely afford to fall out with their mother, who held the purse strings; but in several of the Duke's letters they are mentioned as sending warm messages to Matilda. Later on, one of them at least was known to have joined in the fun and games at the Home Lodge. We do not hear about Lord Henry's reaction.

As to the world at large, it would appear that the Duke was impervious to the censure of society: perhaps the sorry tale of previous scandals, and the public disgrace brought upon him by his perpetual indebtedness, had made him indifferent to the criticism and disapproval of outsiders. Being an incurable romantic, he may have thought the world well lost for love.

Between 1819 and 1823, three daughters were born to Marlborough and Matilda.* In the letters from the Duke written before or after the birth of each child, he expresses touching and anxious solicitude for the mother and baby's well-being. Matilda was attended by a Woodstock surgeon, Mr George Coles, who was expected to furnish the Duke (if he was absent at the time) with

* The dates of the children's births have been calculated from their death certificates, so they may not be quite accurate. No trace has been found in the local parish registers of any records of their baptisms.

detailed reports of his patients. Marlborough was most likely at Blenheim when their first child, Georgina Matilda, was born in the early spring: Matilda herself was only seventeen. Shortly after the birth, the Duke, finding himself in London, suggested to Matilda that she might like a visit to the metropolis. On 13 April 1819 he wrote to her:

> I really think you might come up to town for a week with your Baby & your Mother & in that case I could take a good lodging for you – Tell me what you think of it. I am very glad you liked the handkerchiefs, I hope you will have one made into a Turban . . . Pray write directly & tell me if you would like to come up for a week or so, if you do you must come by a Chaise and not in a Coach, & I think you should bring your Mother with you – but this is as you like best – Most affect: yours,
> My dearest Girl,
> Marlborough.

When their second child, Caroline Augusta, was born, probably sometime in 1821, the Duke was at Whiteknights: it must have been in the last period of his tenure there, before relinquishing the place to Sir Charles Cockerell. Perhaps he was making arrangements for the final folding up of the property, and so could not be at his 'dearest Girl's' side; but he kept in constant touch. It was high summer, and he wrote from Whiteknights:

> W.K. 2 o'clock Friday.

> Since your last letter, my dearest Matilda, I have been particularly anxious about you & I have been disappointed in not hearing today – Charles is now fishing, so I have left him & am come home to write to my beloved Girl. He desires to be remembered to you . . . I hope you got the blackcurrants and that you liked them . . . Pray write often my dearest dear Girl, & beg Mr Coles to give me immediate Notice if you should be brought to bed, but I think you are safe till my return . . .

There is an interesting, somewhat frigid reference to his wife and daughter in this letter: 'I suppose you know that Her Grace & my daughter are gone abroad for a couple of months, & then come back to Blenheim . . .'. Perhaps this jaunt abroad was carefully timed.

The tone in which Marlborough refers to the Duchess from time to time in these letters is markedly different from that which he used when writing to his former love, Mary Anne Sturt. In those days he was obviously still concerned for Susan's well-being, and he still had a liking, if not a love, for her. Twenty years on, there seems nothing left but coldness.

Babies wait neither upon dukes nor dustmen, and the next letter from Whiteknights is full of relief and joy:

> Nine o'clock Saturday Morning
>
> I have just received the intelligence, my dearest Matilda of your safe delivery & of your being as well as can be expected . . . I now have only to pray that my dearest Girl & her Baby go on well & you may guess how happy I shall be to see you . . . Mr Coles says the Baby is very large & healthy. I am so glad that the weather is moderate and not too hot for you . . . Don't write till Mr Coles allows you my dearest Matilda; but when he does *one* line will be most gratifying to your *most affectionate* M.
>
> I long to see our little Baby.

One cannot help wondering if, in years gone by, poor Susan had ever been the object of such care and solicitude.

Their third child, another daughter, to be called Ellen Elizabeth,* was probably born in 1823. We do not know precisely how many children Matilda bore in the following years. Records have been found relating to a son, Henry, baptized at Bladon in October 1831 and buried there a mere two months later; and at least two more sons were born: another Henry, and George, both of whom figure in one of the Duke's later letters. Henry, however, cannot have lived beyond adolescence, for in his mother's Will, made in 1848, she refers to only one son, George – of whom no later record has been found.

After one of her confinements, the Duke sent Matilda to recuperate at some watering place. He missed her sorely:

---

* Ellen Elizabeth grew up to marry, *en deuxième noces*, Lionel Campbell Goldsmid, a Captain in the Merchant Service; their daughter Ellen Georgina married George James Marshall, and from them is descended the family of Mrs Susan Marshall Bernstein, to whom we owe the preservation of the Duke's letters to Matilda Glover.

My dearest Girl, I received your letter last night & I was *most* happy to hear that your ride did you good, as it shows that you are stronger tho' thinner – I have only *2 days* more to pass without seeing you and *I do so long for Monday, I hope* you *are not sorry* . . . Coles thinks the Water [from the Spa presumably] will not lose any of its virtue by being bottled, so I hope, my dear you will settle something about its being sent, about 2 quarts *twice a Week* . . . God bless you my dearest Girl, I shall go and see that your House is comfortable tomorrow or Sunday . . .

Although the Duke was so full of consideration for his young mistress, he could not conceal his impatience to resume their usual life together after the birth of one of the babies. He wrote from London: 'You know where I wish I was, & you know what I wish I was doing up one pair of stairs. Pray wean the young Lady as soon as possible & prepare yourself for Saintliness & kisses . . .'.

As with Mary Anne Sturt, Marlborough was a good present giver; she had received trinkets, gowns, Parmesan and, on one occasion, a carpet. Twenty years on, his letters to Matilda are full of questions as to whether she has received the oranges, coffee, and other like comestibles considered delicacies at that time. When he was staying in the neighbourhood of Bedford, he procured some local lace for her, and on another occasion, on returning from London to Blenheim he told her: 'I bought you as I returned a beautiful Gown *made up* in Oxford Street, your favourite colour Pink . . .'. Interspersed with these delightful gifts were more homely presents: joints of lamb, and 'pork for roasting and some pickles'.

Matilda responded to these attentions as best she could; perhaps she was a good gardener too, because in one of the Duke's letters he remarks: 'I have tried your potatoes and they are very good.' On another occasion, she sent him plants; he sounded delighted: 'Many, many thanks my dearest Girl, for your dear little present, but that I may see them oftener I have planted them opposite to my Window; I did not like to put them so far off as the Pond . . .'.

While this romantic affair was proceeding, with all its passion combined with charming domestication, Marlborough's ducal life continued at the Palace. After the first flush of enthusiasm when he succeeded to the dukedom, Marlborough's affairs, financially, domestically and socially, seem to have resumed their sadly chaotic state.

Fortunately for posterity, the core of the inheritance and the treasures at Blenheim Palace were entailed – only the Duke's personal fortune and possessions could be seized for debt. In 1818 the Duke's disgruntled creditors had relentlessly closed in upon him, and the following year saw the dispersal of the contents of Whiteknights. 1819 must have been a bad year altogether for the Duke and his family, what with the sales at Whiteknights, the scandals surrounding Blandford, and (probably) the departure from Blenheim of the Duchess. We have no indication as to whether Marlborough minded his wife leaving him: deeply involved as he was with Matilda Glover, he may have been glad to be rid of her company and unwelcome supervision – it is unlikely their relationship had been anything of a pleasure in these months of his ever-deepening entanglement.

In the archives, between 1818 and 1823, there are several Notes of Arrears of Taxes, and Inventories and Orders to take possession of Goods and Chattels.[4] In February 1820 there was an execution at Blenheim, when goods were taken 'to and for the use of Thomas Wright of Henrietta Street Covent Garden London Esquire'.[5] Considering the splendour of his inheritance, the list of goods seized to satisfy Mr Wright's claims upon the Duke seems pathetic: from His Grace's private apartments were taken divers paintings (some of them family portraits), and sundry musical instruments and music books. From elsewhere in the house guns were seized; also a rosewood secretaire, a clock, and some ornamental boxes. Outside in the Coach Houses no fewer than six carriages of various types were listed, from 'A Capital Travelling Chariot' to a park phaeton and a garden chair. While from the farm numbers of livestock were taken: six cows, two pigs, five grey horses, a saddle horse, and a pony. It must have all been so humiliating; but perhaps by now the Duke was indifferent to such events.

No doubt as a direct result of the execution described above, and perhaps because of other similar depredations, we find in March

1820 an agreement with a firm of upholsterers in Piccadilly, Thomas Blades and Benjamin Palmer, whereby the Duke is to pay £50 a year (in quarterly sums) for the hire of furniture and effects for use in 'Blenheim House'.[6] The schedule lists carpets, curtains, frame for chimney glass, gilt moulding and rods for pictures with supports, cloth to cover doors, etc. etc. Presumably goods 'on hire' could not be seized in any future raids. It was moreover evident that, whether in consequence of financial stringency or the departure of the Duchess, many changes were being made in the Palace.

Notwithstanding these melancholy and embarrassing events, the Duke seems to have kept up his spirits pretty well, and was not in the least deterred from badgering the Prime Minister, Lord Liverpool (1770–1828), with a series of requests ranging from the Lieutenancy of the County to Lord of the Bedchamber.[7] The Lieutenancy of the County had been in his family since the time of the Great Duke, but we are not surprised to learn that in 1817 Lord Macclesfield had been appointed to that prestigious office; no reaction is recorded to this later request. In March 1821 there is another vacancy (the Duke understands) among the Lords of the Bedchamber: Lord Liverpool 'Is sorry, it is not within his power to meet His Grace's wishes.'[8] Marlborough's requests continually meet with polite 'put-offs'. Finally, in 1824, the Duke asks the Prime Minister if he could be made use of on a foreign diplomatic mission; he would accept 'any Diplomatic appointment not derogatory to my Rank'.[9] Lord Liverpool sends the Duke's request on to Mr Canning, the Foreign Secretary, but tells Marlborough he cannot hold out any expectation of success;[10] and there the matter rested.

Ever a genial host, Marlborough had, as we have seen, started off in fine style with his 'accession party'. Among his frequent family guests were to be Professor Nares and Martha Elizabeth; after staying at Blenheim in January 1818, Nares wrote: 'nothing could have been pleasanter than this short visit . . .'. There had been concerts every evening, and all the heads of the University had been invited to dine.[11] In March, as we know, Professor Nares also visited the Duke at Whiteknights – so he was busy entertaining in both his abodes.

Some three years later, we have a diverting account by Henry Fox, later fourth Baron Holland (1802–59) of a dinner party at

Blenheim, to which to his great surprise he had been bidden: the
Duke may have been trying to widen his acquaintance. It seems that
some of the results of his financial straits were in evidence:

> I dined on the 20th [November 1821] at Blenheim, where
> I was very much amused with the Duke, and surprized at
> the splendor of the establishment. The party were chiefly
> (with the exception of some hungry curates) Oxonians.
> The dinner was good and rather pleasant. The *house ill-
> lighted*; and all the servants, I believe, *bailiffs*. I went with
> Vernon [Robert Vernon Smith, later Baron Lyveden]. I
> was astonished at the invitation, for I never had seen him
> in my life. He is pleasant but looks exactly like a great
> West India property overseer.[12]

Other visitors also continued to come to Blenheim. Readers will
remember how Mrs Arbuthnot, the Duke of Wellington's friend
and constant companion, had paid a visit to Whiteknights in January 1821; some three years later, in April 1824, she and Wellington
toured Blenheim, avowedly 'in a very cursory manner, being pressed
for time . . .' (Mrs Arbuthnot seemed habitually to allow too little
time for her sightseeing – she had also been in a great hurry when
she went to Whiteknights). The Duke of Marlborough himself conducted his eminent guests on their tour (unlike his father in similar
circumstances!). Mrs Arbuthnot's admiration and approval of all
she saw was somewhat tempered by a tinge of envy on behalf of her
heroic companion:

> In going thro' the stately apartments of this splendid
> building I could not but regret the difference of times
> which rendered it impossible for a second Blenheim to be
> erected to the Hero of Waterloo. Such a house could not
> now be built under millions. It is magnificently placed on
> the edge of a hill. It is the fashion to call the style heavy &
> bad, but I confess I could only admire, not criticize.[13]

As to Marlborough's gardening activities, Mrs Arbuthnot was
delighted with them: 'The present Duke, who is gardening mad, is
making a flower garden on a bank which slopes rather precipitately
down to the waterside & which, when finished, will be the most
lovely spot that ever was seen.' Her admiration however had to

stop short at the house and gardens:

> The family of our great Gen is, however, gone sadly to
> decay & are but a disgrace to the illustrious name of
> Churchill, which they have chosen this moment to resume.
> The present Duke is overloaded with debt, is very little
> better than a common swindler, & lets everything about
> Blenheim. People may shoot & fish at so much per hour!
> and it has required all the authority of the Court of
> Chancery to prevent his cutting down all the trees in the
> park. He did melt & sell the gold plate given the great
> Duke by the Elector of Bavaria, substituting ormolu ones
> to deceive the trustees . . .

It is sad to realize the extent to which our Duke had acquired
such a shabby reputation among his contemporaries and equals:
Mrs Arbuthnot was no mere gossip-monger – she was well-informed.
Her strictures, however, with regard to the letting of such amenities
as fishing and shooting – which seems to have shocked her as much
as the taint of swindling – will surely astonish modern readers.

As we know, Lord Blandford had, within a short time of his
father's succession, brought a case against him in the High Court of
Chancery to restrain him from cutting timber at Blenheim; his case
at that time had failed, but not long afterwards, on further applica-
tion, such an injunction was granted. Thereafter, for two or three
years, there was to be a continual tussle between the Duke and his
heir over this matter. The difficulty in which the Vice-Chancellor's
court found itself was to define what, and how much, timber it was
reasonable for the Duke as a landowner to expect to fell in the ordin-
ary course of prudent arboriculture – and even garden planning –
and what was in effect vandalism for financial purposes. It is clear
from *The Times*' Law Reports that the lawyers and judges were
equally at a loss to decide these knotty points. On various occasions
the court was asked to re-define the restraint more precisely, but
despite a petition by the Duke, the injunction was maintained.
Needless to say, His Grace sought and found the means to circumvent
the controls which had been placed upon him. Watchful neighbours
in 1823 commented in a letter: 'What a fellow the Duke is, he is
cutting down Oaks in the park and barking them, pretending for

his use, draws them to the timber yard and then sells them and steers them away . . .'.[14]

Then the matter of the gold plate was undeniably shocking. In 1819, the Marlborough trustees took the Duke and Mr Thomas Triphook to court, requiring them to return (or compensate the trustees for) a large service of gold plate; this service, the gift of the Elector of Bavaria to John, first Duke of Marlborough,* had been bequeathed, with other valuable and interesting items, by the fourth Duke to his son. They had been designated as heirlooms, and an inventory was made which both the fifth Duke and his trustees signed: it was specified that these heirlooms should not be removed from Blenheim Palace without the consent of the trustees. In May 1819 the trustees (their suspicions aroused) caused another inventory to be taken: the gold plate was found to be missing.

According to the Duke, he had placed the gold plate in the hands of a Mr Thomas Triphook, a stationer in St James's Street,† with instructions to take the service to the appropriate craftsmen to have the new Spencer-Churchill arms engraved upon each piece. Subsequently, finding himself in grave financial difficulties (this was the same year as the sales at Whiteknights), he had told Triphook to retrieve the plate and to negotiate loans on its security: Marlborough solemnly avowed he had no intention of parting with the gold service for good, and that what happened subsequently had been without his consent or knowledge.

Over a period of about two years, and some six or seven hearings in the Court of Chancery (how rich the lawyers must have waxed on the Spencer-Churchill family!), the following shameful story emerged: the Duke had used Triphook as his agent for the purpose of raising money by pawning the gold plate; when it was apparent that not enough money would be forthcoming from this expedient, he had decided to have it melted down, and had told Triphook to arrange this. His intention at this time, according to Triphook, was to have ormolu facsimilies made of the service, saying he did not

---

* David Green, in *The Churchills of Blenheim*, wrote that the gold plate was given to the first Duchess by Sophia, Electress of Hanover, but I can find no confirmation of this, and in *The Times*' Law Reports the plate is attributed as above.

† In his bachelor days the Duke had lived in lodgings with a Mr Triphook, a bookseller in St James's Street. This may very probably have been the same individual.

wish it to be known that he was disposing of the gold plate, and that no one would detect the difference between the real and the false. In the event, no facsimile service seems to have been made.

The trustees moved quite quickly, but not as quickly as the Duke, for by the time the case came to court on 8 June 1819 the Elector of Bavaria's princely gift to the Great Duke had been reduced to three ingots of gold, and the proceeds delivered to the Duke. In his defence, Mr Triphook reiterated that he had believed the gold plate to have been Marlborough's property, and not an heirloom, and that he had throughout acted strictly in accordance with His Grace's personal instructions.

The end of the case is obscured by the fact that the issue of the gold plate becomes part of a larger and even more complicated legal debate about whether the Blenheim heirlooms and the Post Office pension could be used for the part payment of taxes. In May 1821, the Lord Chancellor made an Order to the effect that 'It was necessary to preserve the heir-looms at Blenheim-house, for the benefit of those who might hereafter come into possession of the estates . . .'.[15] A decision which – alas – came too late to save the gold plate. This lamentable story, combined with that of the Duke's legerdemain in the matter of the Bedford Missal at the sale of his books, makes it impossible to refute Mrs Arbuthnot's labelling of him as 'little better than a common swindler'.

Some years later, a spoof obituary of the Duke was printed, purporting to appear in 1846, which derided various episodes in his life, including his liaison with 'Mrs Sturt', the supposed sale of the gold plate, and so on, terminating with these lines (said to be copied from his monument) :

> That His Grace is in Debt let it never be said
> Especially now he's no more;
> For all's settled and he his last debt has just paid
> Though he never paid one before.[16]

Marlborough's activities were not only the cause of comment in sophisticated circles: humbler neighbours also observed the comings and goings in the Park. The Richardson family, who lived at Combe, a village not far from Blenheim, vouchsafed the following interesting information in a letter to their brother in London on 13 July 1823:

... there was an old Woman and three young ones lived at
the home lodge a good while and the duke there or the[y]
at Blenheim every night we heard the Marquis fetcht
his Brother away, and the womans are gon all but one
and she lives at the home lodge the Duke have given Miss
Glover a poney and Gig and Miss takes her eldest
daughters there every morning and fetches them at
night. The woman and Miss seems very comfortable
companions both the Misses and the Duke are at the
home lodge most nights to a late hour playing on music
and the[y] say she is a fine singer and so the[y] was all,
we hears she is in the familey way, and Miss Glover is
quite forward in the same way, we hear today the Dukes
son is come to Blenheim again, he's as fond of them as his
father is, the Duke have built a little lodge where old
weakman liv'd between Woodstock and bladon and have
put Misses Mother and her husband in it to lesson the
familey but I don't know what he is to do, we thinks the[y]
are gon from home . . .[17]

From this somewhat garbled account, it is clear that the Home
Lodge was the centre of much conviviality, and that one of the
Duke's sons (probably Lord Charles) had joined in the fun, and that
on one occasion Lord Blandford had descended and removed his
brother from the jolly but manifestly unsuitable company there –
perhaps at the behest of his mother? Marlborough shows up (although in the wrong context) as a good 'family man' – looking after
Matilda's mother and her 'husband' (perhaps not Matilda's
father?). There seems to have been much to-ing and fro-ing between
the Home Lodge and the Palace in Miss Glover's gig: perhaps
Georgina Matilda and Caroline Augusta played at the Palace. We
cannot know who were the other ladies in this *galère*, nor how many
of them were in varying stages of pregnancy (or by whom) – except
in the case of Matilda Glover, who that year gave birth to her third
child by the Duke of Marlborough, Ellen Elizabeth.

While all this 'malarkey', as the engaging expression puts it, was
in train, the Duke's own family had their feasts and funerals. A
cause for feasting was the birth in 1822 of a son and heir to George,
Marquess of Blandford and his wife Jane: the first of their four
children, named John Winston, he was to grow up to be the seventh

Duke of Marlborough (the father of Lord Randolph Churchill and Winston's grandfather). In June of that year, Lady Caroline, her mother's constant companion, was married to Mr David Pennant, a gentleman descended from an ancient Welsh family. One feels this was a love match, and from various letters[18] it is evident that Susan Marlborough maintained a close relationship with her daughter after her marriage and was on good terms with her son-in-law. But, alas, this happy situation was not to last. On 18 December 1823 Caroline Pennant gave birth to a daughter and, just over three weeks later, she herself died; she was in her twenty-fifth year. Her baby daughter was given her name. The solitary Duchess and poor young David Pennant, himself only twenty-six, must surely have been numbed by misery.

Later that year, however, there was a real reason for family rejoicing: Lord Henry, aged twenty-eight, married his cousin, twenty-six-year-old Elizabeth Martha Nares. We have heard very little about Henry; he was destined (as was predictable for younger sons) for the Church, but his health did not allow him to follow this career. Henry and Elizabeth Martha's marriage took place at her home in Biddenden, Kent, where her father, the kindly and delightful Professor Nares, was Rector; Lord Henry's maternal uncle, the Reverend Dr Stewart (next year to become Bishop of Quebec), officiated at the ceremony. Both the Duke and Duchess attended the wedding, but their inevitable meeting was understandably the cause of some anxiety and anguish to Susan beforehand, as we learn from a letter to his father from David Pennant, written from London on 12 July 1824 (the day before the wedding): 'The Duchess sets off in an hour or two to sleep at Maidstone and thus to be in good time for the nuptial ceremony of tomorrow. It will I should conceive be a trial to her – but her mind is much occupied by it and that mind is naturally a very strong one . . .'.[19] She would have had the support of her brother, Dr Stewart, and Blandford had promised also to escort her on what must in the circumstances have been a difficult day for her. One wonders how the Duke brazened it out.

Three years later, that tearaway Lord Charles entered the Holy Estate of Matrimony: at thirty-three, one would hope that he had settled down somewhat. Like others in his family, he had had money troubles (around 1824 he had been officially insolvent);[20] but over

the years his mother, as she was empowered to do, had been instrumental in getting the trustees to pay up his debts. His bride, Etheldred Catherine Bennet, was the daughter of a Wiltshire Member of Parliament. Lord John, their sailor son, was now the confirmed bachelor of the Duke and Duchess's children, but he was making a good career in the navy.

From around 1830, Matilda Glover began to spend much of her time in London, either in lodgings or in a house taken for her by the Duke. We find no recorded reason for this new mode of life, and so we must rely for an explanation on our own intuition and imagination. By now the three girls, Georgina, Caroline and Elizabeth (the 'Ellen' was dropped), would have been eleven, nine and seven respectively, and social life in and around Woodstock may well have posed some problems for them and, indeed, for their mother. Perhaps the Duke and Matilda felt it was easier for them to be educated in London, where Matilda could appear as a married woman with her children. All the Duke's letters to her in the earlier years of their relationship were addressed to 'Miss Glover', whereas in the 1830s there are several extant directed to 'Mrs Spencer Glover' at her London address.

As the years pass, the Duke's letters to Matilda continue in affectionate and domestic vein: indeed, their relationship bears much more similarity to the married state than to an 'affair'. At one point Marlborough set her up with an insurance policy or annuity – he would maintain the policy during his lifetime, he wrote, then she must keep it up. And when Matilda was away at the seaside (salt bathings for sore eyes), the Duke minded the children, taking them for drives to Oxford and such-like ploys.

There is one delightful letter from Marlborough to his Matilda, written almost certainly from Blenheim – evidently she had just departed for a visit without them all. It shows our Duke not only as a fond and solicitous lover, making arrangements ahead for his 'dearest Girl's' enjoyment and comfort, but also in a charmingly paternal light: he seems greatly to have enjoyed the company of this, his second, batch of children.

> My dearest Girl,
>
> I must write, if it is only to tell you what you know, how anxious I have been all day about you, & how delighted I

shall be if the Post tomorrow brings me fair tidings of your
comfortable arrival, & that you found the Wine etc. all
ready for your approval. It has been a lovely day here,
I took a long walk by myself and also two with Elizabeth
& George. We dined at 5 exactly, & we have been very
good Company together. She is not by any means so shy
& reserved as when her older sisters are here. Henry &
George set off nearly as soon as you were gone. Henry
never asked my leave to go, & George *finished his reading*,
& I shall insist on his reading at least one hour with
Elizabeth every morning before he goes out anywhere.
As I do not expect many words from you tomorrow, I hope
you will give me a full account of yourself the next day.
Dull we shall be, dull we must be without you & I shall
cut [count?] the watches till your return . . .

This whole letter breathes the atmosphere of a long, loving and
stable relationship: in all but fact, one feels, it was his second, and
happy, marriage.

Arising out of Marlborough's predilection for the company of
his younger children, we now come to a curious and intriguing incident described in the journal of the great reformer, Anthony Ashley
Cooper, later seventh Earl of Shaftesbury (1801–85). He was the
eldest son and heir of Cropley Ashley Cooper, sixth Earl of Shaftesbury, who had married the fifth Duke's sister Anne. From 1826 to
1830 young Lord Ashley (as he then was) was a Member of Parliament for Woodstock in tandem with his cousin, Lord Blandford. In
early February 1828, he found himself at Blenheim, visiting his
uncle (with whom he can have had very little in common):

Last night I dined with the Duke of Marlborough. Never
did I feel so touched as by the sight of his daughter Susan –
his natural daughter. She is Charlotte, our dear Charlotte
over again, in voice, in manner, in complexion, in feature,
in countenance. I could hardly refrain from calling her
Sister. O Great God, have compassion upon her forlorn
state! What will become of this poor girl? What danger is
she beset with! May *I* have the means of doing her some
real lasting service! Father of mercies, grant thy protection and keep her from the awful perils that are on every
side.[21]

Knowing, as we now do, of Blandford's illegitimate daughter by Harriet Spencer, and the rumours in circulation that she might have been the Duke's child, it would seem that Lord Ashley almost certainly mistook the identity of the child he saw, and believed her to be the Susan Churchill whom he must have known was being brought up by the Lambs at Brocket. In the author's opinion, it is much more likely that she was Georgina, the eldest of the Duke's children by Matilda Glover, who could equally well have shown a strong family resemblance to Lord Ashley's elder sister Charlotte. There is no evidence that Susan Churchill was at Blenheim at that or at any other time, and, since there is no mention of the girl being present at dinner, Lord Ashley may have glimpsed her only briefly, was told by the Duke that she was his daughter, and jumped to conclusions. By nature high-minded and virtuous, Lord Ashley would in any case have greatly disapproved of his uncle's raffish mode of life and regarded Blenheim as a totally unsuitable place for the upbringing of innocent children, legitimate or illegitimate: hence his prayerful recommendations to the Deity.

✳◇✳◇✳

In the earliest days of their relationship, Matilda was too young, and probably too overwhelmed both by the passion and the rank of her lover, to ask herself many questions as to her future. Soon, it must have become quite evident to her that the Duke had no intention of abandoning her: on the contrary, he established her in comfort, and in proximity to him. No doubt the passage of years bred confidence in her: but, as she grew older, concern about the future may well have crossed her mind, perhaps prompted by the concern of her own relations. Marlborough was thirty-six years her senior: if anything happened to him, what would become of her? We have a letter from him which tells us much – it is also, unusually, quite precisely and clearly dated: 22 July 1830. The Duke was then sixty-four, and Matilda twenty-eight years old.

> I am happy, my dear, to do what you wish, which is to assure you of my intention which amounts to a promise & I consider a promise, should I ever prove single to make you my Wife. I do not see what more I can say or do – I must however beg that our intention may be kept to our-

selves, as matters of this sort ever should be, and always
are, while one Person is alive – whom I need not name
[the Duchess, presumably]. It is enough that I promise
all you ask, for what comfort or advantage can there be
in blazoning our mutual intentions to all the world –
These matters should be kept sacred till the time arrives
for legitimately developing them, as they are nobody's
business but our own. Were I to write volumes I could not
say more, & on reflection you must allow that I have said
every thing which you ought to require for the furtherance
of the object you have in view . . .

The last sentence is somewhat ambiguous, but it seems quite clear
that Matilda had been seeking what she now had – a written promise
of the Duke's intention of marrying her, should he be free to do so.
In the light of his conduct to Matilda over a period of time, as well
as his letters to her, there is no reason to suppose that the Duke's
written declaration was other than his true and solemn intent.

There is a French saying that in love '*Il y a toujours celui qui
embrasse, et celui qui tend la joue*': reading through the bundle of letters,
which span more than a decade, this author has been left with the
impression that the Duke led in the accounts of their love, and that
Matilda, as the years went on, was the one who proffered the (no
doubt velvety) cheek to her captive Duke. The innocent and perhaps
gullible village damsel had evolved by the date of his 'declaration of
intent' in 1830 into a clear-sighted and firm personality, the mother
of a growing family, with her future – and theirs – to consider.

That Matilda Glover was deemed by those close to the Duke to
have influence over him is borne out by a letter to her from Mr
Coles, the Woodstock surgeon who had attended her in her confinements. Although undated, the letter must certainly belong to
the later period of the Duke's life, and from its context it would
appear that he and Matilda were absent from Blenheim and that
the Duke had been far from well (gout, perhaps?), and had written
to Mr Coles about it:

Dear Miss Glover,

You will believe that I value the Duke too highly to
hear of His Grace's indisposition without feeling anxious
about him. I trust however, that the attack, from His

Grace's letter this morning, was trivial & temporary, & that my advice will be all that is required, otherwise you will not, I am sure, fail to seek some of the able advice that surrounds you – I have ventured to caution His Grace on the subject of diet – I do really think that he indulges too freely, & that he would be less susceptible of illness, if his diet were more restricted & simple – again I consider a pint of Wine daily, such as His Grace partakes of, more than a prudent quantity – It should be remembered that His Grace does not use the strong exercise he did a few years ago & he cannot therefore enjoy the good things of this world with equal impunity – at his period of life the vessels lose of their elasticity and do not so readily accommodate themselves to a full circulation – We have laughed over the subject of Diet so frequently, that His Grace may think indifferently of it, but I am firmly persuaded it is of some importance that His Grace should moderate his Bill of fare, & my object in addressing you, is earnestly to solicit your cooperation & influence in impressing it on His Grace . . .[22]

Readers will no doubt find that the good Doctor's letter has a certain timelessness about it.

In the last years of the Duke's life, Matilda seems to have come to live in the Palace itself. By the mid-1830s, Marlborough may well have been feeling his age (he would have been seventy in 1836), and perhaps he found it gloomy and lonesome dwelling in the great Palace alone. When he made his Will in 1838, he referred to her as 'now living in my family at Blenheim'.

The Duke's love affair with Matilda Glover would of course have been known to all the neighbours virtually from its outset, when he established her in the Home Lodge and she began producing her family, thus precipitating the departure of the Duchess. That the position was known and accepted locally is clearly illustrated by an extract from the diaries of a Dutch lady, Countess Cornelie de Wassenaer,* a great traveller, who wrote (in French) detailed

---

* Countess Cornelie de Wassenaer (Baronne Heeckheren) had been at one time Maid of Honour to the Princess of Orange (the Grand Duchess Anna Pavlovna of Russia) later Queen of the Netherlands. I am indebted to Mr Igor Vinogradoff for this interesting extract. The Countess was one of his wife's forebears.

accounts of her many journeys. In October 1836, she and some companions arrived at Blenheim; it being a Sunday, the house was closed to visitors – however, by reciting their titles, and the fact that they were foreigners, they persuaded the doorkeeper to seek the Duke's permission for them to visit the Palace, which was duly granted. They were greatly impressed by the splendour of the rooms, and by the pictures and treasures displayed in them. Presently, the party were shown into a room which was clearly used by the residents in their daily existence:

> . . . books scattered about, a piano, a harp, and over two little sofas by the chimney piece – two modern portraits, of which one depicts the present duke, aged 75 years [she has aged him by five years], the other portrait being of a young and pretty woman, who, our guide told me, is Miss Glover. The servant, who was showing us round, informed me that this person is the Duke's mistress, that he lives separated from his wife, and even from his three sons. The Duke had dissipated his fortune by gambling and other means, but that he could not alienate the Palace and estates at Blenheim, which, however show the effect of his profligacy, inasmuch as they are very badly maintained . . .

It is interesting that the servant should say the three sons were at variance with their father. We have seen how previously kindly messages were passed to Matilda by Marlborough from Charles and John, and that one or other of them visited the Home Lodge; but if Matilda by now was ensconced in the Palace itself, this may have proved too much and have caused a real breach with the younger sons as well as with Blandford. There is evidence that other members of the family also shunned Blenheim in these years.

Matilda Glover had her pledge, but she was destined to remain a 'backstreet' wife, for the Duchess was to outlive the Duke by one year. Marlborough had tried to make provision in his lifetime, as best he could, for Matilda – and she had her recognition in his Will, for he bequeathed 'all and singular my Goods Chattels and Effects of what nature or kind whatsoever the same may be unto Matilda Glover now living in my family at Blenheim in the County of Oxford . . . And I do hereby nominate constitute and appoint the said Matilda Glover to be the sole Executrix of this my Will.'[23] There cannot, for sure, have been much to leave; but Matilda may have felt that, as far as she was concerned at any rate, the legend beneath the Spencer-Churchill family's coat of arms – *Fiel Pero Desdichado* (Faithful Though Unfortunate) – had not been betrayed.

XII

Largo

THE DUKE OF MARLBOROUGH'S financial embarrassments were not surprisingly reflected in the general appearance of the great house and its surroundings. When Countess Cornelie de Wassenaer had visited Blenheim in 1836, she had noted that the Palace and the estates showed 'the effect of his profligacy, inasmuch as they are very badly maintained . . .'.[1] Some three years earlier, the critical eyes of Mr Loudon had also remarked signs of neglect, which he had carefully annotated in the account he gave of his visitation:[2] even before gaining admittance to the park, he had noticed that in the courtyard to the Triumphal Gate, 'The outer piers of the narrow entrance are beginning to decay; and out of one of them is growing a young ash tree, 5 ft. or 6 ft. in height, and out of the other a sycamore of about the same size.' Unfortunately, this was only a prelude to the general dilapidation the distinguished 'Conductor' of the *Gardener's Magazine* was to observe on his way towards the Palace: recalling from previous visits the beauty of the reflections in the lake, great was his disappointment on finding that the water's surface was 'quite green from aquatic weeds', and that the level of the lake had sunk to a marked degree; the masonry of Vanbrugh's Grand Bridge was also in need of attention, as were the exterior walls and gateway to the Palace. The great Court of Honour seemed to be in a reasonable state of repair, unlike the side-courts, where the vista through the succeeding arches had been quite spoilt: 'The Duke has turned . . . [the stable] court into a kind of melon, hot-house, or rubbish-ground; and a strange place it is, taken altogether.'

In front of the Palace itself, Mr Loudon's eagle eye noticed that attempts had been made (by both the fourth and fifth Dukes) to improve the terminations of the towers; he was affronted by this tampering with Vanbrugh's work, commenting: 'Indeed, there must be something defective in the arrangement by which the heirs of the great Marlborough hold this property; otherwise neither these alterations could have been made, nor the lake and the building have been suffered to be so much injured by neglect as they now are.' It would no doubt delight his heart were he able to see Palace and Park now – cherished and tended as never before, six generations on.

We have already remarked how little the Duke seemed to care about the opinions of the world at large, and perhaps this indifference derived from the fact that he did not frequent London society, nor was he in conspicuous attendance at the House of Lords; indeed, owing to his dire financial straits (which now seemed a chronic condition), the Duke scarcely dared to show his face outside the Blenheim walls, for fear of bailiffs. Possibly for the same reason, after Marlborough House reverted to the Crown in 1817, neither a country nor a town address is listed for the Duke in *Boyle's Court Guide* for many successive years. But we hear of him being in London in several of his letters to Matilda Glover – perhaps he shared her lodgings; there is also evidence that he made use of the Duchess's address, 16 Grosvenor Place, but probably not after her departure from Blenheim. Being thus largely absent from the London social scene, the Duke could ignore society's contemptuous judgements.

Nor was it only the outside world who had come to deride or shun this foolish but not unlikeable man. Marlborough's own family seem increasingly to have avoided contact with him: the sympathy of such close relations as his brother Francis Churchill and his wife, appear to have been with the affronted Susan; and we know that his own children frequented Blenheim less and less.

Even Marlborough's *cousinage* held aloof: 'Between ourselves 'tis a poor beast, a very shambling animal',[3] wrote George Trevor Spencer to his brother-in-law, John Cam Hobhouse, later Baron Broughton (1786–1869), in 1827, referring to his 'precious Cousin', the Duke. The third son of William Robert Spencer, and brother of the unfortunate Harriet, Spencer was at this time in his late twenties, and an ordained priest (he would later become Bishop of Madras).

He and his wife must at some time have been on friendly enough terms with his considerably older cousin, for there is a plan for Mrs Spencer's garden,[4] carefully drawn to scale, presumably by the Duke, for their Derbyshire home: a nice present – how sad his cousin did not feel more kindly towards him! A year or two earlier, the Duke had been in correspondence with the same John Cam Hobhouse, who had announced his hope of visiting him – at which prospect Marlborough expressed great pleasure, adding, we may think, somewhat wistfully: 'I have not seen one of your good Family for an Age; 2 of your Sisters are within 20 Miles of me, but I might as well be in Jericho for the chance I have of seeing them . . .'.[5] But by this time it was impossible not to deplore the Duke's disordered affairs, his lack of probity, and his scandalous way of life.

One friend at least, however, was to coninue faithful in these later years: Captain Gronow, who has already regaled us with a lively account of a visit to Whiteknights. Gronow was to visit his friend some years later at Blenheim; Marlborough had warned him that he would

> find a great difference between his magnificent way of living at White-Knights, and his very reduced establish-ment at Blenheim. He said that he had from the estate, fish, game, venison, mutton, and poultry in abundance, and had a good cellar of wine; but that he was so involved that he could obtain credit neither in Oxford nor in London, and that his sole revenue (and much of that forestalled) was the annuity on the Post-Office, which was inalienably secured to the great Duke.[6]

Although the Duke, continually pressed for money as he was, had been guilty of neglecting the outer fabric of the Palace, he had lavished imagination, knowledge and money on his private gardens, and on the Rock Garden, with its fantastical touches in the area around the Grand Cascade. Nor were his energies and restless imagination restricted to the great outdoors: in the Palace itself, he

---

73. The fifth Duke and Duchess's grandchildren, by Sanders: John Winston (in plaid), Alan (holding the shell), Alfred (seated) and Louisa. The Galloway connection is strongly represented in this charming picture: the children sport the Stewart tartan, and the background surely depicts the storm-tossed coast of Galloway.

gave rein to flights of his own fashionable and idiosyncratic fancy.
Happily he left untouched the great State Apartments, which still
in his time were resplendent with the art treasures descended through
five generations, but he allowed his uninhibited Regency taste to
frolic through the Arcade Rooms, which lie beneath the Long
Library, running along the west side of the Palace at garden level:
these he arranged most sumptuously. Dr Mavor has described them
for us: the first was a room of some thirty feet in length –

> The sides and the ceiling are of Waterloo blue puckered
> drapery, ornamented at intervals by black rosettes, and a
> large rosette of the same material in the centre of the
> ceiling, from which all the ribs of the drapery diverge . . .
> Two other apartments are now added; the one a With-
> drawing Room, fitted up entirely with a Japan wain-
> scoting, round a painted representation of the Tiger Hunt
> in India, with the landscape of which every beautiful
> plant of that country is given from nature, either on the
> banks, or floating on the surface of the Ganges. The
> Refectory is in imitation of an Italian Dining Room, of
> Verd d'Antique and Sienna marble, with corresponding
> columns and door-cases. The doors are of polished Blen-
> heim oak, and the floors tesselated with similar oak and
> acacia, also grown in Blenheim Park.[7]

Outside, a 'Pavilion of an octagon form' had been erected: its
description takes us right back to the arbours and seats at Whiteknights – it was 'entirely composed of various coloured woods, with
their natural bark. This is supported by columns of yew, with a
covered colonnade around it.' Time (or an 'improving' descendant)
has swept away the Pavilion, but in the Arcade Rooms, now the
restaurant and cafeteria, tourists sip their tea surrounded by the
delights of the Tiger Hunt, and the exotic blooms floating on the
waters of the Ganges.

On the site of the fifth Duke's Arcade flower garden are now the
magnificent Water Terrace Gardens, created between 1925 and

---

74. *Previous page*: 'Blenheim House and Park' by J. M. W. Turner, c. 1832.

75. *Opposite*: A tiger hunt from a wall painting executed by an unknown artist for
the fifth Duke, in what is now the Refreshment Room at Blenheim.

1930 by the ninth Duke, and designed by Achille Duchêne, the French architect. By this time, the gardens by the Grand Cascade, constructed and planted by his forebears, had become wild and over-grown, and the Bernini fountain had fallen into disrepair. The ninth Duke rescued this famous monument from neglect, and installed it, meticulously restored, on the lower terrace; it is balanced by another obelisk, especially designed to match the original one. Gladys, the ninth Duke's second wife,* laboured valiantly with her own hands during the 1920s to restore the gardens by the Grand Cascade, but the task was too great for her, and time was not on her side.

I sometimes wander in the now wild and rugged area which once was the site of the beautiful and unusual gardens created by the fourth and fifth Dukes. One must tread carefully, for boulders and hewn rocks lie concealed in the sea of bracken and brambles – remnants of the Rock Garden; part of a mossy cavern remains – was this perhaps the Druids' Temple? Up above, on a ridge, a forester's house is to this day called 'Springlock Cottage', for hard by was the great revolving stone which, at a touch on the 'magic' spring, admitted visitors to this secret place. Down below, at the foot of the Grand Cascade – 'magician Brown's' *pièce de théâtre*, which has magnificently survived the ravages of time – is the circular stone basin, now cracked and broken, which was the first site of the Bernini fountain: the sound of the torrent fills one's ears, and in the early spring all around are shining drifts of snowdrops.

Climbing up the hill again towards the lake and the Palace, one finds hardly a trace remaining of the fifth Duke's renowned private gardens. Smooth lawns, noble trees, gigantic clumps of rhododendrons, and a classically inspired yew enclosure certainly compose a more harmonious setting for the vast house than did his busy succession of gardens (albeit filled with rare and beautiful species) and the 'spotty frittered appearance'[8] made by his tree and shrub plantings, which earned him such harsh criticism at the hands of contemporary gardening pundits. All the same, one nurses a twinge

---

* Charles, ninth Duke of Marlborough (1871–1934), first married Consuelo Vanderbilt in 1896; she was the mother of the tenth Duke and Lord Ivor Spencer-Churchill. They were divorced in 1921, and later that year Marlborough married Miss Gladys Deacon, the celebrated American beauty. From 1931 they led separate lives; Gladys, Duchess of Marlborough, died in 1977.

of nostalgia for the long straight lines of tulip trees and *Magnolia conspicua* (*Magnolia denudata*), which even won the approval of Mr Loudon. But on the exact site of the fifth Duke's collection of roses, the present Duke and his Duchess have made a beautiful and elaborate 'rosarium', which would surely have earned his ancestor's applause.

Despite his generally dilapidated state, the fifth Duke of Marlborough had a strong sense of the historical significance of the title he held and its heritage. Paradoxically, one may observe that by his feckless lifestyle, both as Marquess and as Duke, he himself did little to support the honour and dignity of the title – but that was not how he saw it. In a long paper submitted to the Lords of the Treasury in April 1824, he expressed his feelings on his tenure of the dukedom and Blenheim with vehemence and eloquence: the Duke was protesting to their Lordships at the rates of taxation levied on Blenheim – the house and its windows – and on the Post Office pension (which, His Grace averred, it was always intended should be exempt from tax). We are not surprised to learn that these taxes were in any case some £2000 in arrears: the Duke hopes very much he can persuade their Lordships either to waive, or at least to postpone pressing their claim: 'It is well known, that the only Income which the Duke possesses is the Pension.' The document reveals the extent of the Duke's financial embarrassments: 'The whole of the Park is in the hands of Creditors . . .', and 'The whole of the Duke's personal Effects, even to his wearing Apparel, are at this Moment, in the hands of a Judgement Creditor . . .'.

At this point the Duke makes an eloquent plea: should the Lords Commissioners proceed with their claim, and allow a further deduction in the Pension,

> then the residue would be wholly swallowed by the claims of other Creditors, and the Duke be left wholly destitute – then Blenheim would cease to be what Blenheim was intended, and hitherto has been – then would the Duke be compelled to clear the land planted by the late Duke – to

drain off the Water and restore the bed of the Lake to Meadow and Pasture – to block up the Windows of Blenheim House, or close the House altogether, and himself remove to one of the Lodges, heretofore the residence of a Menial, for Blenheim the Duke will never quit . . .

After this emotional outburst, the final paragraph of this memorandum provides a classic example of the optimistic nature of the Duke, and of his propensity to indulge in deceiving himself, as well as others :

The differences which have for a long time subsisted between the Duke and his family, are every Day subsiding, and the Duke has confident expectations that at no distant period, his Family will again surround him at Blenheim (a consummation he devoutly wishes) and by their reunion in the Bonds of Harmony give a new life to everything connected with that princely place.[9]

We do not know what was the reaction of the Lords of His Majesty's Treasury to this frantic document, but we do know that the domestic life of the Duke, contrary to his (professed) expectations, was never to re-establish itself as so hopefully described.

Only a few pages back, we had to recount how our Duke had descended to blatant dishonesty in the matter of the gold plate, and how at the insistence of the trustees a court injunction had been obtained restraining him from disposing of any other heirlooms. But, ironically, it is not upon the reckless, feckless 'Regency' Duke and his wild and spendthrift son that the odium must be laid for the sale of the Sunderland Library, and the dispersal of the Blenheim art treasures. The responsibility for these actions lies with the seventh and eighth Dukes – our man's grandson and great-grandson. John Spencer Churchill, seventh Duke of Marlborough (1822–83), first, in 1875, sold the world-famous collection of Marlborough gems built up with such care by the fourth Duke (this collection cannot have fallen within the formal entail) ; five years later, assisted by his friend, Earl Cairns, the Lord Chancellor, a bill was passed through Parliament – the Blenheim Settled Estates Act – which specifically enabled the Duke to dispose of the historic Sunderland

Library. But the Act effectively also broke the entail, and paved the way for his son, George, eighth Duke of Marlborough (1844–92), to sell heirlooms and treasures galore, despite the angry remonstrances of his younger brother, Lord Randolph (1849–95). The list of the famous and beautiful masterpieces from Blenheim which passed through the salerooms in a short space of years makes sad reading.

Ever hopeful, even in his shabby later years, our Duke still nurtured aspirations to public office: in 1834 we find him writing to the new Tory Prime Minister, Sir Robert Peel, asking to be considered for any office: 'I ask no Sinecure, I like employment, & am *above nothing* which a Gentleman can hold . . .'.[10] Even at this distance of time we wince at the rebuff: Sir Robert regrets that claims for official employment are such, and means at his disposal so inadequate, that he 'must deny myself the satisfaction which it would give me to be enabled to hold out to your Grace the prospect that I can avail myself of your Grace's offer of service.'[11]

Perhaps Blandford's political activities rankled within the paternal bosom: after the fiasco of the election in 1815, when Sunderland, as he then was, had been obliged to withdraw his candidature for one of the Woodstock seats, he had, as Marquess of Blandford, three years later entered Parliament as Member for Chippenham, Wiltshire. In his maiden speech he defended the use of spring-guns (crippling contraptions used chiefly to protect properties against poachers); and he was strongly against Catholic Emancipation (which was passed in 1829).

In the two years 1829–30, Blandford took a lively and frequent part in debates, by which time his 'landed proprietor' stance had given way to an increasingly radical outlook. He initiated resolutions on the reform of rotten boroughs, and in favour of enlarging the franchise, together with other reforming spirits promoting radical motions which were to see fruition in the Reform Bill of 1832. His speeches were quite rousing: he called for the repeal of all taxes on labour and industry, and declared: 'They ought to abolish all sinecures, pensions and useless places.'[12] (What about the Post Office pension?) His father can scarcely have applauded such sentiments, especially from his son. A Tory, Mr Croker, encountering Lord Blandford in the vote office in January 1831, had, after some conversation, taken leave of him with: 'Goodbye, Citizen Church-ill.'[13]

Blandford, however, despite these lively beginnings in the House of Commons, which might have augured an interesting political future, lapsed thereafter into public silence – why, we do not know. It may have owed something to his propensity for gambling, for it was during his reforming phase, and while he was vehemently urging economies on the Government, that the Marquess, somewhat ironically, exhibited his predilection for this aristocratic vice by losing an enormous sum of money at Doncaster Races. David Pennant, staying in London with his mother-in-law, wrote to his father in September 1827: 'The Duchess seems quite well and in good spirits, though much annoyed by the news which she had just received of Blandfords having lost fifteen thousand pounds at Don-caster, without having one to pay, and what is to be done no one knows. As this was talked of at Boodles it can be no secret . . .'.[14] The world indeed knew, Mrs Arbuthnot later putting his losses at £26,000.[15]

In 1830 Blandford and his brother, Lord Charles, had been returned together for the two Woodstock seats: perhaps parental disapproval of the heir's radicalism had something to do with the former's replacement by Viscount Stormont in 1831. However, two years on, and the Reform Bill having shorn Woodstock of one seat, Blandford was back, now the family's sole local representative. In 1835, Lord Charles took over from his elder brother, but was himself narrowly defeated in the 1837 election; subsequently the declared victor withdrew (there had been allegations of irregularities). In 1838 there was a bye-election in which Lord Blandford, once more the candidate, was opposed by his sailor-brother, Lord John. The whole campaign was acrimonious: Lord John petitioned the House of Commons that his brother's election was invalid on account of bribery and other electoral misdemeanours; the House disagreed and declared Blandford duly elected. To a latter-day generation, the whole scenario appears unedifying and totally incomprehensible. But Lord Blandford had scarcely two years to run as 'tribune of the people' before his father's death would raise him to a more elevated parliamentary sphere. It is interesting to remark in passing that, as sixth Duke of Marlborough, his radical views were to undergo considerable modification.

◇◇*

Whiteknights must have offered a bleak appearance indeed after the depredations of the auction sales. The Duke, however, still spent a good deal of time there and, despite financial embarrassments, he continued to construct seats and to make improvements in the gardens; he was also busily despatching stocks of trees and plants to Blenheim. In the early time of his love for Matilda Glover, they stayed together at Whiteknights, and it must have been a joy and solace for him to show his 'dearest Girl' the paradise he had created; she no doubt made the perfect audience, with her unaffected wonder at all he had wrought.

We do not know if the Duchess ever returned to Whiteknights – it would seem unlikely – but we have a touching picture of their daughter Caroline visiting her childhood home with her husband David Pennant in the summer of 1823; they had been married exactly a year, and she was expecting a child. She had been about two years old when Whiteknights had become her home, and must have had happy memories of years of childhood happiness there, playing in the gardens and woods with her elder brothers, before the tensions between her parents and their financial worries cast shadows across her guileless pleasure.

David Pennant was much impressed with all he saw, and, writing to his father, he told him that Whiteknights 'had far exceeded my expectations though they were raised very high. I certainly never saw so enviable a spot . . .'.[16] Caroline, for her part, at the same time wrote to her mother-in-law, who was evidently far from well, urging her, as soon as she felt strong enough, to visit both Whiteknights and Blenheim, but principally – and most immediately – the former:

> My dearest Mrs Pennant,
>
> I was extremely sorry to hear of your continued indisposition but hope you have been taking great care of yourself . . . We have made a most delicious excursion to dear White Knights, which is just now in the greatest beauty, do pray if you can alter your route, and go to see

it, I am *sure* you will think it worth the trouble. Blenheim
will improve every year, but poor W. Knights is on the
decline, it makes me quite melancholy to think of it . . .[17]

Having described in great detail how her parents-in-law should
plan their expedition to both Whiteknights and Blenheim, she ends
her letter by telling Mrs Pennant that they had been busy shopping
with an eye to future events: 'We have been purchasing linen at
Wilton's in Bond Street about 150£ worth – and today I have been
choosing patterns of baby linen!' In his letters to his father at about
this time, David Pennant testifies to his dear 'Car's' good health –
her spirits speak for themselves. For us, it is all unbearably poignant –
for we know this was destined to be the last year of Caroline's life,
and the last summer days of their short-lived happiness.

Although Marlborough was to throw himself with gusto into
the creation of his new gardens and pleasure grounds at Blenheim,
he must surely have cast some nostalgic backward glances to the
Whiteknights period and the great area of arboretum, gardens,
woods and wilderness he had been forced to abandon, which were
the creation over twenty years of his imagination, knowledge and
energy. Although he may have been stung by the criticism of some
of his visitors, yet, as the years went on, he must have derived justifiable pride and satisfaction not only from the curiosity displayed
in his gardening activities at Blenheim, but, above all, from the
continuing interest which Whiteknights evoked among the horticultural *cognoscenti* of the day, reports on the gardens there frequently
appearing in the pages of the *Gardener's Magazine*.

In 1828, in a feature entitled 'Calls at Suburban Gardens',
Whiteknights was one of several visited, although the writer of the
report adopted a somewhat *de haut en bas* tone: 'To those who can
distinguish what is rare from what is common in trees and shrubs,
these grounds are well worth seeing; but those who look for the
beauties of landscape-gardening, or the polished picturesque of
English pleasure grounds, will be disappointed . . .'.[18] A year later,
the same publication bemoaned the general condition of the
gardens: 'What a pity it is that this place is neglected! How it must

76. Mrs Arbuthnot and the Duke of Wellington walking out together, 1834
(artist unknown).

A SKETCH IN THE PARK.

grieve a gardener to look at the ruins of so much splendour! Many green-houses, hot-houses, and aquariums, &c., are standing empty; and some remaining plants show the rich collection which has been here in former times [a large portion of which one presumes the Duke removed to Blenheim] . . . but still,' the report continued, 'this place is well worth the greatest attention.'[19]

Sir Charles Cockerell (not intending to bankrupt himself, as had his predecessor) had found it beyond his powers to maintain the glasshouses and other structures in the enclosed gardens, and these had seriously deteriorated over the years; no doubt he had reduced the Duke's workforce, but the head gardener Mr Jones had, despite his limited resources, managed to maintain the collections in good order.[20] About this time, Sir Charles's tenure of Whiteknights had come suddenly to an end. The true ownership of the property had, for some years, been the subject of dispute, and in 1828 the claim advanced by Mr Francis Cholmeley (a descendant of Sir Henry Englefield, the sixth Baronet, through his surviving daughter, Teresa-Anne) was upheld by the courts.[21] Another important change was imminent: Mr Jones – who had been at Whiteknights for the best part of thirty years – would in 1830 rejoin his former employer, the Duke of Marlborough, at Blenheim.[22] Evidently Mr Cholmeley, the new owner, intended to maintain the gardens in a worthy manner, for Mr Jones's place was taken by another high-class head gardener – Mr Ward, from Downton Castle in Herefordshire, the seat of the numismatist and antiquarian Richard Payne Knight (1750–1824), who was the champion and proselytizer of the 'Picturesque' and who had created at Downton gardens on a grand scale following his own principles of garden design.

As we have seen, interest in the Duke's gardening activities did not wane over the years, and, earlier in the same season of 1833 that he visited Blenheim, the 'Conductor' of the *Gardener's Magazine* (Loudon) had made a comprehensive tour of Whiteknights. He found that Mr Cholmeley, with his new head gardener, Mr Ward, had made some changes, no doubt with the saving of labour in view:

---

77. A photograph of Matilda Glover in her later years.

We first went over the house-garden [the Botanic Gardens of Mrs Hofland's account]; the alterations made in which are, the removal of some of the hot-houses, particularly the exotic aquariums; the turfing of a number of the groups of flowers, leaving only the shrubs and trees that were in them; and the removal of all the plants in pots . . . The walks remain as they were, as do a few of the flower-beds which are left unturfed, and the whole of the beds in the botanic garden. The interest excited by the garden notwithstanding all these changes, is still almost as great as ever; because the rare trees and shrubs, which were at all times the only objects of permanent value, still remain.[23]

He then filled several pages with detailed reports on the size and condition of the most remarkable of the shrubs and trees, the progress of whose development he had observed on more than one occasion since his first visit to these remarkable gardens nearly thirty years earlier. The Magnolia Wall – always the object of admiration to visitors – was singled out for comment: Loudon described it as 'magnificent and unique'.

While proceeding through the grounds, Loudon saw signs of neglect and decline: the lake was so covered with invasive plants and weeds that the water was invisible (he was to observe the same effect at Blenheim); the long arcades were in a state of decay, although the covered seats and summer-houses were 'in tolerable preservation'. Two years later, in August 1835, he was once more at Whiteknights, and on this occasion he reported that he had found the collections in excellent order overall. However, he made a general criticism of the original siting of some of the trees, which in consequence were not thriving: 'Such errors in the progress of an art are unavoidable,' he wrote, 'but it is the duty of the rising generation, to turn to account the mistakes of their predecessors . . .'.[24] When Blandford had started his plantings, so new to cultivation in this country were many of the species and varieties he acquired that there was little expertise available as to the soil and situation most suitable for them – other than that many American plants required to be planted in peat beds. However, it is clear that, despite mistakes Blandford may have made in placing certain species, a great many specimens grew to fine maturity, and were the admiration of succeeding generations of plantsmen.

Mr Cholmeley, who had so successfully vindicated his familial claim to Whiteknights, was not destined to remain its owner for very long. Various misfortunes befalling the family, the estate had to be mortgaged in 1839; and in the same year, the house and manor were sold to one James Wright Nokes, a speculator, for the sum of £24,600. Up to this time a serious effort had been made to maintain the gardens and grounds in a seemly state: true, many of the more elaborate flowerbeds had been eliminated, and some of the hot-houses taken down, but attention had been paid to the exotic shrubs and trees, under the supervision of Mr Ward, who was still employed there in 1840. Now, however, began a sorry period for Whiteknights: already in 1835, Mr Loudon had observed that the house stood empty; in 1840 it was pulled down, and there were sales both from the main part of the estate, and of outlying parts. Various speculators were over the next few years to produce different plans for the development and exploitation of the property. One project mooted was for the creation of 'a miniature town, unequalled in the annals of the picturesque . . .';[25] there would be 150 villas – and all in the Elizabethan style. We may perhaps feel it was fortunate that this plan, like the others, had to be abandoned through lack of public support.

When Mr Loudon had made his tour in 1835, he had heard that Mr Cholmeley might sell Whiteknights, and he had expressed anxiety as to what the future might then hold for these important gardens; in 1840, the year of the fifth Duke's demise, and soon after the property had passed to Mr Nokes, the idea was mooted that Whiteknights might be the ideal place for a National Botanic Gardens. There was a body of opinion at this time which thought the founding of such an institution most necessary, owing to the dis-advantages under which the already existing metropolitan botanical gardens – the Chelsea Physic Garden, the Royal Botanic Gardens at Kew, and the Royal Horticultural Society's gardens (then situated in the grounds of Chiswick House) – laboured, in terms of restriction of space, and ever-increasing aerial pollution. In the *Horticultural Journal* appeared the following comment:

> The more we have considered the subject of National Gardens at White Knights, the more we have believed that their formation, or rather their adaptation, would confer a benefit on the science. There never was such an opportunity of commencing a concern of the kind with so little outlay, nor is there to be found in Europe a garden so capable of being made to surpass all others. This, so far as regards hardy exotics, it does already . . .[26]

Unfortunately, this conception, which would have been an ideal solution for Whiteknights, never materialized.*

In 1849, the lands and manor of Whiteknights were conveyed to Sir Isaac Lyon Goldsmid, a bullion broker, and the first Jew to be created a baronet. When he died in 1859, he was succeeded by his son, Francis; Whiteknights was to remain in the overall ownership of this family until 1947, when the University of Reading acquired the freehold of the entire estate – an area of some three hundred acres. It was Sir Francis Goldsmid who built Park House in the 1860s, on the site of the Englefield/Blandford mansion; today the house is used as the Senior Common Room of the University.

In 1867, the park at Whiteknights was divided into six leaseholds, varying in size between fifty and one hundred acres; several houses built on the plots by the famous Victorian architect, Alfred Waterhouse RA, survive today. In 1878, an article appeared in the *Gardeners' Chronicle* describing the gardens of the Wilderness (now demolished), which took in, as the name suggests, a large part of the Woods or Wilderness originally planted by Lord Blandford; the owner at this time, the Hon. Mrs Marsland, was a lady of taste. By the late 1860s, the Wilderness gardens had become thoroughly overgrown; but there still remained, according to the article, 'grand specimens of many rare trees and shrubs that dot the lawn', and also 'noble trees and huge masses of Rhododendrons and other flowering shrubs that border and decorate the extensive pleasure grounds.'

Some amazing relics from the gardens' past were found just outside the Wilderness, in the park: piles of 'gigantic boulders' – the

* In 1904, the Royal Horticultural Society moved its gardening operations from Chiswick House to Wisley in Surrey. In 1965 the Royal Botanic Gardens leased Wakehurst Place in West Sussex from the National Trust as an extension of their gardens at Kew.

'Grey Wethers' mentioned by Mrs Hofland. Mr Lees, the gardener, was a man of intelligence and imagination, and, the *Gardeners' Chronicle* recorded, it occurred to him 'that in these boulders were the elements of a gigantic rock-work or fernery; and therefore all were, with a great expenditure of labour, carted into a hollow place in the pleasure grounds, surrounded with trees and shrubs, and there fashioned into the massive arrangement now presented . . .'.[27] This huge rockery, duly planted up with ferns and other suitable plants, became – as the article put it – 'a fine feature in the place': fern gardens were much in fashion at that time.

In the winter days of 1984, this author had the opportunity to walk the length and breadth of the Whiteknights terrain with Mr Ian Cooke, the Superintendent of the Grounds of Reading University; I had already traversed them in my imagination with my readers, guided by the enthusiastic and effusive Mrs Hofland, in the summertime of 1816. Today large areas are taken up with the University buildings, which represent almost as many styles of modern architecture as there were different species of plants in the Marquess of Blandford's gardens. The whole place throbs with activity, and the campus is peopled with students – walking, bicycling, and generally enjoying themselves in the parkland around the still beautiful lake. Mindful of the botanic and horticultural glories of its past, Reading University has put a high priority on plantings which soften the outlines of the lumbering buildings, and maintains a generous and imaginative programme of tree planting on the campus.

Only the faintest traces remain of the pleasure grounds created by Lord Blandford. Here and there a few veteran trees survive from the days of Whiteknights' fame as a garden: a lopsided line of cedars of Lebanon; a ghostly swamp cypress and some tulip trees; by the upper lake, and near the Plant Sciences block, can be seen a large snow pear tree (*Pyrus elaeagrifolia*), gnarled with age but still an amazing sight in spring with its snowy blossom.

But the area which contains the greatest number of survivors from Blandford's days, and which still faintly shows its former outlines, is the Wilderness. Having been designated a conservation area, and consequently left to nature's own rough devices, it has escaped the depredations of twentieth-century 'improvers'. By 1980, *Rhodo-*

dendron ponticum and other invasive species had overgrown and suffocated the older exotic varieties, and were fast obliterating features and paths remaining from earlier days. At this point, however, the University authorities decided to take action; by 1983 a two-year project was under way to tackle the Wilderness. In a short space of time most gratifying results have been achieved:[28] the massive stone Grotto (described by Mrs Hofland as having 'the appearance of a rocky cavern') has been re-built, and the surrounding banks grassed over. In clearing away the vegetation which smothered the site, a strong group of yew, birch and amelanchier (*Amelanchier laevis*) was revealed; all these trees were mentioned by Mrs Hofland as species planted by Lord Blandford (although, with the possible exception of the yews, these cannot be the originals).

In a World War II rubbish tip, a hexagonal fountain bowl was discovered, probably belonging to one of the two fountains which marked the approach to the Grotto. Elsewhere was unearthed an intricately carved stone, resembling the intertwined roots of a tree. An illustration on the front of a booklet published in 1840, *A Day at Whiteknights*,[29] shows a statue on an identical plinth: perhaps one day the statue will be found. Meanwhile, the lakehead has been dredged, the banks strengthened with timber piles and re-seeded; and the rustic bridge has been reconstructed. It is hoped that money and labour will make it possible to recreate some more of the original features of the Wilderness, for which the restorers can refer to Mr Hofland's enchanting paintings as guides.

During the clearing operations it has been most rewarding to discover many fine specimens of native species such as yew, birch, rowan and cherry, and among these have been revealed much older trees, some of which undoubtedly date from Blandford's time. One such remarkable veteran is a Manna ash (*Fraxinus ornus*): the *Gardeners' Chronicle*, in its 1878 article on the Wilderness gardens, made particular mention of this tree, describing 'the enormous development made of the stock of the common Ash in which it is grafted as compared with the stem of the tree itself; the bark of the stock is rough and uneven, and that of the scion tree perfectly smooth'.[30] When the forestry team recently pulled the ivy off this old ash, the features described above were at once revealed. Likewise a hoary, fastigiate oak.

Expert and much-needed attention is being given to these survivors, and a policy of replanting the areas cleared of unwanted
trees and scrub has been implemented: mature exotic trees are
being replaced, and native species such as oak, birch, rowan, larch,
lime, hornbeam, beech and pine are being planted, to create a woodland which will in due course provide a beautiful and interesting
amenity for modern Whiteknights, where links with its romantic
and fantastical past will have been preserved.

Between 1818 and 1821, Susan, Duchess of Marlborough travelled
abroad on the continent a good deal, taking her daughter Caroline,
now entering her twenties, with her. These are the years that spanned
the collapse of life at Whiteknights, the appearance of Matilda
Glover, and the Duchess's departure from Blenheim. No doubt
foreign travel put a distance between Susan and the domestic life
which had increasingly held for her nothing but unhappiness.
Caroline kept a small green leather-bound album[31] in which, from
the sketches and dated signatures of friends, we can keep track of
some of their travels; while from George Agar-Ellis[32] we know of a
jolly breakfast party. He was in Paris when news was brought to him
one summer morning in 1818 that the Duchess of Marlborough was
at the Hôtel de Londres; hurrying round, he found his aunt with
Caroline, George Blandford, and two friends – they were all having
breakfast, at which, no doubt, he joined them. In October 1819,
Duchess Susan and Caroline were once more in that magic city, and
this time their party was augmented not only by George Blandford,
but also by Jane, his wife (Susan's niece), whom he had married at
the beginning of that year. In 1820, mother and daughter made
quite an extensive tour, lasting most of the summer, taking in
Monaco, Schaffhausen, Naples and Zurich.

With the company of her daughter, the Duchess was not lonely;
also, her relationship with her eldest son and his wife (despite his
iniquities), would seem to have been a good one, for when, in 1823,
she removed from Grosvenor Place to 3 Hyde Park Place, Cumber-
land Gate, Blandford's London address was shown in *Boyle's Court
Guide* to be the same as his mother's. As the young Blandfords'

country home was in far away Norfolk, this must have been a cosy and practical family arrangement.

It will be remembered that Susan Marlborough had been one of sixteen children, and, as she was by nature a very 'family' person, she would not have lacked for company spread over several generations, for she had a veritable tribe of nephews and nieces. Her mother, Anne, Dowager Countess of Galloway, lived in London and also had a 'Grace and Favour' apartment at Hampton Court (her husband had been a Lord of the Bedchamber). Susan's brother, the eighth Earl of Galloway, and his family would have divided their time between the two Galloway houses – the gaunt, grey house on the wave-tossed peninsula in Wigtownshire, and their London abode in St James's. In both places Susan had spent much of her childhood and youth, and even now that she herself was 'getting on', she journeyed north for long summer visits to Scotland – perhaps taking in her sister, Lady Graham, at Netherby on the Borders, in her travels. The Pennants invited her to their home, Downing in Flintshire; and (ignoring Blenheim) Susan no doubt still visited her uncle, Sir Henry Dashwood, and his family at Kirtlington from time to time.

Susan Marlborough was now in her late fifties and after so many trials and troubles one would have hoped that the mellower light of a summer afternoon might illumine these later years. As we have seen, 1822 was a year which gave several occasions for family rejoicings: George Agar-Ellis married Lady Georgina Howard in March; in early June, Jane Blandford gave birth to a son and heir; and later that same month the beloved Caroline was married to David Pennant, with every prospect of great happiness, in which her mother shared. But the sunshine was not to last the day: less than two years later, in January 1824, Caroline died three weeks after giving birth to a daughter, and an icy shadow of grief fell over Susan's life – from this time on, more sorrows than joys were to be her portion. In the seventeen years which remained to her, no fewer than sixteen of her closest relations – mostly much younger than herself – were to depart this earthly scene. After Caroline's death, it does not seem that the Duchess travelled abroad – perhaps the spirit had gone out of her, and foreign scenes would only have served to remind her, yet more sharply, of the beloved companion whose presence had made every place more enjoyable.

Life is, however, lived step by step: over the course of the next few years, one or two further events would have given the Duchess some happiness and satisfaction. Lord Henry's marriage in 1824 to his cousin Elizabeth Martha Nares was one: his mother knew his bride from her visits with her father to Blenheim, and there grew to be a close and tender relationship between Susan and her daughter-in-law. Lord Charles married three years later and was to have five children. Meanwhile, the Blandfords' brood of four – John, Alfred, Alan and Louisa – were growing apace, the younger boys taking names from the Stewart side of the family. Sadly, Lord Henry and Elizabeth were childless; he had never been strong, and was only thirty-two when he died in 1828: his widow Elizabeth turned to his mother to give, and to receive comfort. A few years later, Lady Henry was to find new happiness when she married Mr W. Whately, QC; but she was to care faithfully for her mother-in-law, the Duchess, to the end of her days.

Fortunately, Susan Marlborough had always liked her son-in-law David Pennant, and it seems her affection for him was returned; this must have been a consolation to them both. Although living in north Wales, he often stayed with his mother-in-law when in London, bringing little Caroline with him. In letters to his father, we learn that Susan was a fond and at times over-protective grandmother to this most adored relict of her own daughter. Thus, when Caroline was about three years old, her father writes: 'The dear child is quite well. But although the hot weather is arrived the Duchess still persists in immersing her in a carriage and she hardly ever gets more than one walk a day.'[33] In the autumn of 1827 the young widower married Lady Emma Brudenell, daughter of the Earl of Cardigan, with whom he was to have another daughter, Louisa, born in 1828. Far from resenting his re-marriage, the Duchess was glad for his new-found happiness, and gave him a handsome tea service as a wedding present.

A most winning letter from little Caroline, then just seven, to her grandmother has survived – in a bold hand, and obviously written under the eye of 'Mademoiselle', who has made a correction or two:

My dear Grandmama

I thank you a thousand times for all your presents, the Tippet and the Slippers fit me very nicely, and are so comfortable and warm. Mlle is delighted with her pretty little Souvenir and is much obliged to you for it. I send you the first little pockethandkerchief I have made for my doll. Dear little Louisa is quite well, and does not forget you or Lady Henry & she says 'I will tickle Elizebus when I go to London.' Good bye my dear Grandmama, your most affec[te] Caroline.[34]

A poignant touch is the little doll's pocket-handkerchief, still with the letter, neatly folded. The letter reveals a charming relationship between child and grandparent, but – alas – young Caroline was to die in January 1832, aged just nine; and three years later, her father, David Pennant, also departed this life, only in his fortieth year.

In the eleven years which now had passed since her daughter Caroline's death, Susan had sustained the loss of a younger brother and sister-in-law (General Sir William Stewart in 1827, aged sixty-three, and his wife in 1833); her uncle, Sir Henry Dashwood, in 1828, aged eighty-three; her mother, Anne, Dowager Countess of Galloway, in 1830, aged eighty-seven; and in 1834 her brother, the Earl, one year younger than herself, aged sixty-six. These deaths of her closest kin must have grieved her – but Christian faith and a stoic philosophy may have helped her to accept their departure. But how deep must have been the grief of losing a second child, Henry; and then a few years later her friend of so many years and vicissitudes, George Agar-Ellis,* both in their thirties. But the greatest of all her bereavements must have been the deaths of little Caroline and her son-in-law David – the last precious links with her beloved daughter, Caroline.

The passage of time, and the sorrows which it had brought – of which the hardest to bear were mutual – do not seem to have made for any *rapprochement* between George and Susan Marlborough. Not even such an important event as a royal visitation, in the form of a visit from Queen Adelaide and her sister, could lure the Duchess back to Blenheim to make an *acte de présence*.

Queen Adelaide (1792–1849), the Consort of William IV, accompanied by her sister, the Duchess of Saxe Weimar, had spent two days being fêted by the University and town of Oxford, and on

* He had been created Baron Dover in 1831, and died in 1833.

21 October 1835, they drove from Oxford to Blenheim Palace. We hear all the details of this visit from Frances, Lady Churchill, who the following day wrote a long letter to the Duchess. It is quite clear that Lady Churchill felt that some explanation was owing to her sister-in-law for the presence of her husband and herself at Blenheim – a clear indication that, in normal circumstances, they did not visit the Duke, thereby demonstrating their sympathy with the Duchess's situation.

After enquiring anxiously after the health of Lord Blandford, whom she had heard was ill, Frances Churchill wrote:

> I now proceed to my original object which was to give you some detail of Her Majesty's visit and reception at Blenheim yesterday, all of which I know will be interesting to you, and to explain the share we have all had in it . . . Lord C. received a letter from his Brother on Saturday last, particularly desiring that we would come over to assist him in his reception of Her Majesty on Wednesday morning. He appeared at this time to be in a state of much anxiety and difficulty, & we felt it would really be extremely awkward, if not impossible, to decline a compliance with his request, on an occasion so important. I must however at the same time, express the sincere regret which was felt by us all, that you, my dear D^{ss}, as Mistress of Blenheim, were not present to do the Honors of it in a more proper manner, to Her Majesty . . .

Lady Churchill then gave her sister-in-law a very full account of the day: the Queen had arrived soon after eleven; Lord Churchill and an escort had met her on the way, and brought her to Blenheim: '. . . Lord Churchill's Band were stationed in the Court & played God Save the King . . . which had a good effect . . .'. The Queen had been welcomed at the Palace steps by the Duke and his brother. After a tour of the house, 'paying much attention to the Pictures', the royal party went 'by the Saloon Door into the Gardens – where everything appeared to much advantage, the day was so beautifully fine . . .'. Afterwards the Queen 'found a handsome Luncheon set out to which she sate down between the Duke and Ld. C & made us all partake with her . . .'. Before Her Majesty departed, the Duke read an Address from the Borough of Woodstock, 'which she answered very graciously . . . on the whole every thing went off surprisingly well, & she saw more, & did more, than most other people could without fatigue.' Concluding this long letter, Lady Churchill hoped 'that when you write, you will mention yourself, it is a long time since we have heard any thing of you my dear Duchess . . .'.[35]

The Duchess moved house twice more: in 1829 to 5 Grosvenor Gate, Park Lane, and in 1836 to 24 Park Lane, where she was to end her days. Her mother's apartment at Hampton Court had after her death been continued to her daughter-in-law, Sir William Stewart's widow, and when she died in 1833, it was granted to Susan Marlborough: it may have made a pleasant retreat and change for her from town life, when in these latter years she may have found the long journey to Scotland too much.

George and Susan Marlborough both achieved the biblical span of life of three score years and ten – a venerable age, by the standards of their times. It is melancholy to have to record that even in these last years of their lives, fate had reserved yet further blows. In December 1839, Etheldred, Lord Charles's wife, died; four months later, in April 1840, he too, aged only forty-five, joined her in the grave.

On 5 March 1840, George Spencer-Churchill, fifth Duke of Marlborough, died at Blenheim Palace after a short illness. During his last years he had lived in seclusion, and had hardly left Blenheim except for an annual visit to a watering place: 'a melancholy instance', the writer of the Duke's obituary in the *Gentleman's Magazine* improvingly opined, 'of the results of princely extravagance.'[36]

They buried him in the frigid Chapel at Blenheim, alongside his forebears; his eldest son, George, now sixth Duke, with his three sons, and Mr Whately (Elizabeth Martha's husband) were present – but no women. Lord John was absent: he was on service in the China Seas. A Captain now – the senior officer in that station, commanding HMS *Druid* – George and Susan's 'tarpaulin son' (as George Agar-Ellis had long ago sneeringly dubbed him) had done rather well in his chosen younger son's profession. He was in his forty-third year, and still unmarried; perhaps he would have risen still higher in rank but in early June 1840, three months after the death of his father, he died in Macao Roads; he was buried in the cemetery at Macao, where there is a handsome tomb.

After all the blows which had been dealt her, the death of her long estranged and negligent husband can scarcely have deeply affected Susan Marlborough. But Matilda Glover (his sole beneficiary) and her children must have mourned him, and the passing of the good times.

Time was running out also for Susan Marlborough, but even now, although wearied by the burden of sorrows and years, she leaves us with the impression of a practical, thoughtful, kindly person. In February 1841 she made her Will:[37] no doubt it replaced an earlier document, but even in the last year deaths had occurred which made changes necessary. It is a long, most detailed document, remarkable for the consideration for individuals it reveals rather than the amount of riches Duchess Susan had to bestow.

Her foremost concern was clearly for the children of her deceased son Charles. There were four of them: the eldest, Charles (twelve years old) received the residue of her estate and effects, and oil paintings of his parents; John, £100; the two girls, Susan and Caroline, £700 each and her grand piano. The children of George, her eldest son, were left much smaller bequests: John (Blandford) received £40; Alfred and Alan, £30 each; and Louisa, £100, and the miniature of her mother and a turquoise anchor brooch. It is interesting to notice her generosity to the girls: perhaps one of the lessons life had taught her was how agreeable and useful it is for women to have some independent means. Devoted Lady Henry (now Mrs Whately) received £200, the Japan Cabinet from her apartment at Hampton Court, and the bookcase (with its contents) from her London house; to her husband, William Whately, the Duchess left a picture.

Her two brothers, Montgomery and Edward, received £100 and £50 respectively; but only one of her surviving sisters was remembered – Charlotte, Lady Crofton, who received £100. There were also bequests to a number of her nephews and nieces on both sides of her family. To most of the pecuniary legacies were added specific objects, all carefully detailed: a pair of candlesticks; miniatures; brooches; the new *Botanical Magazine* in four volumes, etc. The

Duchess also remembered several servants, the amounts she left them varying from £150 to one James King and ten guineas apiece to Mrs Haven and Rumbold.

Not vast amounts, not a treasure-trove, but when Susan laid down her pen, having signed her last Will and Testament that February day, she could with justice feel she had set her affairs in order: she hoped she had remembered everyone she should. Now she could rest, and quietly await her turn: Death, after all, was no stranger.

Susan, Dowager Duchess of Marlborough died on 2 April 1841, in her seventy-fourth year. She was buried in the Chapel at Blenheim – it was her rightful place – but perhaps she would have preferred a tomb by the sounding sea in Galloway with her forebears. Of her six children only one, George, Duke of Marlborough, survived her. And of her own large family, only two of her brothers, Montgomery and Edward Stewart, were still alive, and three sisters, Anne, Elizabeth and Charlotte. In the next generation, eight of her grandchildren were living.

If one considers the respective legacies these two – George Spencer-Churchill and Susan Stewart – left, in a real sense, to their unborn descendants, one is struck by an element of ironic justice. For despite his many talents, only vestigial shreds survive of all the fifth Duke's artefacts and activities: a few hoary old trees alone bear witness to the wonderful gardens he made; a mere book or two from the amazing collection he amassed – and lost; some printed sheets of music that no one plays or sings; no storied monument – only the tales of his debts, profligacy and fecklessness live on.

But that nice if unexciting woman, Susan, fifth Duchess of Marlborough, who throughout this chronicle of their lives has remained an elusive figure – yet she has a distinction which none of her predecessors, nor her successors so far, can claim. In the Chapel at Blenheim – where God Himself must mind His precedence – high up on the wall opposite the towering monument to the Great Duke, is a seemly marble memorial tablet to Susan, placed there by her only surviving child, her eldest son, George, sixth Duke of Marlborough:

no other Duchess is so commemorated, not even the tremendous
Sarah. It is a monument also to filial piety – and, maybe, remorse.
  Translated, the inscription reads:

> Below in the vault of the chapel has been placed whatso-
> ever was mortal of Susan, Duchess of Marlborough, most
> noble by birth, dignity and virtue.

> She lived for 72 years, 11 months and 22 days and was laid
> to rest in placid death on the second of April eight days
> before her birthday in the year of deliverance 1841. If any
> other above all she was a true christian woman, pious,
> honest, kind and must be commemorated by the grateful
> remembrance of her mind, rather than by a monumental
> structure and splendour. For her epitaph is the sacredness
> of all life. For her pyramid the mass of her good deeds. For
> her effigy is her example.

> However you, who enter this building whether a visitor
> or a worshipper, must know that the eldest son of this
> woman, also now the only survivor of her six children,
> placed the marble, which you see, mourning for the best
> of parents, in order that he might commend to posterity
> so great a constancy of his mother's faith.

> Farewell, farewell, most loving mother, but the hope of
> your family is in Christ, that they will enjoy with you
> eternal life without sorrow and without tears.

  And Susan, Duchess of Marlborough has yet another – and more
joyful – epitaph: for, to a later generation, she has bequeathed the
series of exquisite flower paintings, folded away in the Library at
Blenheim for nearly two hundred years – unfaded, they retain the
freshness of the day she laid them aside.

78. Susan, fifth Duchess of Marlborough's memorial plaque in the Chapel at Blenheim.

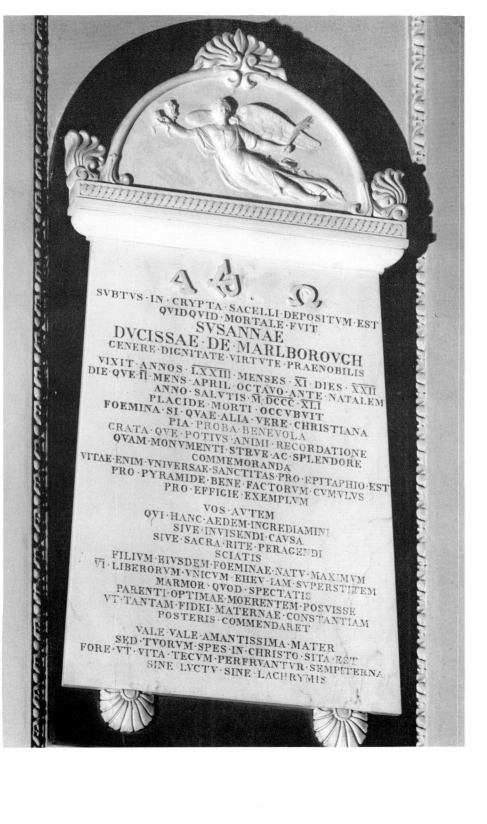

A · Ω

SVBTVS · IN · CRYPTA · SACELLI · DEPOSITVM · EST
QVIDQVID · MORTALE · FVIT

SVSANNAE
DVCISSAE · DE · MARLBOROVGH

GENERE · DIGNITATE · VIRTVTE · PRAENOBILIS

VIXIT · ANNOS · LXXIII · MENSES · XI · DIES · XXII
DIE · QVE · II · MENS · APRIL · OCTAVO · ANTE · NATALEM
ANNO · SALVTIS · M · DCCC · XLI
PLACIDE · MORTI · OCCVBVIT
FOEMINA · SI · QVAE · ALIA · VERE · CHRISTIANA
PIA · PROBA · BENEVOLA
GRATA · QVE · POTIVS · ANIMI · RECORDATIONE
QVAM · MONVMENTI · STRVE · AC · SPLENDORE
COMMEMORANDA
VITAE · ENIM · VNIVERSAE · SANCTITAS · PRO · EPITAPHIO · EST
PRO · PYRAMIDE · BENE · FACTORVM · CVMVLVS
PRO · EFFIGIE · EXEMPLVM

VOS · AVTEM
QVI · HANC · AEDEM · INCREDIAMINI
SIVE · INVISENDI · CAVSA
SIVE · SACRA · RITE · PERAGENDI
SCIATIS
FILIVM · EIVSDEM · FOEMINAE · NATV · MAXIMVM
VI · LIBERORVM · VNICVM · EHEV · IAM · SVPERSTITEM
MARMOR · QVOD · SPECTATIS
PARENTI · OPTIMAE · MOERENTEM · POSVISSE
VT · TANTAM · FIDEI · MATERNAE · CONSTANTIAM
POSTERIS · COMMENDARET

VALE · VALE · AMANTISSIMA · MATER
SED · TVORVM · SPES · IN · CHRISTO · SITA · EST
FORE · VT · VITA · TECVM · PERFRVANTVR · SEMPITERNA
SINE · LVCTV · SINE · LACHRYMIS

Source Notes

CHAPTER I

1 In Sarah, Duchess of Marlborough's 'Green Book'. There are two copies of this letter, dated 2 January 1721, in the Blenheim Papers: BM Add. MSS 61450, f. 144, and 61451, f. 116
2 Walpole to Sir Horace Mann, 10 September 1761. *Correspondence*, ed. Lewis, vol. 21, p. 530
3 *Ibid.*, 29 August 1762. *Op cit.*, vol. 22, p. 73 and fn. 31
4 Green, *Blenheim Palace*, p. 184
5 Walpole, *op. cit.*, vol. 12, p. 253; Burney (D'Arblay), *Diaries and Letters*, vol. 2, p. 328 (16 December 1785)
6 Mavor, *A New Description of Blenheim*, 1789, pp. 46–7
7 White, *A Versatile Professor*, p. 101
8 Undated [3 July 1759]. Blenheim Papers, BM Add. MS 61668, f. 72
9 Undated [1781]. Herbert, *Pembroke Papers*, p. 174
10 [2–8] April 1779. Herbert, *Henry, Elizabeth and George*, p. 163
11 Rowse, *The Later Churchills*, p. 143
12 Auckland, *Journal and Correspondence*, vol. II, p. 301
13 Quoted by Watney, *The Churchills*, p. 59 (no source given)
14 Moore to Duchess of Marlborough, 30 September 1780. Blenheim Papers, BM Add. MS 61670, f. 117
15 10 March 1789. Auckland, *op cit.*, vol. II, p. 300
16 29 November 1782. Blenheim Papers, BM Add. MS 61670, f. 134
17 Jesse, *Memoirs of the Life and Reign of George III*, vol. III, pp. 7–8
18 White, *op. cit.*, p. 100
19 Powys, *Diaries*, p. 197

20 25 June 1770. Blenheim Papers, BM Add. MS 61672, f. 137
21 Calvert, *Alice Elizabeth Blake, An Irish Beauty of the Regency*, p. 84
22 19 September 1781. Herbert, *Pembroke Papers*, p. 152
23 Rosenfeld, *Temples of Thespis*, p. 109; from which the rest of this account of the Blenheim theatricals is largely drawn
24 Reynolds, *Life and Times*, pp. 6–9
25 Erskine, *Lady Diana Beauclerk*, pp. 286, 292. (Letters to her daughter, Mary, Countess Jenison of Walworth, 3 March and 8 July 1802)
26 Blunt, *Mrs Montagu*, vol. I, p. 365
27 Quoted by Watney, *op. cit.*, p. 60 (no source given)
28 Oman, *Nelson*, pp. 502–3
29 The account of Lord Nelson's visit to Blenheim is taken from Marshall, *Early History of Woodstock*, supplement, pp. 45–6, and Rowse, *op. cit.*, pp. 159–60
30 Gronow, *Reminiscences and Recollections*, vol. I, pp. 314–15
31 Walpole to Henry Seymour Conway, 3 July 1765. *Op. cit.*, vol. 39, p. 3

CHAPTER II

1 Blenheim Papers, BM Add. MS 61670, f. 56
2 Herbert, *Henry, Elizabeth and George*, p. 82. Quoted in letter Coxe to Lady Pembroke, 12 July 1776
3 Blenheim Papers, BM Add. MS 61670, f. 76
4 *Ibid.*, f. 78, 4 October 1778
5 *Ibid.*, ff. 135–6, 12 August 1783
6 *Ibid.*
7 17 March 1783. Herbert, *Pembroke Papers*, p. 217

8 Farington, *Diary*, vol. VIII (1815–21), p. 286
9 *Jackson's Oxford Journal*, 4 June 1784
10 *Ibid.*, 6 March 1787
11 Gronow, *Reminiscences and Recollections*, vol. I, p. 314
12 *Ibid.*
13 *Jackson's Oxford Journal*, 7 August 1790
14 3 June 1789. Marshall Papers
15 This account of the 'Gunninghiad' combines information gleaned largely from Walpole, *Correspondence, ed. cit.*, Rowse, *The Later Churchills*, Gantz, *The Pastel Portrait*, and Gunning, *Letter . . . to the Duke of Argyll*
16 Walpole to Miss Mary Berry, 9 October 1791. *Op. cit.*, vol. 11, p. 366
17 *Ibid.*, 29 July 1790. *Op. cit.*, vol. 11, p. 104
18 *Ibid.*, vol. 11, p. 108
19 9 August 1790. *Op. cit.*, vol. 39, p. 479
20 Walpole to Miss Mary Berry, 22 October 1790. *Op. cit.*, vol. 11, p. 123
21 *Ibid.*, fn. 12
22 *Ibid.*, p. 136
23 13 February 1791. *Op. cit.*, vol. 11, p. 200
24 Walpole to Miss Mary Berry, 27 March 1791. *Op. cit.*, vol. 11, p. 229
25 Gantz, *op. cit.*, p. 124
26 Walpole to Miss Mary Berry, 18 February 1791. *Op. cit.*, vol. 11, p. 202
27 *Ibid.*, 21 February 1791. *Op. cit.*, vol. 11, p. 205
28 *Ibid.*, p. 201
29 *Ibid.*, 21 February 1791. *Op. cit.*, vol. 11, p. 204
30 Walpole to Miss Agnes Berry, 13 February 1791. *Op. cit.*, vol. 11, p. 197
31 Walpole to Miss Mary Berry, 19 March 1791. *Op. cit.*, vol. 11, p. 225

79. The Marlborough and Galloway coats of arms, from the brass locks on the doors of the main entrance at Blenheim, probably installed by the sixth Duke.

32 *Ibid.*, 27 March 1791. *Op. cit.*, vol. 11, p. 229

33 *Ibid.*, 4 July 1791. *Op. cit.*, vol. 11, p. 307

34 *Ibid.*, 11 March 1791. *Op. cit.*, vol. 11, p. 220

35 *Ibid.*, 28 February 1791. *Op. cit.*, vol. 11, p. 208

36 *Ibid.*, 2 June 1791. *Op. cit.*, vol. 11, p. 279. This is but one of several versions in circulation at the time.

37 *Op. cit.*, vol. 11, pp. 348–9

CHAPTER III

1 Earl of Galloway to James Nish, 4 December 1801. Galloway Muniments, Scottish Record Office, GD 138/3/21/5

2 Quoted by Lindsay, *The Burns Encyclopaedia*, p. 344

3 Young of Harburn, MS memoir of Burns. Quoted in Kinsley, *The Poems and Songs of Robert Burns*, vol. III, p. 1434

4 Quoted by Namier and Brooke, *The House of Commons 1754–1790*, p. 481 (no source given)

5 1 December 1766. Quoted in Namier and Brooke, *op. cit.*, p. 482

6 *Gentleman's Magazine*, November 1806, vol. LXXVI, pp. 1085–6

7 Information provided by Professor R. H. Campbell, from Galloway MSS, Scottish Record Office, Edinburgh

8 Quoted in letter from Williams to Garlies, 2 June 1788. Williams, *English Works of the late Rev. E. Williams*, Appendix

9 Lady Stafford to Granville Leveson-Gower, 21 May 1794. Quoted in *Complete Peerage*, 1926, vol. V, p. 607

10 2 August 1790. Williams, *op. cit.*, Appendix

11 Hylton, *The Paget Brothers*, p. 213

12 Walpole to John Chute, 4 August 1753. *Correspondence*, ed. Lewis, vol. 35, p. 71

13 Quoted by Rowse, *The Later Churchills*, p. 195. Not traced in rearrangement of Blenheim Papers at British Library.

14 29 September 1791. Auckland, *Journal and Correspondence*, vol. II, p. 391

15 *The Times*, 15 September 1791

16 Auckland, *op. cit.*, vol. II, pp. 398–9

17 *Ibid.*, vol. III, p. 112

18 Powys, *Diaries*, p. 252 (25 July 1791)

19 Letter to his father, David Pennant senior, 12 July 1824. Pennant Papers CR 2017 TP 431/160

CHAPTER IV

1 Installed *c.* 1774. Green, *Blenheim Palace*, pp. 250, 289

2 'Landskip' or picturesque gardening: spelling used by the poet William Shenstone (1714–63), *Unconnected Thoughts on Gardening*. Hadfield, *Gardening in Britain*, p. 203

3 Jacques, *Georgian Gardens*, p. 163

4 Royal Botanic Gardens Archives, Kew, Inwards Book 1793–1809, p. 44

5 [?] November 1797. Royal Botanical Gardens Archives, H 4474/65

6 Dawson MS 45, f. 18–20 [British Library]. DTC 10(1)210–13 [British Museum (Natural History), Dept. of Botany]

7 4 December 1797. Dawson MS 45, f. 21. DTC 10(1)214–16

8 DTC 10(1)217–19

9 Berkshire Record Office D/ESv (M)B11

10 Dormer, *The Parish and Church of Saint Peter, Earley*, pp. 39–40; *Victoria County History: Berkshire*, vol. III, pp. 210–11

11 Dormer, *op. cit.*, p. 40. (The source given is to the Cowslade MS in R. Dioc. Archives, Plymouth, but the present location has not been traced.)

12 Common Pleas 43/966, plea 448–470

13 Dormer, *op. cit.*

14 Walpole, *Correspondence*, ed. Lewis, vol. 35, p. 71

15 Smith, *Memoir and Correspondence of the late Sir James Edward Smith, M.D.*, vol. I, p. 435

16 Details concerning the Hoflands are derived principally from the thesis by Denis Butts, 'Mrs Barbara Hofland, 1770–1844'. See also, by the same author, 'Barbara Hofland the Sheffield Skylark', *Antiquarian Book Monthly Review*, vol. X, no. 7, pp. 252–7, and Phyllis Bell, 'The Hoflands at Richmond', *Richmond History*, no. 2 (December 1981), pp. 2–7

17 11 October 1817. L'Estrange, *Life of Mary Russell Mitford*, vol. II, p. 14

18 Mary Russell Mitford to Sir William Elford, 10 February 1819. Letters, Reading Central Library

CHAPTER V

1 Hofland, *A Descriptive Account of the Mansion and Gardens of White-Knights*. Unless otherwise indicated, all quotations in this chapter are from this source.

2 Jacques, *op. cit.*, p. 193

3 Attention is drawn to the Aquarium Greenhouse in Hix, *The Glass House*, p. 48. It was among the earlier glass houses designed specifically for aquatic plants.

4 Reading University Library, Plans drawn by George Tod, Surveyor and Hot-House Builder, 1806. Hot water heating came into wide use after 1816. See also Jacques, *op. cit.*, p. 190

5 *Gentleman's Magazine*, vol. IX (1833), p. 665

CHAPTER VI

1 *Report of the Cause between Charles Sturt Esq., Plaintiff, and the Most Noble the Marquis of Blandford, Defendant, for Criminal Conversation with the Right Hon. Lady Mary Anne Sturt*. Details of the Blandford/Sturt love affair, including extracts from their correspondence, and the ensuing lawsuit are derived both from this pamphlet and from *The Times'* Law Reports, 28 and 29 May 1801.

CHAPTER VII

1 *A Descriptive Account of the Mansion and Gardens of White-Knights*. Unless otherwise indicated, all quotations in this chapter are from this work.
2 Mary Russell Mitford to Sir William Elford, 9 November 1819. L'Estrange, *Life of Mary Russell Mitford*, vol. II, p. 75
3 Gantz, *The Pastel Portrait*, p. 35
4 *English Interiors 1790–1848: The Quest for Comfort*, p. 110
5 *The Later Churchills*, p. 199
6 Dropmore Papers. BM Add. MS 58990, f. 56
7 17 February 1806. *Ibid.*, f. 58
8 *Ibid.*, f. 68
9 *Ibid.*, ff. 72, 74
10 30 November 1806. *Ibid.*, f. 79
11 Royal Society Miscellaneous MSS 6.67
12 BM Add. MS 33981, f. 216
13 *Ibid.*
14 Jacques, *Georgian Gardens*, pp. 173, 187
15 29 May 1807. L'Estrange, *op. cit.*, vol. I, p. 66
16 *Ibid.*, vol. II, p. 14
17 *Ibid.*, p. 16. The text of the sonnet has been corrected from the manuscript letters at Reading Central Library.
18 Loudon, *Arboretum et Fruticetum Britannicum*, p. 127
19 *Gardener's Magazine*, vol. IX (1833), p. 665
20 Loudon, *op. cit.*, p. 127
21 Wheeler, *Sportsascrapiana*, p. iv
22 L'Estrange, *op. cit.*, vol. I, p. 271
23 Mary Russell Mitford to Sir William Elford, 5 July 1814. Letters, Reading Central Library
24 Arbuthnot, *Journal*, vol. I, p. 63

CHAPTER VIII

1 Gronow, *Last Recollections*, pp. 186–7; *Reminiscences and Recollections*, vol. I, p. 314
2 In the Marshall Papers
3 Dr James Blackstone to Lord Auckland, 24 October 1811. Blenheim Papers, BM Add. MS 61674, ff. 101–2
4 *Ibid.*, 24 November 1811, ff. 103–4

5 Dover, *Diaries*, 18 December 1814, Annaly (Holdenby) Papers, Northamptonshire Record Office, X 1384
6 *Ibid.*, 23 December 1814
7 *Ibid.*, 28 December 1814
7 *Ibid.*, 29 December 1814
9 *Ibid.*, 30 December 1814
10 *Ibid.*, 2 January 1815
11 *Ibid.*, 12 September 1815
12 *Survey of London*, vol. XXV, pp. 76–80
13 Dover, *op. cit.*, 7 October 1815
14 *Ibid.*, 23 October 1815
15 *Ibid.*, 20 April 1817
16 *Ibid.*, 27 July 1815
17 *Ibid.*, 31 July 1815
18 *Jackson's Oxford Journal*, 5 August 1815
19 Dover, *op. cit.*, 1 August 1815
20 *Ibid.*, 3 August 1815
21 *Ibid.*, 17 September 1815
22 *Ibid.*, 21 September 1815
23 *Ibid.*
24 *Ibid.*, 22 September 1815
25 *Jackson's Oxford Journal*, 14 October 1815
26 BM Add. MS 34459, f. 58
27 Gronow, *Reminiscences and Recollections*, vol. II, pp. 51–2. The incident is difficult to place precisely, but it is likely to relate to the latter years of the Duke's life.

CHAPTER IX

1 Details of the history of the Pantheon are drawn chiefly from the *Survey of London*, vol. XXI, chapter XVIII.
2 Walpole to Sir Horace Mann, 6 May 1770. *Correspondence*, ed. Lewis, vol. 23, p. 210
3 Berkshire Record Office, D/ED OT3. The deed is dated 22 February 1812.
4 Dover, *Diaries*, 29 October 1815
5 *Ibid.*
6 *Ibid.*, 2 December 1815
7 *Ibid.*, 1 March 1816
8 Gronow, *Reminiscences and Recollections*, vol. I, p. 315
9 *Ibid.*, p. 316
10 Rowse, *The Later Churchills*, p. 202
11 Gronow, *op. cit.*, vol. II, p. 226
12 *Ibid.*, vol. I, pp. 208–9
13 *Ibid.*, vol. I, p. 301
14 The account of the *affaire* Law is taken from *The Times'* Law

Reports of 10 and 23 November 1838, unless otherwise stated.
15 Dover, *op. cit.*, 30 March 1817
16 *Ibid.*, 27 April 1817
17 *Reading Mercury*, 25 August 1817
18 *Ibid.*
19 Dover, *op. cit.*, 21 April 1817
20 White, *A Versatile Professor*, p. 250
21 Rowse, *op. cit.*, p. 231
22 White, *op. cit.*, p. 250
23 Farington, *Diary*, vol. VIII (1815–21), p. 286 (5 June 1821)
24 Undated [early October 1817]. Letters, Reading Central Library
25 *Letters* (ed. Chorley), vol. I, p. 40
26 27 February 1819. L'Estrange, *Life of Mary Russell Mitford*, vol. II, p. 55
27 Mary Russell Mitford to Sir William Elford, 8 April 1819. Letters, Reading Central Library
28 *Ibid.*, 27 February 1819. L'Estrange, *op. cit.*, vol. II, pp. 55–6
29 Mary Russell Mitford to Barbara Hofland, 17 April 1819. *Letters* (ed. Chorley), vol. I, p. 58
30 Letters, Reading Central Library
31 Edwards, *Libraries and Founders of Libraries*, p. 385
32 L'Estrange, *op. cit.*, vol. II, p. 74
33 *Gardener's Magazine*, vol. IX (1833), p. 668
34 Mary Russell Mitford to Sir William Elford, 9 November 1819. L'Estrange, *op. cit.*, p. 74
35 *Ibid.*, p. 75
36 *Ibid.*
37 *Ibid.*

CHAPTER X

1 Dover, *Diaries*, 3 March 1817
2 Undated, but clearly early 1817. *Letters* (ed. Chorley), vol. I, p. 78
3 BM Add. MS 61677, ff. 103–4
4 28 July 1817. Marshall Papers
5 *Ibid.*, 30 July 1817
6 Dover, *op. cit.*, 13 April 1817
7 BM Add. MS 61677, f. 102
8 *Ibid.*

9 Dover, *op. cit.*, 26 March 1817
10 *Ibid.*, 27 March 1817
11 Counsel's Opinion, 29 January 1818. BM Add. MS 38367, f. 244
12 Dover, *op. cit.*, 18 September 1818
13 *Annual Register*, 1818. Vice-Chancellor's Court, Saturday, December 19. The Attorney General, at the Relation of the Marquis of Blandford and the hon. Agar-Ellis *v.* his Grace the Duke of Marlborough.
14 The details of this decree etc. emerge from documents in the Hautenville Cope Papers at the Bodleian Library, Oxford, MSS D.D. C 1–4
15 The greater part of the account of this episode is based on Dorothy Howell-Thomas, *Lord Melbourne's Susan.*
16 *Journal*, vol. I, pp. 12–13 (9 April 1820)
17 Mavor, *A Description of Blenheim*, 10th ed., 1817, p. 65
18 Mavor, *op. cit.*, 12th ed., 1835, p. 58
19 *Ibid.*, pp. 60–61
20 *Ibid.*, p. 65
21 This and subsequent extracts quoted from *Gardener's Magazine*, vol. X (April 1834), pp. 99–104
22 *Gardener's Magazine*, vol. IV (1828), p. 87
23 Loudon, *Arboretum et Fruticetum Britannicum*, p. 127. (Loudon actually wrote 'fourth' Duke, but it is clear he was referring to the fifth Duke of Marlborough.)

CHAPTER XI

1 Farington, *Diary*, vol. VIII, p. 286 (5 June 1821)
2 Marshall, *Early History of Woodstock*, supplement; McKinley, *Surnames of Oxfordshire*, p. 252
3 Marshall Papers, from which all the Duke's letters quoted in this chapter are taken, unless otherwise stated.
4 Blenheim Papers. BM Add. MS 61677, ff. 112–18
5 *Ibid.*, BM Add. MS 61678, f. 184
6 *Ibid.*, ff. 182–3

7 Duke of Marlborough to Lord Liverpool, 11 June 1820 and 27 March 1821, BM Add. MSS 38285, f. 222; 28380, f. 122
8 28 March 1821. BM Add. MS 38289, f. 123
9 17 November 1824, BM Add. MS 38299, f. 210
10 22 November 1824, BM Add. MS 38299, f. 209
11 White, *A Versatile Professor*, p. 249
12 Fox, *Journal*, p. 88
13 Arbuthnot, *Journal*, vol. I, pp. 304–5 (29 April 1824)
14 John and Mary Richardson of Combe to their brother, Mr C. Richardson, of London, 18 May 1823. Oxfordshire Record Office, Coombe I/1, f. 52
15 *The Times*, 16 May 1821
16 *The Age*, 21 March 1826
17 J. and M. Richardson to C. Richardson, 13 July 1823. Oxfordshire Record Office, Combe I/1, f. 57
18 Pennant Papers, Warwickshire Record Office, CR 2017 TP 431
19 *Ibid.*, CR 2017 TP 431/160–70
20 Arbuthnot, *op. cit.*, vol. I, p. 305
21 Journal of Lord Shaftesbury, 6 February 1828. Quoted in Hodder, *The Life and Work of the 7th Earl of Shaftesbury, K.G.*, vol. I, p. 81
22 Marshall Papers
23 PCC Wills, Public Record Office, PROB 11/1939

CHAPTER XII

1 See Chapter XI, p. 212
2 *Gardener's Magazine*, vol. X (April 1834), pp. 99–104
3 Undated [1827]. Broughton Papers, BM Add. MS 36463, f. 415
4 Marshall Papers
5 Undated [early September 1825]. Broughton Papers, BM Add. MS 36461, f. 247
6 Gronow, *Reminiscences and Recollections*, vol. I, p. 316
7 *A Description of Blenheim*, 12th ed. (1835), pp. 58–9
8 *Gardener's Magazine*, vol. X (April 1834), p. 102
9 6 April 1824. BM Add. MS 38371, ff. 9–10

10 21 December 1834. BM Add. MS 40407, f. 28
11 22 December 1834. *Ibid.*, f. 111
12 *Hansard, Parliamentary Debates*, vol. XXIII, p. 805
13 Croker, *Correspondence and Diaries*, vol. II, p. 100
14 26 September 1827. Pennant Papers, CR 2017 TP 431/167
15 Arbuthnot, *Journal*, vol. II, p. 334 (16 February 1830)
16 Undated [1823]. Pennant Papers, CR 2017 TP 431/145
17 *Ibid.*, CR 2017 TP 431/146
18 *Gardener's Magazine*, vol. IV (July 1828), p. 176
19 *Ibid.*, vol. V (1829), p. 383
20 *Ibid.*, vol. VI (1830), p. 655
21 *Victoria County History: Berkshire*, vol. III, p. 215, and Common Pleas 43/966, plea 448–470
22 *Gardener's Magazine*, vol. IX (1833), p. 664
23 *Ibid.*
24 *Ibid.*, vol. XI (1835), p. 503
25 Robertson, *A Day at Whiteknights*, introduction
26 Vol. II, new series (1840), p. 260
27 28 December 1878, p. 814
28 I am indebted not only to Mr Ian Cooke's personal guidance on my tour of Whiteknights, but also to an article by him, 'Secret Garden', published in *GC & HTJ*, 7 September 1984, for information on Whiteknights grounds, and particularly the state of the Wilderness at the present time and the work taking place there.
29 Robertson, *op. cit.* Illustration by H. C. Pidgeon
30 28 December 1878, p. 814
31 Pennant Papers, CR 2017 TP 622
32 Dover, *Diaries*, 9 July 1818 and October 1819 (various dates)
33 12 June [1827]. Pennant Papers, CR 2017 TP 431/165
34 28 December 1830. Pennant Papers, CR 2017 TP 548
35 22 October 1835. Blenheim Papers, BM Add. MS 61677, ff. 173–7
36 Vol. XIII, new series (May 1840), pp. 537–8
37 PCC Wills, Public Record Office, PROB 11/1946

Bibliography

MANUSCRIPT SOURCES

Annaly (Holdenby) Papers, Northamptonshire Record Office, Dover
  diaries
Auckland Papers, British Library
Banks Papers, British Library and British Museum (Natural History)
Berkshire Record Office, various documents on Whiteknights
Blenheim Papers, British Library, BM Add. MSS, various (as cited in
  source notes)
Broughton Papers, British Library
Butts, Denis, 'Mrs Barbara Hofland 1770–1844', M.Phil. thesis,
  University of Sheffield, 1980
Common Pleas, Public Record Office
Dawson MS, British Museum (Natural History)
Devonshire MSS, Chatsworth
Dropmore Papers, British Library
Galloway Muniments, Scottish Record Office, Edinburgh
Hautenville Cope Papers, Bodleian Library, Oxford
Johnston Stewart, Gavin, 'From Out the Storied Past: The Galloway
  Family and their Houses', thesis submitted for degree of BA (Hons),
  Edinburgh College of Art, 1983
Marshall Papers (collection of Mrs Susan Bernstein)
Mitford, Mary Russell, Letters, Reading Central Library
Oxfordshire Record Office, parish registers etc. for Woodstock and
  surrounding parishes
PCC Wills, Public Record Office
Pennant Papers, Warwickshire Record Office
Royal Botanic Gardens, Kew: Archives
Royal Society Miscellaneous MSS
University of Reading Library and Archives, various documents on
  Whiteknights

PRINTED SOURCES

Age, The, 1819, 1825–6
Annual Register, various dates
Arbuthnot, Harriet, Journal 1820–1832, ed. F. Bamford and the Duke of
  Wellington, 2 vols, London: Macmillan, 1950
Auckland, Lord, Journal and Correspondence, 4 vols, London: R. Bentley,
  1860–62

Banks, Sir Joseph, *The Banks Letters* (Calendar of the manuscript correspondence, ed. W. R. Dawson), London: British Museum, 1958

Battiscombe, Georgina, *The Spencers of Althorp*, London: Constable, 1984

Beavan, A. H., *Marlborough House and its Occupants*, London, 1896

Bell, Phyllis, 'The Hoflands at Richmond', *Richmond History*, no. 2 (December 1981), pp. 2–7

Bigham, Clive, *The Roxburghe Club: Its History and Its Members*, London: Oxford University Press, 1928

Blenheim Papers (British Library Catalogue of Additions to the Manuscripts), 3 vols, London: British Library, 1985

Blunt, Reginald, *Mrs Montagu, 'Queen of the Blues': Her Letters and Friendships 1762–1800*, 2 vols, London: Constable, 1923

Boyle's Court Guide, 1792– (various dates)

Burney, Fanny (Mrs D'Arblay), *Diaries and Letters 1778–1840*, 6 vols, London: Macmillan, 1904–5

Butts, Denis, 'Barbara Hofland the Sheffield Skylark', *Antiquarian Book Monthly Review*, vol. X, no. 7 (July 1983), pp. 252–7

Calvert, Hon. Mrs Frances, *Alice Elizabeth Blake, An Irish Beauty of the Regency*, London and New York: J. Lane, 1911

Cavendish, Harriet, *Hary-O: The Letters of Lady Harriet Cavendish 1796–1809*, ed. Sir George Leveson-Gower and Iris Palmer, London: J. Murray, 1940

Chambers, Robert, *The Life and Works of Robert Burns*, Edinburgh and London: W. & R. Chambers, 1896

Charlton, John, *Marlborough House*, London, HMSO, 1978

Complete Peerage, vol. V, London: St Catherine Press, 1926

Cooke, Ian, 'Secret Garden', *GC & HTJ*, 7 September 1984, pp. 33–5

Cordeaux, E. H., and Merry, D. H., *Bibliography of Printed Works relating to Oxfordshire*, Oxford, 1955; supplement, 1981

Cornforth, John, *English Interiors 1790–1848: The Quest for Comfort*, London: Barrie & Jenkins, 1978

Cowles, Virginia, *The Great Marlborough and His Duchess*, London: Weidenfeld & Nicolson, 1983

Croker, J. W., *The Croker Papers*, ed. L. J. Jennings, 3 vols, London: J. Murray, 1884

Dormer, Ernest W., *The Parish and Church of Saint Peter, Earley*, Reading: C. Nicholls, 1944

— 'White Knights, Reading: A Short History of the Ancient Estate' [Cactusville Facsimile no 14, 1982], reprinted from *Reading Mercury* and *Berks County Paper*, 2 July 1904

Edwards, Edward, *Libraries and Founders of Libraries*, London, 1865

Erskine, Mrs Steuart, *Lady Diana Beauclerk*, London: T. Fisher Unwin, 1903

Farington, Joseph, *Diary*, ed. J. Greig, 8 vols., London: Hutchinson, 1922–8

Fisher, John, *The Origins of Garden Plants*, London: Constable, 1982

Fox, H. E. (later fourth Lord Holland), *Journal 1818–1830*, ed. Earl of Ilchester, London: Butterworth, 1923

Gantz, Ida, *The Pastel Portrait*, London: Cresset Press, 1963

Gardeners' Chronicle, 1878

Gardener's Magazine, vols IV–XIII (1828–38)

Gentleman's Magazine, various dates

Gloag, John, *Mr Loudon's England*, Newcastle upon Tyne: Oriel Press, 1970

Green, David, *Blenheim Palace*, London: Country Life, 1951

— *Blenheim Park and Gardens*, Woodstock: Blenheim Estate Office/Alden Press, 1972; reprinted 1980

Green, V. H. H., *The Oxford Common Room*, London: E. Arnold, 1957

Gronow, Captain R. H., *Last Recollections*, London: Selwyn & Blount, 1934

— *Reminiscences and Recollections*, 2 vols, London: Nimmo, 1889

Gunning, Susannah, *A Letter from Mrs Gunning Addressed to His Grace the Duke of Argyll*, London, 1791

Hadfield, Miles, *Gardening in Britain*, London: Hutchinson, 1960

Hansard: Parliamentary Debates, various dates

Herbert, Lord (ed.), *Henry, Elizabeth and George: Letters and Diaries of Henry, Tenth Earl of Pembroke and his Circle (1734–80)*, London: Cape, 1939

— *Pembroke Papers 1780–1794*, London: Cape, 1950

Hill, Constance, *Mary Russell Mitford and her Surroundings*, London: Bodley Head, 1920

Hix, John, *The Glass House*, London: Phaidon, 1974

Hodder, E. *The Life and Work of the 7th Earl of Shaftesbury, K.G.*, 3 vols, London: Cassell, 1886

Hofland, Mrs [Barbara], *A Descriptive Account of the Mansion and Gardens of White-Knights, A Seat of His Grace the Duke of Marlborough, illustrated by T. C. Hofland*, London, 1819

Horticultural Journal, 1839, 1840

House of Lords, Journal of the, vol. XLV (1805–6)

Howell-Thomas, Dorothy, *Lord Melbourne's Susan*, Old Woking: Gresham Books, 1978

Hylton, Lord (ed.), *The Paget Brothers 1790–1840*, London: J. Murray, 1918

Jackson's Oxford Journal, various dates 1781–1835

Jacques, David, *Georgian Gardens: The Reign of Nature*, London: Batsford, 1983

Jesse, J. H., *Memoirs of the Life and Reign of George III*, 3 vols, London, 1867

Kinsley, James (ed.), *The Poems and Songs of Robert Burns*, 3 vols, Oxford: Clarendon Press, 1968

L'Estrange, A. G., *Life of Mary Russell Mitford*, 3 vols, London:
R. Bentley, 1870

Lindsay, M., *The Burns Encyclopaedia*, New York: St Martin's Press;
London: R. Hale, 1980

London Gazette, June 1817

Loudon, John Claudius, *Arboretum et Fruticetum Britannicum; or the Trees
and Shrubs of Britain*, 8 vols, London: Longmans, 1838

— reports (various dates), *Gardener's Magazine*, 1828–38

McKinley, Richard, *Surnames of Oxfordshire*, London: St Leopard's Head
Press, 1977

Marshall, E., *The Early History of Woodstock*, Oxford and London, 1873;
supplement, 1874

Mavor, William Fordyce, *A [New] Description of Blenheim*, Oxford (various
publishers), 1789–1835

Maxwell Lyte, Sir H. C., *A History of Eton College (1440–1910)*, London:
Macmillan, 1911

Millman, Thomas R., *Life of the Right Reverend, The Honourable Charles
James Stewart, D.D. Oxon., Second Anglican Bishop of Quebec*, Ontario:
Huron College, 1953

Mitford, Mary Russell, *Letters* (ed. R. Brimley Johnson), London: Bodley
Head, 1925; *Letters* (ed. H. Chorley), 2 vols, London: R. Bentley,
1872; *Life* (includes letters), *see above*, L'Estrange, A. G.

Montgomery-Massingberd, Hugh, *Blenheim Revisited*, London: Bodley
Head, 1985

Namier, Sir Lewis and Brooke, John, *The House of Commons 1754–1790*,
London: HMSO, 1964

Neale, J. P., *Six Views of Blenheim*, London, 1823

Oman, Carola, *Nelson*, London: Hodder & Stoughton, 1948

Oracle, The, September 1791

Pevsner, Nikolaus, *Berkshire*, London: Penguin Books, 1966

Plumb, J. H., *The First Four Georges*, London: Batsford, 1956

Porter, Roy, *English Society in the Eighteenth Century*, London: Penguin
Books, 1982

Powys, Caroline, *Passages from the Diaries of Mrs Philip Lybbe Powys,
1756–1802*, London: Longmans, Green, 1899

Priestley, J. B., *The Prince of Pleasure and His Regency 1811–20*, London:
Heinemann, 1969

Reading Mercury, various dates

Reynolds, Frederic, *Life and Times of Frederic Reynolds*, 2 vols, London,
1826

Roberts, Henry D., *Royal Pavilion, Brighton*, London: Country Life, 1939

Robertson, J. G., *A Day at Whiteknights*, Reading: J. Snare, 1840

Rosenfeld, Sybil, *Temples of Thespis*, London: Society for Theatre
Research, 1978

Rowse, A. L., *The Later Churchills*, London: Macmillan, 1958

Satirist, The, 1808–14

Scots Magazine, 1767–85

Smith, Ernest, *A History of Whiteknights*, Reading: University of Reading, 1957

Smith, Lady Pleasance (ed.), *Memoir and Correspondence of the late Sir James Edward Smith, M.D.*, 2 vols, London: Longman, 1832

Smith, Sydney, *Selected Letters*, ed. Nowell C. Smith, London: Oxford University Press, 1956

Spain, Nesta, *George III at Home*, London: Eyre Methuen, 1975

Stroud, Dorothy, *Capability Brown*, London: Faber, 1975

— *Humphry Repton*, London: Country Life, 1962

Sturt, Charles, *Report of the Cause between Charles Sturt Esq., Plaintiff, and the Most Noble the Marquis of Blandford, Defendant, for Criminal Conversation with the Right Hon. Lady Mary Anne Sturt*, London, 1801

Survey of London, vols XXIX and XXXI, London: Athlone Press/University of London for the LCC/GLC, 1960, 1963

Times, The, various dates

Tod, George, *Plans, Elevations and Sections, of Hot-Houses, Green-Houses, An Aquarium, Conservatories, &c., recently built in different parts of England, for various Noblemen and Gentlemen*, London, 1823

Townsend, James, *The Oxfordshire Dashwoods*, Oxford: Oxford University Press, 1922

Victoria County History: Berkshire, vol. III, London: Dawson, for University of London Institute of Historical Research, 1972

Vickers, Hugo, *Gladys, Duchess of Marlborough*, London: Weidenfeld & Nicolson, 1979

Walpole, Horace, *Correspondence*, ed. W. S. Lewis, 48 vols, Oxford and New Haven, USA: Oxford University Press and Yale University Press

Watney, John, *The Churchills*, London: Gordon and Cremonesi, 1977

Watney, Vernon James, *Cornbury and the Forest of Wychwood*, London: Hatchards, 1910

Watson, J. Steven, *The Reign of George III, 1760–1815*, Oxford: Clarendon Press, 1960

Wheeler, C. A., *Sportsascrapiana*, London, 1867

White, G. Cecil, *A Versatile Professor: Reminiscences of the Rev. Edward Nares D.D.*, London: R. Brimley Johnson, 1903

Williams, St George Armstrong, *English Works of the late Rev. E. Williams (with a memoir)*, London: Whittingham, 1840

Willson, E. J., *James Lee and the Vineyard Nursery, Hammersmith*, London: Hammersmith Local History Group, 1961

Index

John
Duke of Marlborough   m. **Sarah Jennings**
1650–1722   1660–1744

John
Marquess of Blandford
d.s.p. 1703

**Henrietta
second Duchess of Marlborough**
1681–1733   m. Francis second Earl of Godolphin

Anne   *m.* 1699 Charles Spencer third Earl of Sunderland
1684–1716   1674–1722

Elizabeth
1686–1714
m.
first Earl of
Bridgewater

Mary
1689–1751
m.
John
Duke of Montag

William
Marquess of Blandford
d.s.p. 1731

Robert
fourth Earl of Sunderland
1701–1729
d.s.p.

John   m. 1733   Georgina
1708–1746   dau. of Earl Granville

**Charles Spencer
third Duke of Marlborough**
1706–1758   *m.* 1732   Elizabeth dau. of Lord Trevor
d. 1761

Diana
d.17

John   m. 1755   Georgiana Poyntz
first Earl Spencer   1734–1814
1734–1783

Diana
1734–1808
m. (1) Frederick
Visc. Bolingbroke
(2) Topham Beauclerk

Elizabeth   *m.* tenth Earl
1737–1831   of Pembroke

Charles   *m.*   Mary
(of Wheatfield)   dau. of Lord Vere
1740–1820   *d.* 1812

Robert
1747–1831
m. Mrs Bouverie

**George Spencer
fourth Duke of Marlboro**
1739–1817

George John
second Earl Spencer
1758–1834

Georgiana
1759–1806
m. fifth Duke
of Devonshire

Henrietta
1761–1821
m. third Earl
of Bessborough

George
Herbert
1759–1827
eleventh Earl
of Pembroke

John
1767–1831
m. 1790
Elizabeth Spencer ✳
d. 1812

William Robert   *m.* 1791   Susan Spreti
1769–1834   1769–*c*1840

Harriet
1798–1834
m. 1819
Count Charles
von Westerholt

3 sons and
1 other daughter

Susan Churchill
1818–*c.* 1882
m. Aimé Timothé
Cuénod

**George
sixth Duke of Marlborough**
1793–1857

m. (1) 1819 Jane Stewart
dau. of eighth Earl
of Galloway
1798–1844

m. (2) 1846 Charlotte Flower
dau. of Visc. Ashbrook
d. 1850

m. (3) 1851 Jane
dau. of Hon. Edw
Richard Stewa
d. 1897

**John Winston
seventh Duke
of Marlborough**
1822–1883

Alfred
1824–1893

Alan
1825–1873

Louisa
*d.*1882

Almeric
Athelston
1847–1856

Clementina
Augusta
*d.*1886

Edward
1853–1911

George
**eighth Duke
of Marlborough**
1844–1892

Randolph
1849–1895

3 other sons and
6 daughters

Charles
**ninth Duke
of Marlborough**
1871–1934

Winston
Spencer Churchill
1874–1965

John
**tenth Duke
of Marlborough**
1897–1972

John
**eleventh Duke
of Marlborough**
1926–